SO LONG GUYS, GOODBYE IS FOREVER

*A Memoir of Bombardier
Lt. Albert La Chasse*

Jane R. Edwards

To order additional copies of this book, contact:
Xlibris Corporation
1-888-7-XLIBRIS
www.Xlibris.com
Orders@Xlibris.com

Dedicated to the Memory of
Lt. Commander Mark Ulin Edwards

.

CONTENTS

I want to thank Jane Edwards for writing this story. I find the portrayal of Al authentic and memorable.

Dorothy LaChasse

ACKNOWLEDGMENTS

Thank you to Al, who is now with "his guys," for his superb recollections and to his wife, my dear friend, Dorothy, for putting up with the months Al and I spent recording his experiences. Gratitude to my beloved, late husband, Mark Edwards, for encouraging me to complete this project. Loving appreciation to my daughter, Catherine, for saving me from the "macros" and preserving this history on disk and to her twin, Matthew, who captured the spirit of this book by his cover art of the eternal B-17, the Flying Fortress. I am indebted to and sincerely envious of Austrian-born Eve Allsbrook, my editor, who knows English so much better than I do. A special thank you and blessings to Jenny and Jim Krusoe for their inspiration to get this book published. Finally, a note of belated thanks to my teacher at UCLA, the late, great *Los Angeles Times* Literary Critic, Robert Kirsch, who told me that this book was "engrossing and publishable." Twenty years later, I believe him.

SO LONG GUYS, GOODBYE IS FOREVER

The B-17F Flying Fortress, the type of plane flown by Al La Chasse and his crew. The men who flew the Fortress described her as "rugged" and "the Greatest." (Photo is courtesy of the Boeing Company.)

But, with the advent of the Americans, the battle of course grew enormously in scope—and in human cost. The extraordinary devotion to duty of the men who flew the bombers is indicated by the fact that more awards and decorations were won by them, than by men of any other army and more cruelly by the fact that of the men who died, over 25,000 have no known grave. That many died in the early days without themselves having inflicted much more than discomfort on the enemy is undeniable, for they had not the weapons to do more; but their experience and their very needs led eventually to the provision of equipment of a standard to match their courage.

Barrie Pitt,
BOMBER OFFENSIVE, The Devastation of Europe

Excerpted from.introduction of *BOMBER OFFENSIVE,*
The Devastation of Europe, by Noble Frankland
(New York, 1970)

1

MISSING

San Diego, California
November 8, 1944

The details of the mission were two years in reaching me but were still a terrible blow: "The pilot and copilot were killed, slumped over dead in their seats"—what a picture to carry with me the rest of my days. And the final blow—"I heard the plane explode." Well, they couldn't touch his soul . . .

> Nanette Bailey, mother of
> Lt. Joseph Norman Gates
> Copilot

White Plains, New York
September 12, 1944

On October 12th, 1942, I received a telegram that my son was "missing in action" over Western Europe October 9th—nothing else until January 1st, 1943—a second telegram from the War Department that my son previously reported missing had been killed on October 9th. No details, no identification—nothing definite or tangible—several weeks later we received the Purple Heart.

I do not believe he is dead. I have the strangest feeling that he will come home to us again.

> Florence A. Dynan, mother of
> T/Sgt. Thomas W. Dynan, Jr.
> Radio Operator

Hyde Park, Massachusetts
October 10, 1944

It is hard to believe that my son was killed but I have heard now from several of the boys' folks so I guess it must be true.

My son, Walter (John), spoke so many times of his crew members and told us what a fine group of young men they were. I am sorry so many of them had to go down with him.

. . . I know there could not have been any prolonged suffering for any of them for which I am very thankful.

Brenda M. Olson, mother of
Capt. John W. Olson
Pilot

American Battle Monuments Commission Cemetery
Maddingly, Cambridge
England
October 7, 1982

Umbrellas popped open, like small, black parachutes as we stepped out into the blustery, rain-soaked morning. There were two busloads, about 120 people. Most had come from the States. Among us were English and American television crews sent to cover the "first-ever" reunion. The station wagon carrying their equipment had arrived before them.

I knew only a few of these 306th Bomb Group people. The one English fellow I did know was Cyril Norman, a World War II history buff from Bedford. We had corresponded for years.

The dedication at my old base in Thurleigh had been made earlier in the week.

The townsfolk had erected a granite monument with the inscriptions "First Over Germany," and "ALWAYS FIRST," commemorating the 306th Bomb Group that had been stationed there. The people were friendly and sincere, but like the weeds that broke the white line of the old runway, there was very little that was familiar. I had paid my respects to Thurleigh when I made it back from Stalag right after the war. Even then, all the people I knew were gone, all left behind that morning in '42, along with my laundry and the silver tea service that I had bought for my mother. No, the tug in my gut was coming here, to this Air Force Cemetery in Cambridge, to see my guys. As I approached it, that pull, that clutch of memories, intensified.

In the Visitor's Building, the superintendent briefed us on the Monument's history. Beyond him, through the windows, I could see, on a backdrop of green, infinite arcs of white. Somewhere close were Olson, Gates, Kaylor, Dynan, Nicholson and Wilder. They were not buried, of course. That was impossible. There couldn't have been anything left in that shattered, burning coffin of a plane that tumbled out of sight below me. But outside this building, I would find their names imprinted on the Wall of the Missing. It would carry their epitaphs—my guys, party to the very beginning, now barely remembered. This was their Memorial, their Shrine, the irrefutable. I was impatient to get to them.

Immediately upon stepping outside, I was startled. The cemetery, of an enormous size, was opulent in its simplicity; in its sweeping curves of crosses and Stars of David; in precise half circles, row after row on a luxuriant manicured bed of grass, magnificently green and iridescent in the dark reflection of the storm. In the biting, pelting frost of rain, I was warmed. I was back with my Group, my Team.

The official ceremony began just outside the Visitor's Building. In front of the seventy-two foot flag standard, young American Air Force men and women presented the Colors. As Taps played, the flags, whipped by the wind, saluted the thirty acres of honored dead: 3,811 graves, 5,125 names on the Wall of the Missing. Six of those were my guys. I was about to see and touch them, run my fingers over the indented permanency. A wreath was laid at the base of the flag. The formal tribute was over.

The Wall extended down the south side of the cemetery from the flagpole and ended at the Memorial Building. It measured 472 feet in length and was built of Portland Stone, limestone quarried on the south coast of England. In a confusion of eagerness, it took a few moments before I realized the names were alphabetized and that from where I stood, I was approaching it from the end.

"Wilder," I said loudly. My English friend, Cyril, caring enough to want to be a part of it, helped me look for him. We hunched over the Ws, looking for Sgt. Truman C. Wilder, the ball turret. He was such a little guy, but then he had to be to fit into the tight space of that position. We couldn't find him. I felt frightened that I misspelled his name. No, I told myself, as I plainly pictured his name *and* face.

"The Wall's screwed up," I announced.

Cyril was puzzled. "I don't understand it," he said. "Maybe we should search for the 306th Group first, the 367th Squadron, and then the name."

We found we were taking a lot of time looking through the Ts and Ss. Some of the wives had already gone back to the bus.

The columns began with the surname, middle initial, given name, squadron, and the bomb group. I found no Olsons. I checked and rechecked but there was no one from the 367th Squadron, no one from the 306th Bomb Group. I thought to myself, this isn't important because my guys are here somewhere, I know it. Their names are probably listed on a separate monument, a special commemorative all by itself. I dismissed the doubt from my mind. This place was too perfect. There could not be, absolutely could not be, any SNAFU.

"There must be an answer," Cyril announced solemnly.

Clouds, like black smoke, drifted across the sky. Winds buffeted the rain, slapping it in my face. The two of us stood so close in front of the Ns that the rain dripped on us from between the umbrellas. We were looking for Nicholson, S/S Bruce Nicholson, gunner. I never even saw the guy. He was a last minute replacement for Luck Talbot who was sick that day. I remember at our first crew meeting Captain Olson saying, "Private Talbot, welcome aboard." I wonder what ever became of him?

A TV cameraman, who had been following me down the Wall, was wasting a lot of film. "Find anyone?" he finally asked.

With no one to tie onto I picked a name at random. "Yeah," I replied weakly, "there's a guy from the 369th."

I couldn't believe it. Still, I was positive they were there. They *had* to be there. But we couldn't find them. There was no Nicholson; no S/S Bert Kaylor, tail gunner; no Lt. Joseph Gates, copilot; no S/S Thomas W. Dynan, radio operator. Dynan was a nice kid and a talented artist. He drew a beautiful Pluto—Disney's version—on the nose of our ship.

"We'll check back at the office in the Visitor's Building," Cyril promised. "They'll tell us something."

The Memorial Building at the end of the Wall had huge maps of the Air Force missions and stained glass windows. I didn't give a damn.

The pavement of English Yorkstone was slippery. It took a long time to walk back past five thousand names to the entrance. Water had seeped into my shoes. Doubt mixed with outrage had seeped into my soul. Surely, I thought, someone here will know and will give me the directions to that plaque edged in gold.

The superintendent, a man in his thirties and wearing a conservative blue suit, regarded me with amazement.

Trying to be calm, I told him, "I have six members of my crew that for all these years have been listed as MIAs; people from this Group, the one that you are hosting here today. And I'm telling you, Sir, that they are missing from the Wall of the Missing. I'm really disturbed. My guys were among the first in the whole Eighth Air Force." My voice carried enough that the three other staff members came into his office.

"Uh, when was that?" one of them asked.

" '42."

" '42?" They looked at each other.

"Yes, 1942, over Lille, France." Impulsively I pulled out a yellow, paperback book from my pocket. "See this? *The 306th B.G. History in Review.* Here," I showed them, "on page five. '9 Oct. '42-Group flew its first combat mission in European Theater. The Group lost its first B-17F. Number 41-24510.' That was *my* plane. My guys went down in it."

For a moment, I was choked with the injustice. My breath caught in my heart, rolled into a knot and climbed to my eyeballs. Tears mingled with the rain on my face.

"I want an answer. If they're not here, then damn it, where are they? I want to know. Where are my guys? MY GUYS. WHERE ARE THEY?"

Cyril and I were silent as the coach motored toward the Imperial War Museum Airfield at Duxford. My English friend was feeling somehow responsible. As for me, I was devastated. I'd kept the bus waiting half an hour because I was so determined to get some information. They didn't have any. The superintendent had finally offered, "You can get in touch with the Battle Commissions in the States." Well, hell.

The personnel at the cemetery appeared stunned at my question. Like, "Who is this old guy and what's he screaming about? Why isn't he complimentary like everyone else?" But, then, except for the original crews, no one could understand or relate to my guys and what they went through. In 1942 they were sacrificed— thrust into battle for the sake of propaganda, with no real training, no adequate weapons, no experience, no protection. Many of them knew their fate. They made their mission.

In 1943, a B-17 gunner who had hung out there, who had experienced the lumbering exposure in a "Heavy" Fortress, the eternity of that straight line over target, the shocking rush of bullets and flak, said:

> I read a very nice piece in a magazine about us; it says we've got nerves of steel. We never get scared. All we want is just to fly all the time and get a crack at Jerry. I never heard anything so brave as us. I read it three or four times to try and convince myself that I ain't scared.[1]

World War II—it's been called "the last popular war"; war that had not even been declared when I was on my way to it.

Al in his U.S. Air Corps Flying Cadet Program uniform,
Santa Maria, California, 1939-40.

2

SEMPER FIDELIS

Edged in black, the communication was brief: "TUESDAY, JULY 15, 1941, YOU WILL REPORT TO THE MARINE CORPS RECRUIT DEPOT AT SAN DIEGO OR DISCIPLINARY ACTION WILL BE TAKEN."

Under military arrest? Me? These guys were serious. The bastards. And I thought I had been discharged. They had only filed me away in the "inactive" drawer. Now, after all my experience, I was on my way to boot camp!

Clang, Clang, CLANG, Clang, Clang . . . the wigwag signal jangled DANGER as the train sped across the intersection.

The Clayton-Knight Committee will get me out of this. They're just too anxious to get qualified pilots. Guys like myself are the sole purpose of their organization; to contact American pilots to fly as Eagle pilots for the Royal Air Force. The Committee must have a lot of influence and a lot of money behind them—while they were interviewing, to wine and dine us like that at the ritzy Hollywood Roosevelt Hotel. I suppose they get a lot of private contributions. It's one way, under our Neutrality Law, that the people in the States can help England fight Nazi Germany.

I'm willing to help, yeah, but not as a marching Marine. I WANT TO FLY.

On both sides of the tracks, silky, golden poppies and green crops feasted on the California sunshine. Walls of orange groves, their limbs sagging in ripened fruit, bowed in the wind from the passing "San Diegan."

I was a fool to sign up with the Marine Reserves in the first place. That recruiter at Glendale College made it sound so patriotic. "Now, if you guys on the football team will join, a lot of others will follow your example." That "occasional" meeting with a bunch of fellow athletes—what a bore that turned out to be.

"I can't make it to the meetings anymore, fellas. I've got a night job. I resign."

Resign? My ass. That's good for one belly laugh. Resign a contract with a reserve unit of the military? How stupid could I be?

What a hassle it was turning back the uniform. I had to drive all the way to Van Nuys to turn in one lousy canteen. I bet it took two whole gallons of gas; 36 cents I didn't have.

The train whistled the familiar crossing code—two long, one short, one long—as we approached Fullerton. The wheels rumbled over tracks set in asphalt, while automobiles waited in trapped observation. Slower, slower, the engine wheezed to a stop.

If I hadn't washed out of the Army Air Cadet Flying School last year at Santa Maria, I wouldn't be here now. I was a good pilot, too. So were Pappy Lutz, Jim Williams and Pat Carey. SHIT. We passed the physicals. That was the biggest hurdle. But we didn't have a chance. Not with all those West Point graduates. There were over eighty applicants, with a maximum enrollment of fifty-five students. Guess who had to go? West Point graduates never wash out of anything. Damn them.

Clickety clack, clickety clack, the wheels bumped over the lines of jointed steel.

Eucalyptus trees, with shredding bark and tapering leaves, stood in straight rows, like giant sentinels, wind screens to the orchards of avocados and oranges. Tall spikes of mustard seed and blue lupine and stalks of wild oats rimmed the railroad tracks. Small white farmhouses peeked out from clusters of shade trees, the unassuming heartbeat to acres of precision cultivation. A fruit stand in the shape of a giant orange advertised roadside produce.

"I sure would like to send my folks back home a box of those oranges."

I had hardly noticed the kid sitting next to me, but as I looked at him, at his round, happy face, it hit me. He was the image of the fat "Big Boy," the trademark of Bob's Coffee Shop in Glendale.

"Where's home?"

"Iowa. Perry, Iowa, outside Des Moines." His chubby face glowed. "My name's Archibald Turner. You can call me Archie."

"Al La Chasse. You heading for the Marine Base in San Diego?"

"Yep."

"Lucky you."

"Yeah. I got a buddy there. He's been in more'n a month. I can't wait to see him."

"Well, Archie," I tried to sound casual, "unless you bump into him in the Saturday morning parade, forget it. You won't see him until after boot camp. And then you'll be lucky."

"Oh, I'll see him all right. I c'n spot him a mile off."

"That's about how far it will be, too."

"You've been through boot camp, huh? You're a Marine?"

"No, and kind of. I've been in the reserves for a couple of years and I've heard stories about boot camp longer than that. It's no fun."

"Aw . . . hey," the kid sat up and pointed out the window, "What'n the world are those little green plants out there? Must be millions of 'em."

"Those, Archie, are strawberries."

"Strawberries? Miles of strawberries! Whoee. My Momma wouldn't believe it. But she'd love it. She makes the best pies in the whole world. I think I'll send her a big box of those, too. Jest as soon as I get my first pay." Dreamily, he settled back in his seat.

First pay, shit. All he'll be able to afford is one of those hand-sized crates of candy oranges like the souvenirs they sell in Olvera Street in L.A.

Side by side, tiny wooden houses blinked through half-opened window shades as we ground to a halt in Santa Ana. Lines of people waited outside the stucco depot. There were lots of children, too. It was summer vacation. They were probably going to the San Diego Zoo. Wish I were.

Archie sat up. "Think I'll get me a window seat while I can. Nice t' meet'cha, Al. See ya in the Marines."

The coach jerked forward. In the excessive acceleration the wheels slipped . . . then grabbing the rail, the train began moving . . . chug . . . chug . . . chug . . . chug . . .

I guess I'll go have a Coke.

The couplings tugged at each other, wrenching the cars sideways. From door to door, I fought for balance as I went forward to the parlor car.

Coca-Cola was one of the addictions I picked up at Santa Maria. We sat next to the Coke machine, waiting for the fog to lift and the orange flag to come up, with nothing to do but drink Cokes until it did. Then, with the flag raised for "go," we climbed into those cute Stearman PT-13As with Lycoming radial engines, light blue bodies, yellow wings and red-and-white striped tails. What a thrill! We all became addicted to flying. We did all those things we weren't supposed to do: Stealing a buzz over the chicken ranch to see if the chickens really did drop their eggs on a dead run—they did; or formation flying in simulated dive bombing over fishing boats.

We were damn good pilots, all of us. The problem was not enough room for everyone. The expanding Pilot Training Program didn't have enough personnel and facilities. And those fields, in turn, had to feed their graduates into Randolph Field in Texas, the West Point of the air. It, too, had a limited capacity.

Bob Chilton wouldn't have washed me out. He wouldn't have washed any of us out—not Pappy, Jim, or Pat. We were all doing too well. Chilton's nose wasn't in the military. He was one of us. He was a terrific instructor; so good he had us soloing in two weeks. He was too good. Just as we were going into aerobatics, he was assigned to train the new instructors.

Al poses next to a "cute" Stearman PT-13A.

I felt like *I* was teaching his replacement.

Then, along came Captain Deering. He said he wanted to take me up for a "check ride." I didn't know that #20 was the Washing Machine, but it was. That was the plane he took me up in. That was my washout flight, my elimination. "Discharged because of flying deficiency."

Flying deficiency, bull. I shouldn't have asked for that pro-phylactic treatment. That was dumb. Still, they made such a point about venereal disease and how important it was to take all the necessary precautions. I thought I was being conscientious when I woke up the Sergeant early that Sunday morning and asked for a treatment. Naïve, that's what I was. Standing there like a little boy, with my pants down around my feet while he cleaned me up. I could just hear the Review Board: "He's not that interested in flying, not officer material." Crap! They would have laid the same girl if they had had the chance. With my own Prophylactic Kit and eighty hours of flying time, it was goodbye to the Allen Hancock Flight Academy in Santa Maria.

Back in the coach, I lit up an El Roi Tan cigar.

Beyond the truck gardening, beehive farming and fields veined in irrigation ditches, were rolling hills, the last barricade to the

Pacific. The green slopes were hugged by families of broccoli-topped California live oaks.

The big, green cars of the Santa Fe Railroad hurried by more miles of orange groves whose smudge pots, like small lighthouses, lay idle in the warm weather.

From the inland fields, we plunged into a vista of the Pacific Ocean at San Juan Capistrano.

So I didn't make it at Santa Maria. Why not join up with the Marine Corps Flying Cadet Program at Long Beach? I knew I could pass the physical and mental tests, and I had the two years of college. I was "in like Flynn"—until the Review Board.

Oh, that withering feeling, when they asked about the U.S. insurance policy that the government had provided for me as an Army Air Corps flying cadet. I stood there with a pen, poised, ready to sign.

"Tell us, Mr. La Chasse, do you have any relative in the military service?"

"No, Sir."

"Then how do you explain this government insurance policy with the same name and address as your own?"

I gave it all the silence I could, but they were going to have an answer.

"Well, that must be the one from the Army Air Corps . . ."

"YOU WASHED OUT OF THE ARMY AIR CORPS?"

I dropped the pen without lowering my hand, like a bomb, did an "about face" and walked out. They didn't have to tell me. I knew what they were thinking. If I wasn't good enough for the Army, I sure wasn't good enough for the Marines. I was lucky they didn't prosecute for fraudulent enlistment.

A margin of summer cottages separated the highway from the beach, their porches draped in towels and bathing suits. Among them, in careless profusion, were magenta bougainvillea and wild geraniums in violet and white.

Beachcombers and children playing in the sand, stopped to wave as the heavy duty coaches roared by at seventy-nine miles an hour.

Brushing a cinder from my suit pants, I took a last puff of my cigar and put it out.

What a beautiful suit, and *I* owned it. Single breasted, light-blue, herringbone tweed, it was the latest style with broad, padded shoulders and soft, wide pleats in the trousers. My shoes were black, wing-tipped with 30-cent steel wedges on the heels. In my white shirt and blue knot tie, I was impressive. Handsome was the word.

Seagulls paced the breaking tide and a white sheepdog raced us into San Clemente. Far out from the shore, I saw Capitol ships at anchor.

Quietly, the seaside apartments and shoreline auto-courts slid by as the train rolled on its way. Purple ice plant oozed down the side of sandstone cliffs and tentacles of seaweed sprawled over mounds of sand. Tumbleweed drifted across the sand dunes and bands of bamboo fenced the inlets in the rocky shore of peaceful San Onofre State Beach.

I am twenty-four. Hell, I'm too old, too mature, too sophisticated for this. I was marching and had learned the Manual of Arms when today's boots were giving apples to the teacher, over six years ago.

What a sweet deal, getting paid seven cents a mile and then hitchhiking up to the Presidio in Monterey to be cadre for the Summer Camps. Those World War I officers cared more about their squads winning a football game than competing in military maneuvers. The camp was more like a sports program that netted me thirty dollars a summer; a bundle in '38 and '39.

We had arrived in Oceanside. It was only thirty-seven miles to San Diego. I felt good. I'd been around. I had my private pilot's license. The CPTP—Civilian Pilot Training Program—was a piece of pie. After Santa Maria, taking the flying course at Grand Central Terminal in Glendale was a cinch. Yeah. I was way ahead of the Marines. Me? A licensed pilot? The Committee wouldn't let me go. I was too valuable.

Al as a part of the cadre of the CMTC Camp
at the Presidio in Monterey, California, 1938.

The CMTC Camp where the cadre were housed in tents.

We left the stands of pine trees, the empty hopper cars, the small cement station and the Oceanside Pier, and traveled south through Carlsbad. We passed lagoons, solitary churches with Spanish bell towers, spiny cactus and fallow fields of wild daisies.

I could hear Bing Crosby singing, "Where the turf meets the surf," as we passed the racetrack and pulled into Del Mar's train depot. There was a loneliness about the station, about the brick wood-framed building and the empty slat-back benches. The metal lampshades elbowed off of the roof like spider legs. It was a perfect backdrop for an evening with film star, Peter Lorre.

Clickety-clack, clickety-clack, semper-fidelis, semper-fidelis.

I reached into my breast pocket and took out the envelope that the Clayton-Knight Committee had given me. Inside were a twenty-five dollar food voucher and a one-way ticket to Vancouver, B.C. There in my hand was the proof, my passport to the Spitfire. It was a good feeling to know the RAF was on my side. "Nothing to worry about," someone from the Committee assured me over the phone when I told them of the notice I had received from the Marines. "You go on down to San Diego and we'll get you out in a matter of days."

Ahead, I could see the train's engine puffing steam, worming around the canyons in an uphill climb. White and pink oleanders blossomed, and stands of sycamore and eucalyptus brushed the tops of the coach cars. Expansive live oaks diffused the morning sunlight over dried, bewhiskered hillsides. I swayed in my seat as the cars lurched on winding tracks through the rough terrain.

I put the envelope back in my pocket. It would be only a few days before I joined Pappy Lutz in Canada. Soon, very soon, I would be flying in the Dominion's Service.

Smoother now, the tracks straightened, passing the outskirts of San Diego and the empty beaches and private rowboats docked in Mission Bay. After a two and one-half hour ride, the black locomotive screeched to a standstill. The myriad of tracks terminated ahead. San Diego was the end of the line.

Unhurried, I took my bag down from the rack, walked up the aisle and stepped out from the opened door that was on the right side of the train. What I thought had been another coach parked beside us was a bus. There were two buses parked together, only a few feet from the train. In front, bridging the small gap between train and bus, was a Marine sergeant.

Uh, oh. I stopped cold.

The sergeant had a face like an English bulldog. His jaws were menacingly set. His eyes glowed like the sinister lights of a German tank. He stood in front of the bus that was parked no more than an arm's length from the train. He wasn't going to let *anyone* get away.

The prick. *He* was happening to me? If there hadn't been so many guys behind me, I would have done an "about face" and marched right off the San Diego Pier.

In an ape-like stance, his feet at 45° angles, the sergeant opened his mouth. Bellowing from his bowels, he screamed, "ALL RIGHT MEN, YOU HAVE JUST FOUR SECONDS TO GET INTO THAT BUS AND TWO ARE ALREADY GONE. MOVE IT! MOVE IT! MOVE IT!"

A shudder throttled my insides as the foreboding shot into focus: eight weeks of boot camp and all the rigors of a buck-ass private, imbued in the Marine Motto: SEMPER FIDELIS, ALWAYS FAITHFUL. I had the feeling, right then, it was all going to be mine.

3

SYMPATHY IS WHERE YOU FIND IT

One deep sigh and we were there. My world had ended.

The buses bounced through the enormous chain link gates and on to the far south end of the base. We got off. The buses disappeared. Gone was our last link to civilization.

No longer in control of our lives, all responsibility was now assumed by the Corps. As intelligent individuals, we were eclipsed in the regime of military organization.

We huddled together, but not for long. The bulldog sergeant was still with us.

"All right, you people, line up four deep."

The group pushed and stumbled into position. I stayed in front so that I would have clear visibility when the Spitfire swooped down out of the sky to rescue me.

"Drop your bags," the sergeant growled. The suitcases, the cardboard boxes tied in string, the zippered satchels, fell to the ground and with them, "home," "Momma," and "I can't."

"Now, I'm gonna give you your first drill command. PLA-TOON, that means all of you, take two steps forward. HUT, TWO.

"Look at me. Right face. Get that? READYYYY? RIAYT, FACE!

"Now we're gonna march. Start with your left, remember, always your left."

We shuffled off to the quartermaster. We were issued a duffel bag, white skivvies and sick green, hanging coveralls initialed USMC.

Eyeballed for size—"Hm-m, you look like medium"—the issue flew at us like it was coming from a machine. Changing clothes was the beginning of tearing us down and building us back up the Marine way.

I folded my beautiful suit, tucking the pants and shirt lovingly inside my coat, buttoned it and buckled my belt around them. PHFFT—into the bottom of the duffel bag.

While waiting in our underwear, we were directed to a temporary infirmary. As we stood outside, we could hear the ouches and screams as kids for the first time received inoculations. I'd been through it before.

One needle plunged into my right arm, someone grabbed my left and stabbed it. "Pull down your shorts and lean over." Bent over the padded table, I was slapped twice and given two shots in each cheek.

Smarting from a creeping soreness, I pulled on my coveralls. They complemented my sagging spirits.

Tenderized like meat, we were herded into another line. I hung back, staving off as long as possible the inevitable. Where was the guy in the RAF uniform with the message from the King?

What was this line? I saw the barber pole up ahead. The line moved fast. For haircuts? Bald heads came out the side door. Oh, no. My beautiful hair. My heart sank, lower and lower, until it got caught on the waistband of my shorts.

The kid in front of me went in and sat down.

The barber asked him, "Do you want to save your sideburns?"

"Yeah," he replied, "I'd sure like that."

"Then hold out your hands, palms up."

There were twenty barbers. These were not tonsorial artists. They were mechanics. There was no sweet smell or steam, no combs, no scissors, and there shouldn't have been any mirrors.

I sat down.

The barber began, "Do you want . . ."

"Don't shit me," I interrupted, "just go ahead and do what you have to do."

He laid the electric shaver on one side of my forehead, zzzzzz down to the back. And zzzzzz down on the other side. From the crown he circled the rest of my head.

I was sheared like a sheep. There was a small tuft of hair left in front, a little ski chute to hang my hat on. It was just enough to leave me looking like a ding-ding. In less than two hours they had done it. I was so transformed, if I had been standing on my front porch, my own mother would not have recognized me.

Bald and baggy, we were hustled back to the sandy boot area. Like the Army summer camps, we were now going to strike our own tents.

Duck walks, like flat ladders, humped across the sand, forming streets, each to be named for its respective platoon. On each side of the "street" were numbered lots, railed in 2-by-4 fences. In the middle of the squared area, compactly rolled and tied, was a tent. By two's, we were assigned a numbered area.

"Pitch your tent," the order came, unencumbered by any instruction.

The engineering was easy enough, especially if you'd done it before. Sink the mast, center the canvas over it, tie the sides to the railing and unroll to the ground.

To the right and left, masts tumbled and tents enveloped the struggling recruits.

The drill instructors sat in their well-constructed quarters at the end of the "streets," watching.

The six of us who had been in the Reserves helped the others strike their tents. It was good to know we could help. Besides, if we didn't, we might be there all night.

When all the tents were secured and the "guide-ons" were posted, identifying the platoons, we were rewarded with a march to the PX where we were given a pail and a list of items to purchase. The inventory included a sack of Bull Durham tobacco for those who smoked; a box of long Marine matches; shoe polish; shoe brush; brass polish; toothbrush; tooth powder; and a sewing kit called "Mother's Helper."

Just what I always wanted!

But to most of the recruits this was a new world and they relished it. Ninety percent of them had spent life milking cows and taking Saturday night baths. Some of them didn't know what underwear was. All these kids wanted were the Dress Blues, the blue pants with the red stripe up the sides. They didn't know those were a long way off.

But for me? Well, I'd been around! I knew what it was like to be treated with respect as a cadet. I'd been courted by the Royal Air Force. I had some brains and here I was taking this shit from guys who joined the Marines to escape the Depression. It was like sitting in your own stuff!

Reveille was at 4 a.m. Taps was at 9 p.m. In between, we marched and marched. Outfitted in heavy-duty shoes and fortified with good food, we were kept hopping all day long. All day long! Wow, they didn't let us go. When one drill instructor got tired, another took over. But the boots kept right on going. During five-minute smoke breaks it was easy to fall asleep. Town? There was no such thing as town. NEVER. Town was marching by two's up to the PX to get two cookies and one piece of gum. Disciplining mind and body, we coped with three harsh elements: the asphalt, the sand and Corporal Gemoets.

Corporal Gemoets was our permanent drill instructor. He was the ugliest and rottenest human being alive. Three hundred pounds of TOUGH, he looked like a baby hippopotamus, both from the back and the front. His face was memorable for his ears that poked out beneath his campaign hat and stiffly pursed mouth. A smile would have pained his face. The guy was all muscle. He worked as a bouncer in a bar in San Diego on Open Post weekends. He had arms like thighs. An American flag was tattooed on his right upper arm. When he flexed his muscle, the flag waved. His specialty as a drill instructor was marching. Some kids didn't know their right from their left. Corporal Gemoets taught them. On the heels of the Corporal's shoes were big steel plates like horseshoes, and he carried a doweling stick, one-half inch wide and thirty-six inches long.

"Hut, Who, He, Hor; Hut, Who, He, Hor; Cadence Count . . ." If someone was out of step, Gemoets was tuned to it.

"All right, who's the shithead?" (One time I recognized it was Archie, the kid I'd met on the train. His face and sense of humor were noticeably thinner.) Gemoets stepped out of the count of our march and into one of his own, his shoes sounding like a drum roll, KA-DUME, KA-DUME, KA-DUME. Moving in on the offender, the Corporal would take his stick and rap the kid sharply on the calf, or the leg, or the ass.

"Pick-em up, pick-em up, pick-em up." OR, he would knock the boy down and march right over him. Glaring down at the young recruit, Gemoets blasted, "If it's sympathy you're looking for, you can find it between shit and syphilis in the dictionary!"

While learning the Manual of Arms, a recruit dropped his rifle.

Gemoets cried, "What did you drop?"

"My gun."

"Your what?" warned Gemoets.

"My gun."

"In the Corps we refer to it as your Piece, your Rifle, and you will pick it up NOW."

Then Corporal Gemoets marched us off the parade ground and to the boondocks into the porous sand near the water. He drilled us in a continual "about face" until we dug ourselves into deep holes. Hardly able to pull up our feet, we labored to follow the repeating order. That night the kid who dropped his rifle got the hell knocked out of him behind the shithouse. He never dropped his "Piece" again.

Two weeks passed and I received a "Dear John" letter from the Clayton-Knight Committee.

"We're sorry, but with the tightening of the Neutrality Laws, we can't interfere with the personnel in the branches of the U.S. Services."

SHEEIIT. It was a form letter completely ignoring the fact that I had already been accepted. That blew a hole in me. I was going to have to stick it out and stay with the Corps until the end of my enlistment in '42.

By now, we were all integrated into the Marine regimen.

We rolled our own cigarettes and smoked with the announcement, "The smoke lamp is lit." When we finished, we stripped the cigarette butt, breaking open the paper and tossing the tobacco into the wind. The paper was rolled in a tight ball and dropped.

Smoking was not an arbitrary decision. One boot smoked a cigarette after lights were out. The next day, Gemoets handed him a full pack of cigarettes and told him to smoke them all. Then Gemoets covered the kid's head with a bucket.

We shined our shoes to a mirror finish.

We learned to care for our clothes, to keep them clean. I put trousers on by holding the cuffs to the waist so neither cuff would touch the floor. We washed our clothes in outdoor basins with brown Marine soap and hung them on lines over the sand to dry. The ironing room was close to the latrine at the end of the Platoon Street. Using newspaper as dampening clothes, we ironed the pleats into the suntans, three pleats in the back of the shirt, one over each breast pocket and center pleats in the trousers.

We moved fast. One whistle meant to jump into assembly in the front of the tent. Two whistles and you grabbed a pre-tied tie, pulling it on over your head, ready to march to mess hall. Three whistles and in "zoom" it was a Class A uniform, the tie clip and *all* buttons buttoned.

Buttons were a specialty of Platoon Sergeant Land. He was a passive 118¾ pounds. He didn't bark orders or become physical with the boots. He got even by pulling off the unbuttoned buttons.

We were lectured on the Corps tradition and history—the oldest branch of the U.S. Military Services—how to handle the flag and respect rank. We were taught identification of ships. We were acquainted with mechanized equipment, including the new type of motor vehicle called a "jeep." We were instructed on the use of gas masks, and how to discover and disarm land mines. We had "chats" about venereal disease and how, if you expose yourself to it, to get to a first aid station for a PRO treatment. No PRO Kits were distributed. We weren't going anywhere.

We were drilled on the Manual of Arms, the care and handling of our "Best Friend," our "Pal," our weapon, the Springfield Thirty-Ought-Six (.30-06) Rifle.

Along with the tightly made beds, parades on Saturday, church on Sunday, and the mashed potatoes and gravy, was the one unalterable constant . . . marching.

"Bing, bing, bing, bing," in our hobnail boots we marched over the endless macadam, more than a mile and one-half of parade ground, from one end to the other, always looking straight ahead. Always. Even when someone made a mistake.

On the command of "forward march," a trainee did an "about face." I heard the people behind me falling like dominoes.

"HULT!" Gemoets barked. "STACK YOUR WEAPONS."

We stacked our rifles on their swivels in groups of threes.

"FOW . . . WAD!" The Corporal was going to discipline the whole platoon. He marched us straight ahead into the San Diego Bay waters. We were in up to our necks before Gemoets gave two "column left" commands that marched us out. The kid who screwed up would get it that night and Corporal Gemoets and Sergeant Land would be watching through the shithouse window.

Mail Call was usually after lunch. Sergeant Land would stand in front of the platoon, call out the name and toss the mail aimlessly on the ground. The boot would pick it up and snap back in line.

On one occasion, as Land threw out the mail, he saw a letter that caused him to stop. He put the letter underneath the stack of mail. When all letters were distributed, he called, "La Chasse, two steps forward. The rest of you, dismissed."

"Come with me," Land ordered. I followed him into his tent.

"I know, I know," he began, "every now and then, in order to know how good their recruit program is, the Corps sends through a shavetail. YOU, you're a shavetail." He handed me the piece of mail that had been forwarded to me by my parents.

It was a renewal notice from GEICO—Government Employee's Insurance Company—car insurance I had taken out last year as a cadet. Assuming I had graduated, it was addressed, Lt. A.W. La Chasse.

Nothing I could say would dissuade Land from his conclusion. He, respectfully, looked down his nose at me.

Still, he knew I was experienced. I could train and march the platoon, which I often did. I was a proficient marksman. I *was* a good soldier.

I decided that was the only course to take the moment I saw Gemoets. I didn't want any part of that fighting behind the latrine, or bruises from Billy sticks or steel shoes. No, Sir. I made up my mind from the beginning. Gemoets would never wave his flag over me.

The Corporal was genuinely hated. One night he came close to being murdered.

My bunkmate was a hot-blooded kid who had probably lied about his age. He looked younger than seventeen. That day, while drilling in the Manual of Arms, Robert had anticipated a command.

"Right shoulder . . ." The completion of the command, "arms," had not been given. Robert had already thrown his rifle forward from his left shoulder towards a "port" position. Realizing his mistake, he reached for the rifle and dropped it on the boot in front of him.

"NEVER ANTICIPATE A COMMAND!" Gemoets screamed. He punished the boy by having him take his eleven-pound rifle and do "up and on shoulders," front and back, until he couldn't hold the rifle any longer and dropped the end of it on his head.

I was lying in my sack when Robert came in and got down on his knees next to me. The words squeezed between his teeth—"I'm going to kill him, I'm going to kill that goddamn Gemoets. I'm going to take my bayonet and twist a hole right through his heart."

"Hey, kid, sit down and let's talk it over," I urged him. "Listen, I know how you feel. We have all felt that way. But this is no solution."

Trembling and on the verge of crying, he said, "I've talked to some of the other guys. They're with me."

"What do you care about the other guys?" I asked. "You're the one that'll pay. And you will, too, because you know damn well you can't get away with it. You have a lot of fences to hop to get out of here. A short 150 feet from this bunk and you're off limits and anyone would know you're a recruit. You look like a recruit. Hell, you'd get an ass full of lead from a riot gun."

Robert remained on his knees looking at me while he thought about it.

"C'mon," I urged him. "We don't have long to go. Why don't you wait until we get to town and we're all in civvies. Then you can go for him. Besides, Gemoets is so tough he'd bend your bayonet."

Without a word, Robert got up and climbed into his bunk.

I tried to keep one eye open. I decided if he started for his bayonet I would fall off of my bunk and create a commotion, distracting him. He didn't get up. I fell asleep.

Coincidentally or not, a day or two later during a "rest break," Gemoets spoke to us, his single effort in personal communication.

"Now hear this," he began. With all eyes on him he paced in front of us slowly, as if he were taking an exact number of steps. Smartly, he turned around. Starting back, he said, "I know, I know, you're tired. I know that some of you are sorry, now, to be here." He stopped and turned to look at us. Holding his doweling stick behind him, his legs straddled, theatrically he went on.

"You don't like me. Some of you hate me, maybe enough to want to kill me. I've had threats before. Lots of 'em. Different kinds. I've been around a long time and it doesn't cut a damn with me. I'm tellin' ya, this is my job. I know it. You know it. And it's gonna get done." He squared his jaw and added emphatically, "That's the way it's gonna be."

Snapping his feet together and folding his arms above his belly, he concluded, "You won't find sympathy from me. From me you'll get discipline and respect for the Corps. If any of YOU don't like it, I'll put the gloves on with anyone of YOU, any time YOU want, any place. It's all right with me." He stood in a motionless amen. Satisfied, he went off by himself and rolled a cigarette.

The effect was profound. The guy was human *and* he had guts. Gemoets had epitomized the Marine Corps, but, more, he had regarded his boots as men. In a few short minutes, the little boys had grown up.

Training became easier. We slept until 5 a.m. and were allowed tailor-made cigarettes.

"Pick up your left, pick up your left . . ." We were marching better every day. We became the front platoon of new recruits. In perfect cadence, we marched before the review stands, sixteen people in step, in sweeping flanking movements, the feet moving up and down simultaneously.

Gemoets had taught us to march.

Physically honed into a Marine, mentally I was determined to fly. I stayed alert to all possibilities.

In a package of mail sent from home, I received a letter from the Army Air Corps. Using my ground school grades and my deportment reports from Santa Maria as references, the Army had invited me back into their branch of service, offering such fields as meteorology, navigation, bombing and photography. "I'd love to," I wrote back, "but there's this problem . . ." Whoever transferred from one service to another? No, I thought, it was an impossibility. My ambition, my goal, my dream to fly again had to remain in the Marine Pilot Program. Hoping for this, anticipating the return to an air arm of the Corps made it easier for me to tolerate the last weeks of boot camp including the "dirty" overnight camp-outs, bivouac.

The last ten days of the boot program were spent at the Marine rifle range in La Jolla. With full gear, we were marched in a route step, four feet apart, in single file to the range. Even though the La Jolla Camp was self-contained, an extension of the Marines Depot, it was a welcome change of scenery.

We all assembled for the first indoctrination by the permanent party, the rifle instructors. The sergeant outlined the training with a hard sell on the invaluable—-our best friend—the Thirty-Ought-Six (.30-06) Rifle.

"Picture a platoon of Japs coming over the hill, if you have to aim at Charlie in order to hit Harry, another Nip will already have shot *you*."

The instructor addressed us like a fatherly coach, so positive in his attitude that it was inevitable that we would become expert marksmen.

"After these ten days of training, you will have learned how to save yourself. You will have accomplished your mission."

A week to go. It was noon on Saturday. We had just finished practice with twenty-two calibers and I was back in my tent. One whistle blew. "TENSHUN!"

We jumped outside and stood erect in front of our tents. Someone was coming up our Platoon Street. That, by itself, was unusual, because we, the cadre, were at least one hundred yards away from the camp entrance and no one had anything to do with us.

Down the line I heard, "He's in uniform." "It's an officer." "An officer?" "He's wearing pink pants . . ."

I shook the sweat from my head, grabbing a look down the duck walk. It was an Air Corps Officer. Out of the corner of my eye I saw the familiar swagger, his feet with it, of my friend, Homer Worley.

"Hi ya, Al," he said, smiling as he walked by me.

I was so frozen, my mouth made a noise upon opening. Pop-eyed, I turned my head fully, looking after him. "Ho . . . Ho . . . Homer? Oh, Homer."

Corporal Gemoets, Sergeant Land and Sergeant Crockett stood in a brace, saluting 2nd Lt. Homer Worley, who outranked every-one on the rifle range.

I couldn't believe it. Homer out here? My eyes were watering. Homer talked to the DIs who were so astounded they forgot their men standing at attention. Homer turned around and gave the command, "At ease, men." Then he came back and followed me into my tent, the most prestigious tent on the post!

"I've arranged for a thirty-six hour pass for you. C'mon Al, let's go have some fun."

"But how did you know where to find me?" I asked. This was incredible.

"Your folks told me you were at the Marine Depot. When I got there, they sent me over here. O.K.? Now, get ready. We're set to go." His blue eyes laughed, his square, handsome face rested in a dimpled smile. He was delighted at the furor he was causing. I was dumbfounded.

The quick, short steps of Sergeant Land came down the duck walk. He peeked inside the tent and, in a prayerful posture, addressed Worley.

"Lieutenant, Sir, you're quite correct, Sir. The base had O.K.'d the pass. Thank you, Sir."

In my green wool Class A uniform, russet belt and shoes, I was out on a pass. I was happy and unhappy.

I was happy to leave the military and happy to be with Worley. We were close high school and college buddies. We had attended the CMTC Camps at the Monterey Presidio together. We had worked at the Ahwahnee Hotel in Yosemite. Homer had insti-gated my love for flying. He always wanted to fly way back in '36 when they were flying Jennies and little Porterfields. We all thought he was crazy. What? Fly in those dangerous things? But Worley

went right from Glendale College to Randolph Field and graduated from Flight School in 1939, an Army Air Corps Lieutenant.

I was unhappy because there I was, in that crappy green uniform, with my hair like a five o'clock shadow, a buck-ass private
and I was *his* football captain. It hurt my pride.

It was near midnight, Sunday, when Homer drove me back to
the camp in La Jolla. His black '31 Ford hummed along at fifty-
five miles per hour along the Coast Highway where for long stretches
it was the only car on the road.

"Boy, the weekend sure went fast," I said, with the deepest
regret. "It was great shooting the shit with Clell and Ace and
Jimmy."

"Yeah. We gotta do it again, soon."

"Oh, Homer. I hate going back. Thank God there's only one
more week. Do you want a cigarette?"

"No, thanks. I'm all smoked out."

"Guess I don't really want one either."

"So what happens, Al, when you finish boot camp? Where do
you think you'll end up?"

"I say my prayers every night. There are a lot of rumors going
around. Some people have requested Sea School. I never cared
enough for the water to be a bellhop for the Navy. Of course, I
don't want to be sent to Pearl Harbor nor to the Philippines,
either. If I did get an opportunity to fly and I was that far away it
would be "to hell with me.""

"Well, what are your options then? Or are there any?"

"Oh, sure. I can finish my enlistment, stay in until August
'42 or I might be accepted for Sgt./Pilot training."

"What are the chances for the last one, or should I ask?"

"You know the military, Homer. Keep your fingers crossed.
All of 'em."

"And your toes, Al. I know only too well. I keep putting in for fighter pilot and I'm still stuck in photo reconnaissance. Just like driving a truck."

"You, Homer, with all your training? Hey, can we stop at that diner up ahead? I'd like to take something back to the guys."

"What are *you* doing out there?" The guard at the rifle range was totally surprised.

"I'm in Platoon 86," I answered, feeling my independence diminishing along with my gift of two gallons of vanilla ice cream.

"It's O.K., Corporal," Homer reassured the guard, "he was with me." With a military flourish Homer signed me in. The guard stood there, perplexed and unmoving. "See ya, Al. Keep in touch." He corked me on the shoulder as he went by, his footsteps crunching on small rocks as he walked back to the Ford.

"Stay where you are," the guard ordered as he began phoning all over the post. He rang and rang but couldn't wake anyone. It was long after the taillight on Worley's black coupe disappeared down the road that I was still waiting to be admitted. The guard was irritated as hell that he couldn't get any response. He fumed at the situation. It was not in the Procedure Manual. I could have walked down the side road of the compound and across the ground to my barracks. It was as simple as that. I had no respect for a guy whose MP arm band was the biggest thing about him, but everyone had more authority than a boot and I was bound to wait just as long as he decided I would. By the time a jeep rattled out of the dark to pick me up, the ice cream I was holding had begun to ooze out of the cartons onto my shoes and into puddles on the gravel. As it melted in the warm September evening, so did my exuberance for the wonderful weekend that was now over.

But the pass and my association with Homer left me with a reputation, a prestige, a temporary fame, which I embellished to the hilt during that last week of training. I told everyone who would listen, how Worley, a talented drummer and superb swimmer, and I worked as box ushers at the Santa Anita Race Track; how we showed the motion picture stars to their box seats reserved for them by the movie studios—people like Judy Garland, Bing Crosby, Betty Grable, Rita Hayworth, Tyrone Power, George Raft, Jackie Coogan, Mickey Rooney, and the famous boxer, Slapsy Maxie Rosenbloom. I described how Homer and I swam relay races and played football in the Rose Bowl.

Al and Homer Worley working as box ushers at
Santa Anita Racetrack, Arcadia, California, 1939.

My fellow boots were awestruck. Even Corporal Gemoets and Sergeant Land were uncharacteristically subdued. They looked at me askance, a phenomenon in their military midst.

The following Friday, we were driven by truck to the Marine Base in San Diego. The next day we would graduate.

Saturday, September 13th, dawned in clouds.

We dismantled our tents and drilled in our last exercise, a march in the weekly morning parade. After lunch, without ceremony, we broke up. I threw my duffel bag into the waiting truck and climbed in, ready to go.

The truck drove slowly across the parade ground towards the front gates of the Marine Corps Depot. I surveyed, for the last time, the sinking sand and bleak, black asphalt.

With no regrets, it was goodbye to all that "sympathy."

4

"MIRACLES TAKE A LITTLE LONGER"

The Marine Air Arm was attached to the Eleventh Naval District based on North Island, across the bay from San Diego.

The pocket of my overalls sagged down my leg, heavy with my military history. I was waiting at the end of the line to plead my case to Major Kreiser who was dispatching people fast. I wanted to make damn sure that he knew I wanted to fly, that I *could* fly. I knew that once I was placed in the machinery of the infantry, I would be there forever.

"My God, fella, you've got more papers than I have," he said, as I handed him the sheath of material stacked in chronological order.

"I would like to sign up for Officers' Pilot Training," I blurted.

The Major shook his head. A private right out of boot camp? A private anywhere. No, that was impossible. Those people were handpicked. Gently, he tried to discourage me from flying.

"Well," I insisted, "then I want to sign up for Sergeant Pilot Training."

Pondering my qualifications, he concluded that, "Yes, well, that might be acceptable."

"When do I leave?"

The Major didn't know. He had never had occasion to request that category before.

Sergeant Pilot Training was spawned to protect the selectivity of officers. It was a convenient pocket to stash second-rate people, the men who could fly but were not considered officer material by the Corps. Flying was so new, very few people had applied.

After a lengthy telephone research, Major Kreiser advised me that the next training program was projected more than nine months ahead. I was willing to wait.

Officially assigned to Communications, I was part of a "casual" group awaiting permanent orders. Radio school, codes, Navy parlance, and sound equipment was the basis of my instruction. I also took messages and was available for emergencies, such as observer for lost aircraft. But the majority of the time I spent working out in the base fifty-yard swimming pool. For the military, war in peacetime consisted of inter-organizational athletic competition between the Services and their branches. Athletes were pampered and had access to special privileges.

Swimming a couple hours every day, practicing for one hundred-yard freestyle sprints, was a great way to keep in shape. I appreciated the gunnery sergeant who was our swimming instructor. He had the ability to coach us into a winning team.

The workouts gave me a chance to arrange my own time— time that could be extended into lazy afternoons of drinking beer in the recreation hall.

On weekends I turned to my first love, flying. For four dollars an hour, I rented planes from a private airfield. They were tandem-seated Porterfields and side-by-side Sylvair Luscombs.

Friends would pay for meals and transportation to go up with me and for the chance to fly. In each plane the steering column would be removed from the passenger's seat so we took a 2-ft. long screwdriver and stuck the one-inch handle upside down into the base where the steering column would be attached. With the screwdriver fitted in tightly, the passenger could then steer the ship with the blade. Looking through the mirror in the Porterfield, I could see that "shitty" grin come over the guy's face as he maneuvered the plane over the Imperial Valley with his makeshift "joystick."

For all the excitement of flying and occasionally dropping down into Tijuana, nothing pleased me more than my invasions into the Officers' Club.

Bunking next to me in my barracks was an Italian with the rank of corporal. He was small and slight, with a swarthy complexion, watery, romantic eyes, and big floppy feet. He and I often went to the mess hall together. I called him "Itie" for Italian and he called me "Frenchie" for La Chasse. He was an introvert, subdued, and acted like an inexperienced little boy. *Except,* it was uncanny the way he could match my stories about flying. In the right vernacular, he described his air experiences. Reluctantly, without trying to sell me, it became evident that Itie's own flying accomplishments buried mine. Even the planes I had only seen, the P-36s and P-40s (I had never heard of a B-17), had been flown by him. And then one day, he showed me his uniform. Itie was a major in the Italian Air Force!

The fact that Itie could fly rings around me was annoying, but the fact that he could be admitted into the North Island Naval Officers' Club delighted me.

As often as we could arrange it, Itie and I went to the club.

The base required that personnel enter and leave the premises in uniform. I would take the "nickel snatcher" across the bay and, storing my uniform in a rented YMCA locker, would change into the resurrected blue tweed suit. Catching the ferry back to North Island, I would meet Itie. Decked out in his black uniform swathed in gold braid, a little slit hat with the bakery ribbon, Itie was totally transformed. No longer the inexperienced, shuffling boy, he now carried himself erect and moved in the confident manner of an aristocrat.

Time and again, the Italian major and his civilian friend were admitted to the club, to the elaborate, inexpensive food, the good booze at fifteen cents a drink and to the girls. There were so many girls, *they* were ready to pay for it.

In the subdued lighting, with my hair grown out to the short cut everyone wore, my presence was never questioned. Of course, I was vague about my military status and I used all the air lingo I knew. When an officer that I had seen at the base asked, "Haven't I seen you before?" I'd answer, "Gee, I don't know. I'm from up north." Another questioned me, "I remember you from somewhere. Do you fly?" I admitted, "Civilian, yeah." When I felt I was stuck, I'd talk about the Clayton-Knight Committee.

Confident that I had all the qualifications of an officer, yet convinced that I would achieve no higher rating than a noncom, as a "civilian" I enjoyed beating the military caste system. Conversation was easy and with husbands out at sea, so were the women. As a private in the Marines, receiving invitations from officers' wives gave me a perverse satisfaction. They wouldn't have looked at me sideways if they had known my rank.

By early October, I had settled into a cushy existence.

I was swimming every day and our team was winning. In the afternoon, as a reward, I drank beer, shot the breeze and bowled. Duty was light and even exciting when we flew "Emergency Flights" in search of lost aircraft. Guard Duty was not my idea of fun, but compared to boot camp, totally acceptable.

By now, I was one of the "regulars" at the Officers' Club. I was booked well into the next year for weekend flying lessons and I had established home base with a couple of very cute dolls.

Besides the easy routine, the food was always the best. Navy provisions were first-rate and that included their food. It was while I was attached to the Marine Arm of the Navy Base at North Island that I learned to eat and love fresh, Eastern oysters. The Navy always had a plentiful supply.

Then, one afternoon, once again, my whole life changed.

I was on my second tour of Riot Squad weekend guard duty from 4:30 p.m. on Friday afternoon to 9 a.m. Monday morning, when I received a seventy-two word wire from Washington, D.C.

It ordered me to report for duty to the Army Air Corps at March Field Air Base the following Tuesday. I was to be sent to the Norden Bombsight Factory on the East Coast to take bombing instruction.

A MIRACLE! Heaven was knocking. But how was I to get out of there?

I ran all over the base. Everyone had left for the weekend. Only a skeleton crew remained. This was urgent. URGENT. I wanted to scream: "LISTEN TO ME. SOMEONE LISTEN! I'VE BEEN DRAFTED. WASHINGTON IS CALLING."

Feeling that I was falsely imprisoned, I ran from one corner of the base to the other looking for help. From a labyrinth of heedless motion I ended up at the desk of the weekend's duty officer. He just happened to be Maj. A.W. Kreiser, the commanding officer I had reported to the day I had arrived.

"Too bad you don't know your congressman," he said, half seriously. He made suggestions where I might call to get some information on transfer procedure, if, indeed, there was any.

I called March Field Air Base. I called the Commandant of Recruits in Los Angeles. I called everywhere and got nowhere. With every nerve popping, I had to relinquish the effort. There was nothing more I could do. I *had* to leave it in the hands of the Major.

To ascertain rank as a major in peacetime was so difficult the guy practically had to be born into the military. Still, Major Kreiser did not have the authority to release me from my enlistment.

If he hadn't cared, he could very well have let it ride, perhaps deny it on Marine priority or just postpone me indefinitely. I didn't know, maybe he respected my achievements: my college degree, my pilot's license, my two flying ratings, 1-s land and 2-s land, and that I had passed the flight test of the Clayton-Knight Committee. Perhaps it was because our first initials were the same. Whatever his reason, he came through.

Exactly one month before Pearl Harbor, after five weeks of communication with Washington, D.C., Maj. A.W. Kreiser signed my "ON POST DISCHARGE:"

UNITED STATES MARINE CORPS
Semper fidelis
fideli certa merces
TO WHOM IT MAY CONCERN:
Know ye, That Albert W. La Chasse, a Private of the
MARINE CORPS RESERVE
Who was enlisted at Glendale, California, on the 30th day of
August, 1938, to serve four years, is hereby—HONORABLY
DISCHARGED—by reason of
"special order of the Major General Commandant"
GIVEN under my hand and delivered at—NAS, San Diego,
California
this 7th day of November, 1941.

A.W. KREISER
MAJOR, U.S.M.C.R.
Commanding BAD-2, NAS

That same day I was driven by jeep to March Field, where the
Marine Police escort signed me out of their care and into that of
the Army Air Corps. As I walked through the field's gates, a glorious flush filtered through my body. Thank, God. I was back. It
felt so good.

Near Headquarters Receiving Station, I saw a sign posted over
the Engineer's Building that said it all. Nothing could have been
more appropriate. It read:

"The impossible we do right away. Miracles take a little longer."

5

BECOMING A GENTLEMAN

"Who are you?" the 1st sergeant asked.

Standing before him in my green, heavy wool, Marine uniform, I was an authentic unknown.

"What the hell is this?" he asked again, when I presented my cadet number 6586321. "Only seven digits?"

Impeded by the rapid expansion, the Air Corps was not able to cope with the hundreds of incoming recruits, including myself. Almost immediately after arriving at March Field Air Base, I was sent home on an undetermined amount of leave.

Comfortably based at home, employed, with plenty of time, it was the purest vacation of my life.

In the company of old friends and my favorite gal, Rheva, we made the familiar rounds to Hoover High School, Glendale College, the homes of Bud Hunter and Jack MacKenzie, the Arsenal Restaurant, Damon's Steak House, Raven's Malt Shop and Bob's Big Boy Diner.

Bob's Big Boy owner, Bob Wian, opened his twelve-stool lunch counter in 1936. He originated the double-deck hamburger and had the gift of never forgetting a face. Stepping inside the diner to the décor of eight-by-ten glossies of race cars, fifteen-cent hamburgers and endless refills of five-cent mugs of coffee, Bob would greet you by name. Any time we found him busy behind the counter, we would help wash and dry the stacks of utensils and coffee cups.

From Laughton's drive-in, to the bowling alley, to the sandwich houses and beer bars, to all the haunts of twenty years, in those several weeks we surrendered to the nostalgia of our youth. Nebulous to the times, no one knew that for us it was end of the season. Soon my friends and I separated to make our individual contribution to history. Some of those friends touched greatness. One was Homer Worley.

Homer came in on leave the weekend of December 7th. He flew into Glendale's Grand Central Air Terminal. He was with me Sunday morning when we heard the news.

"Any more pancakes, bacon, applesauce? What else would you boys like?"

My little German stepmother had fed us stacks of fluffy pancakes, at least a pound of bacon and plates of scrambled eggs. She couldn't pour enough milk, serve enough melted butter or hot maple syrup, and moved continuously, in and out, through the kitchen swinging door. In her white cotton apron, with her graying hair piled in braids, she hovered over us like we were visitors or important guests, almost in anticipation of times to come. Perhaps it was the recognition that our years of growing up were over.

And how we were comforted in the surroundings of crocheted doilies and overstuffed chairs, the smell of brewed coffee and fried bacon. There was security in those small, familiar rooms. Homer and I felt a warm insulation, like it was "Maple Street, U.S.A."

"I see where a lot of your friends are being drafted," my father said, peering over the Sunday morning paper. "You boys are lucky that you're where you want to be, in the Air Corps."

"Yeah, I'm happy, Pops. But I'm damn proud of being a Marine. That's the best military training anyone can get. I'll vouch for that."

"Oh, come on now, Al," Homer restrained himself. "You think that's military the way that guard handled you in La Jolla? He didn't know what to do."

"Aw, that was a first. I wasn't in his orders. No, I firmly believe that the Marines are the most disciplined arm of the military. Really."

"I'd argue with you, Al, but I've got more interesting things on my mind, like the Smith sisters. How 'bout going over to their house today? I'd love to spend some time with Billie. She's some doll. You think that maybe they'd like to see a movie? What's playing, do you know?"

"I think there's a new Abbot and Costello at the Alex. I'll call to make sure."

"Laura," my father called to the kitchen, "will you bring me some more coffee? And Al, is there someone at the door?"

"I'll see, Pop." As I walked to the front room my thoughts were on the Smith sisters and Christmas shopping. "Hey, it's Sylvia from next door." Our neighbor was always ladylike, neatly dressed and wearing lipstick. But, today, even though it was late in the morning she was standing at our door wrapped in a bathrobe with her hair in big, metal curlers. "Hi, Sylvia, is there some . . ."

"Turn on the radio, quick!" she screamed, as she rushed past me. "There's been some kind of bombing at Pearl Harbor. The Japanese!"

My mother, holding the pot of coffee, stood like the rest of us, in complete astonishment.

It was impossible. The Japanese? Sylvia *had* to be wrong. How could they fly all the way to Hawaii? The Magnavox console heated up past the static to the clearly audible ". . . that Pearl Harbor has been attacked. All military personnel will immediately report to their respective bases. I repeat . . ."

Homer was instantly transformed. Dramatically, his attitude, his body, his whole being, squared into an Air Corps Officer.

"Drive me to Grand Central, will ya, Al? I've got to get back."

Within one-half hour I had driven him to the air terminal, across the field to his parked plane. I watched him take off.

His ship, a high wing DeHavilland Observation craft, was so ungainly it seemed to defy all natural laws of aerodynamics.

Expertly, he maneuvered the craft into the air. Circling around me, he waggled the wings and then headed to his base in Northern California.

Homer was a hell of a soldier. He flew all kinds of aircraft from Fortresses to fighters during his tour in the Pacific Theater. I saw him after the war. He named a son after me. In 1946, while receiving aircraft for March Field, enroute over the Mojave Desert, Homer Worley cracked up in a P-80.

On December 8, I arrived back at March Field. The open and loosely protected base of a month ago was now locked and heavily guarded. Sentries in helmets, carrying rifles, patrolled the inside gates. Outside, work parties were constructing another barbed wire fence. It took me over an hour to be screened and admitted to the field.

California was panicky over the possibility of a coastal invasion. Yet, even with the threat of momentary enemy attack we were so unprepared, it took a month before I received my assignment.

> "Aviation Cadets . . . will proceed without delay to Ellington Field, Texas . . . for further instruction in specialized bombardier training . . . I certify that the above listed Aviation Cadets were last rationed at this station to include the noon meal and departed this station January 9, 1942 at 2 p.m."
>
> Mark P. Manion
> 1st Lt., Air Corps
> Assistant Adjutant

Ellington was preflight Ground School for bombing. The primary instruction was in mathematics. Starting in arithmetic, we went through logarithms and into spherical trigonometry.

Spherical trigonometry? Lucky for me and others in our class there was an intelligent kid who reduced the complicated headaches to five or six formulas. He was heavy in candy bars and cigarettes while we were lightened by memorization of those formulas that enabled us to make the corrections in height, drift and altitude, resulting in an accurate calculation for the proposed bomb drop. Actually, the mathematical instruction served as conditioning to appreciate the sight, for it would compute the problems automatically. Other courses in Ground School were logistics, history, intelligence *and* another round on venereal disease.

Local families tried to do their part in the war effort by opening their homes to cadets and entertaining them in a "home away from home." While waiting for a bus to take us back from one of those family dinners in River Oaks near Houston, I saw a newspaper headline that startled me:

"AIR CORPS TO INCREASE PERSONNEL TO 2,000,000."

Lots of guys named Jones. We had our share at Ellington: Shedrick Jones, Davey Jones, "Casey" Jones and Kenny Jones. Butterball, I called him. If you couldn't like Butter, you couldn't like anyone. I met him at the La Mar Hotel in downtown Houston. Everyone at our table was on the dance floor but us.

"Looks like we're left to buy the next round of setups," I said.

"Yeah, looks like we're stuck all right," he agreed.

Reaching over to shake his hand, I introduced myself. "Hi, the name's Al. Al La Chasse."

With a solid handshake he responded, "Glad to meet you, Al. I'm Kenneth Jones. Call me Kenny."

"Where you from?"

"Alva, Oklahoma," he beamed.

"You look it."

"Where you from?"

"Glendale, California, just north of Hollywood. Hope I look it."

"Yeah, but don't worry. Youth is on your side." The large, brown eyes betrayed the poker face. Kenny Jones was game for any snot-nose remarks I had. He egged me on.

"Glendale, hmmm," his blond eyebrows creased as he asked, "Isn't that where all those movie stars are buried?"

"At Forest Lawn, yeah, but there are plenty of other attractions."

"I wouldn't call that a very lively town," Kenny punned, happily.

"Listen, there are plenty of live stars around Glendale. I suppose from the sticks of Oklahoma you've never heard of Bing Crosby?"

"Bing Crosby? The Crooner? He lives in Glendale?"

"Well, no, but he almost ran over me once. It was on the corner of Wilson and Central avenues, next to the Gilmore Gas Station. I started to cross the street and he drove through the intersection just as the traffic signal's semaphore raised to stop. He was driving a yellow La Salle. The roadster convertible had black trim, big wheels and a compartment next to the seat above the running board where the golf clubs were stored. In his hat, scarf and pipe he was as recognizable as any California landmark and was probably on his way to the Oakmont Country Club for a round of golf."

The waitress stopped at the table. In her abbreviated cowboy costume she epitomized the cute and perky girls of Texas.

"Ya'll ready for another setup?" she drawled.

"Bring a round for the whole table and more ginger ale for me. How about you, Kenny, do you want another Coke?"

"Thanks, Al."

"And another Coke."

"Ya'll don't go 'way now, hear?" Walking away, she winked at Butter.

"But," I continued, "there are stars, big stars, that live in Glendale. Marion Davies, for instance; she poured me a glass of lemonade."

"When was that?" Kenny asked, intrigued.

"When I was a Parcel Post truck driver. She had a big Spanish home on Riverside Drive that backed up to the waterless Los Angeles River. Her neighbor was Jean Parker. Anyway, I was always delivering packages to her. Tobacco companies used to send her cartons of cigarettes and hotels were constantly returning personal items she had left in their rooms. One package fell apart as I handed it to one of her servants. 'Oh, not again,' the maid said as a pair of panties and a bra fell out."

"What size bra?" Kenny inquired eagerly.

"38 D. Cripes, I'm sure I was going to grab it and check the size. Now, can I go on?"

"O.K. O.K."

"So, one day when I delivered a package, she was having a swimming party. Marion Davies came out to the big iron gates herself, to let me in. She took my hand and led me up to the bar and poured me a drink. She looks just like she does in the movies: little, pretty and very charming."

"Did you grab a feel?"

"You, Kenneth Jones, have no class."

"You, Al La Chasse, were a delivery boy. What else did you do?"

"I grew up on the Warner Brothers Studio in Burbank. A bunch of us kids used to play on the movie props in the back lot. We rang the bell in the train engine, climbed over the riverboat and chased each other as we played cowboys and Indians in the towns of empty building fronts. When we saw the security guard coming down the dirt road, we'd hide."

The petite brunette served the fresh setups. It was cheap enough that I didn't mind paying for it. After all, I was from Southern California.

I poured some bourbon from the bottle of Four Roses to stiffen my ginger ale.

Kenny drank his Coke straight.

Glibly I went on advertising my hometown. "You know, in Glendale, major studio previews are shown at the Alex Theater. When a "sneak preview" is shown at night, they turn on the lights of the spiral needle on top of the theater and the huge klieg lights on the front sidewalks. I worked the parking lot adjacent to the theater. I've parked the cars of stars like, uh, Victor McLaughlin,

Alan Jenkins, Warner Baxter, Clara Bow, Joan Blondell, Ted Lewis and oh, yes, Errol Flynn."

"Errol Flynn?" Kenny asked in disbelief.

"Yeah. Good lookin' guy. He tipped me a buck."

Jones was entranced and so were the others who had come back to the table. They were pulled by the names of stars. I was on stage, live from California.

"Oh," I bragged, "I've seen more movie stars than you've seen on the screen. Why, you can bum a ride on Hollywood Boulevard and nine times out of ten the guy will have been in the movies. Hell, you can bump into the stars right on Hollywood Boulevard, or even at the beach."

"No kidding?"

"No kidding. Some buddies and I were doing flips on Muscle Beach at Santa Monica, when Jimmy Durante came out of his house to watch us. The 'Schnozz' had on a small, gray T-shirt and shorts. His legs looked like gangly tree branches. I remember when he stepped over the sidewalk's curb it took awhile for the knobby joints to get it together. We asked him, 'You Jimmy Durante?' He angled his face and shook his tongue against the side of his cheek and said, 'The one and only.' He invited us into his home to make ourselves a sandwich."

"But I've told you enough about where *I* come from. How about where you're from, Kenny. Any movie stars there?"

"Well," Kenny paused.

Obnoxiously, I teased, "I know, I know, it's a one-horse town where the flies take turns on the horse and the police force is a swell fellow."

Kenny shrugged. "Sure, and all those oil fields . . ."

"California has Signal Hill."

"And cattle," Kenny added, undiminished.

"We have herds of them on location in Calabasas . . ."

"And waving fields of wheat," he contended, ebullient.

"Sounds like Fresno. Oh, Kenny, give up. From the blue waters of the Pacific Ocean to the snow-capped peaks of the high Sierras, there *is* no place like California."

Kenny leaned over and corked me on the shoulder. "Wait until you visit Alva, Oklahoma, Al. You'll change your mind."

I called Kenny "Butterball," not because he was fat. He wasn't. He was a little under-conditioned for a young guy with a protruding waistline and a round face. In a drill the officer said to Butter, "Draw your hips level." I thought, "He'll never do it." The officer went on, "When you're at ease, you should look the same as when you're at attention. Don't worry, we'll get that off." It didn't matter how much weight Kenny put on or took off. Whenever he did push-ups, his gut stayed on the floor.

Some kids sweated all the time; about classes, about the way they looked, about flying. Not Kenny Jones. He entertained the moment and was always hanging out for the bright tomorrows.

". . . the following named Avn Cadets . . ., Class 42-7, 8, 9, this sta, will proceed from this sta immediately to ACAFS, "Air Corps Advanced Flying School-" Albuquerque, New Mexico . . .

". . . Aviation Cadets listed on this order were last rationed to include SUPPER March 18, 1942 and departed this station 8 p.m., this date."

For the Commanding Officer:
WILLIAM N. REESE
2nd Lieut., Air Corps,
Assistant Personnel Officer

It was shivering cold when we arrived at the training center in New Mexico. But it was dry and clear, perfect weather for the Bombardier School's flight phase.

Outside the rural community of Albuquerque, in the desert, were a group of marked ranges, each having one or more targets. It was the job of the bombardier to select, navigate to, and bomb the assigned target. The aircraft we flew were twin-engine Beechcraft, AT-11s. Equipped with a greenhouse nose and bomb bay doors, it was a neat little aircraft, often used as limousines for officers.

Al, showing the imprint of a bombsight circle around his right eye, with a friend, coming off flight line on bombing range field.

Our commanding officer, Major Borecky, had been a commander at the CCC Camps and knew from experience how to handle young men. As opposed to Marine Corporal Gemoets' use of fear and muscle, the major used positive psychology. One week after we got there, he relaxed mess hall privileges to provide his officers, including those of us who were one-half officers, with a limited amount of beer. Less than one-third through the program, he urged us to order our "pinks," our officers' uniform, in the face of the accelerated schedule.

To some cadets, the rewards would make no difference. Some men simply couldn't take flying. That was the paradox of the training program. After spending thousands of dollars on each cadet in Ground School, the management was now going to find out if the kid could fly.

In the Marines, if you couldn't make it as a marksman, you were a "shithead." In Bombardier School, if you couldn't take flying, you were a "dog face" or a "mud hen." And in this school, too, the only sympathy was found in the dictionary.

In a practice flight out over the Rio Grande, the other cadet flying with me became ill.

Activated electrically, the solenoids release their pins and, with the whine of the gears, the bomb bay doors opened. A mass of particles blew through the cabin. The boy took one look and vomited his Friday lunch of fish and tomatoes. Red masses flew across the cabin, splattering against the bulkhead, the seat and me. In the cold air the undigested matter bubbled and began freeze-drying. I pulled the Klaxon Horn. I saluted and, pointing to my classmate, screamed, "Sickness back here, Sir." The master sergeant instructor and the pilot looked back at the blotches of red and the pale, sick kid. Restrained by his safety belt, swaying in his seat with his tongue hanging out, he continued to regurgitate.

The pilot was madder than hell. The kid was not air material and *that* was unforgivable. Swearing loudly, the pilot turned the plane around and headed back to the field. Diving down to the runway and pulling to a jolting stop, the pilot got out and blew a whistle. Buckets of water were brought to the plane for the sick cadet to clean up his own mess.

Many of the pilots were unnecessarily hostile, so intently did they dislike their assignments of flying training ships in training commands. It was obvious some of the pilots were screw-ups who barely made it. They had little patience with the trainees. Their attitude was difficult to take, especially since we were all plagued with the fear of washing out. I was not spared.

The bombing targets were numbered in Roman numerals with a large letter N placed at one end of the range to indicate direction. There could be as many as four numbered targets to one range. At night the bombsight field was circled in lights. One night's bombing practice I had planned the logistics and navigated to the selected target. Just as I got ready to bomb, I saw a plane below me dropping its bombs on my target. My pilot was furious. "Goddamit, you've picked the wrong target! I'll have you in the Walking Man's Army for this."

I didn't think I was wrong, yet the accusation was very disturbing. The whim of a pilot could end the career of a cadet.

He reported me. I was called out of class the next day to give an account of the incident. The course I had chosen was proved accurate by the films that were taken in the ship's camera. I was not teamed with that pilot again. After that, school went smoother.

The pilots of that Bombardier School were of another breed. They were led by a commander who was more hotshot, more daring and perhaps more hostile than any of the others.

Flying near the Rio Grande, the commander, who was a classmate buddy of my pilot, settled his plane over ours. With the right wing of his craft positioned on top of the left wing of ours, I could see from the nose that he was no more than a few feet above us. I had enough flying experience to know how dangerous that was. Ground thermals—hot or cold masses of air—could instantly move a craft up or down. But, if that wasn't bad enough, the command pilot dropped into the river's canyon with us following directly behind. Was there enough room for the wings? What if someone was flying in the opposite direction? Negotiating the sharp turns, we flew low over the curling water. For more than two minutes at a speed of 125 miles an hour, as I watched the jagged edges above me, the multi-colored fringe of bluffs and the green beds below, I repeated to myself over and over, "If we can just get out of here." Climbing out, the two aircraft resumed formation until, closing towards the base, they broke apart. I knew I did dumb things when I flew at Santa Maria, diving in and out of clouds and flying between oil derricks when I couldn't tell the distance between them, but the difference was that then *I* was the pilot.

When we were not flying in the air, we were flying a bomb trainer on the ground day or night. The trainer was about fifteen feet high and looked like scaffolding on four wheeled legs. Electronically energized, it was steered by another person. As we drove over a huge map on the floor, following a specific mission target, sometimes a sea-craft, we would simulate precision bombing with the Norden bombsight.

Easing the tribulation of Bombardier's School was the college town of Albuquerque.

It was a small town. Two blocks from the main road there was nothing but farms and open spaces. Private girls' schools, established in Albuquerque because of its isolated environs, invited cadets to their dance. The girls were horny, but the dances, held in the gyms, were heavily chaperoned. The high doors were bolted and chained except for a smoking exit and that was guarded.

The happiest times I had in Albuquerque were provided for me by Butterball's aunt and uncle.

"How is your mother, Kenneth?"

"She's fine, Aunt Gloria."

"Is she still making those wonderful patchwork quilts of hers?"

"Oh, yeah," Kenny nodded.

"I haven't seen Aggie for the longest time; ten, maybe eleven years now." A sigh exaggerated the thin lines around the aunt's eyes and mouth. "Time goes by so fast." She patted the perspiration from her forehead and smoothed the lap of her apron. Folding her arms, she reminisced: "You know, Al, Kenneth's mother and I look quite a bit alike although I'm somewhat taller. We are, in fact, similar in many ways. We always liked the same things, but Aggie has something I don't: a knack with a needle. My lands, how that girl can sew!" The smile at the recollection broadened as she looked around the table, as if she was counting her blessings: her two daughters, Elma Mae and Florence; their friend, Janet; Kenny and myself. Then, snapping back to duty, she urged, "Now don't be shy, boys, help yourselves. Kenneth, have another pork chop. Al, how about you? Have some more chicken? Corn? Biscuits? I have some hot in the oven."

"No thanks, Mrs. Williams," I declined. "You're a wonderful cook. Everything was delicious." And it was becoming more so. Fortunately, Janet was seated next to me. Smiles had passed between us and I now had my hand resting on her leg. The fact that she didn't push it away was very inviting.

"How is training going?" Elma Mae asked. "Is it awfully scary?"

"No," Butterball said, swallowing a mouthful of mashed potatoes. "Nothing's scary except maybe the instructors. Some of them are kind of hard to get along with."

"Yeah," I agreed. "Most of them act like they've been out of high school for two months. They all want to be fighter pilots. Some of them pretend they are, the way they hedgehop to the bomb sites."

"Florence," Gloria addressed her youngest daughter, "pour the boys some more lemonade and chip some more ice. That'll cool us down. Then you two girls can clear the table."

"You do a lot of flying?" Janet asked, wide-eyed.

"Oh, sure," I answered casually, my fingers making smooth little circles just above her knee, "but there's indoor training, too. They have these contraptions that move around the floor, supposedly to simulate bomb runs. I call them 'Rube Goldbergs' because they're always breaking down."

"Well, it's just wonderful having my sister's little boy here!" Aunt Gloria reiterated her pleasure, her dark eyes beaming familial love on a fidgeting Kenny. "I have some pictures of you and your brother, Clyde." She started to rise from the table. "Why don't I get some of them and we can . . ."

"Mother," Elma Mae interrupted as she removed her plate, "it's so hot. Why don't we take the boys to the plunge today? We can look at pictures another time."

"Well, all right." Kenny's aunt sat back down. "Yes," she nodded, "you boys will come often. Your uncle, Kenny, will be back the first of the week and I know he'll expect a lot of visiting."

Florence set the rhubarb and peach pies in front of her mother who began slicing them. "You know, Al, Kenny was a big baby. Over ten pounds! His mother sent me a picture of him and described him as the roundest, pinkest, most adorable . . ."

Graduation of Bombardier Class West Coast 42-8 took place on Saturday morning, June 13, 1942, at ten o'clock. We were presented our diplomas by Col. Frank D. Hackett, AAF, and were administered the oath of office by Maj. Antone Borecky, AAF.

Of the eighty-seven men sent from Ellington to Albuquerque, all of whose names began with the initials J-Z, seventeen did not graduate.

Between March 18 and June 13, 1942, the Army Air Corps became the Army Air Force.

With my commission in hand, dressed in uniform "pinks," I had finally made it. I was now declared by an order of Congress, not only a 2nd Lieutenant in the U.S.A.A.F., but a gentleman as well.

Al, (kneeling) and Kenny Jones, (Butterball) behind him
in dress uniform with friends.

6

WENDOVER

... Wendover, Utah ... It's out there on the west side
of what is known as the Great Salt Lake Desert, smack on
the Bonneville salt flats where all the fancy high speed auto-
mobile activity has taken place through the years. Good
place to land and take off; that was about all you could say
for it. In fact you just *looked,* and you wanted to take off
right away.

General Curtis LeMay [2]

"... Wendover Field ... more like Leftover Field ..."
Bob Hope

Wendover would become a training ground for the giant B-17s,
the B-24s and B-29s. For forty-eight months during WW II, it
would contain five thousand to fifteen thousand Air Force trainees. It was the field on which the atomic bomb crews would train
for their Hiroshima and Nagasaki missions.

On June 15, 1942, I received orders to report to AB, Salt Lake
City, Utah, ... "there-to without delay," ... On June 19, I was
assigned to Wendover Air Base ... "reporting upon arrival to the
CO there-at for duty." My CO was Lt. Col. Curtis LeMay.

There were only a couple of us who reported to the base that
morning. With all my Marine and Air Corps Cadet training fused
into one salute, I announced with pride, "Lt. Albert La Chasse
reporting as requested, Sir." Along with the other officers, we stayed

at attention until he looked up from his desk, returned the salute and put us at ease.

"O.K. gentlemen, sit down. We're sure glad to have you fellas here. How was your trip?"

Thick neck, set jaws, piercing eyes that looked right through you, with a head of hair like swirled chocolate frosting, Curtis LeMay exuded command and determination.

"We're putting something together here that's going to do a lot for America. It's going to take hard work, but we'll get the job done."

Holding a stubby cigar the size of his fingers, his tie loosened and papers massed on his desk, he continued.

"There are some old-timers here, by old-timers I mean the people who had their problems out at Pearl. But the rest of us are new and we are all getting started together. Now, for the time being, there won't be much of a schedule, not until we get more personnel. In the meantime, you can pick up your assignments in the outer office."

He concluded our meeting by inviting us to "a little party at Stateline, tonight. We'd like to buy you a drink."

The party was generally a get-together to show that the brass could get along with the underlings. And it worked. Everyone got along great. The brass stayed together and the underlings stayed together. I really didn't know how to go up to a colonel and tap him on the shoulder, nor did anyone else. It was like, "Sir, may I speak now?" That was no party. I'd rather get a drink and find a shavetail like myself, someone I could relate to.

"What class are you?" "What field? Randolph? Albuquerque? Santa Maria? Grand Central? Alamogordo?"

LeMay walked in chomping on a cigar, surrounded by high-ranking officers. With a drink in his hand, he moved around, deep in conversation. He was still at the base, at his desk, working.

I didn't know what to expect, but I did look forward to some kind of formal welcome. I kept within earshot of the circulating LeMay, hoping when he made some announcement I'd be able to hear it. I never tried to get too close, not that you could if you wanted to, with his aides always around him. Just as you fly in formation, they walked in formation; one was two steps behind, the other three steps behind, and they'd kick you out of the way to stay precisely in that order.

Still, when the CO moved, I'd move and then I'd find he was just going over to say hello to Charlie. One time I thought he was really getting ready to do something and he went into the john.

I waited all evening for the party to jell. It never did. There were no names, no introductions, no organization. It was scary. If this is the way they run the Air Force, what had I gotten myself into?

The base was almost as formless. Poor LeMay, he needed all the help he could get.

Formerly an emergency landing field, Wendover had been used primarily as a practice-bombing target for the Salt Lake Base. As opposed to March Field and Ellington, Wendover was so loosely put together even Hitler could have walked in. Everything from chain-link fencing to sideboards had been thrown up in an attempt to cut it off from the main road. There was a checkpoint at the front gate, but the rest of the base was wide open. The only security Wendover had was its own isolation.

Though the Army Corps of Engineers had posted their sign and was at work, the base was still primitive.   .

A couple of old flying socks flapped in the salty wind, remnants of its recent civilian past. There were tents and a dozen single-story barracks, so quickly thrown together they were hardly more than shells. They had wood slats on the outside and tarpaper inside— the only insulation against occasional squalls. They kept out the water, but the wind played hell with them. At night it wasn't unusual to see some guy's blanket being buffeted through the room by gusts of chilly wind.

A few of the barracks had adjoining toilet facilities and communal showers. Those were taken on a first-come, first-serve basis. The men that came later were assigned barracks that had none and they had to use separate facilities that were scattered over the post.

A utility buildir   vas used as a combination PX and church. Four mess halls were under construction. Headquarters was housed in an old wooden building with a big front porch, a convenience for temporary parking of the B-4 bags. There were some maintenance buildings for aircraft, a couple of ammunition dumps and a post theater, the one substantial structure on the base.

Down at the flight line, an impoverished assortment of aircraft edged the taxi strip. About ten aircraft in all, there were several Douglas A-20s, a B-18A, some very worn B-17s, a twin-engine cargo C-46 and two sleek Beechcraft used for ferrying in brass. There were two landing strips, one runway, and a second runway under construction.

The "eyes and ears" of the airfield was located just off the flight line. Accessible by stairways, Wendover's Tower was a second-story glass room built on top of a storage building. The radio equipment was technically undependable so that the big, faded orange windsock was a visual necessity and so, too, were the red and green flares that signaled stop and go to the aircraft.

Wendover was a lonely, skeletal post with no vegetation, and only the sound of the train running between the base and the highway was a reminder of the civilized world I had known. To me, it was what a Foreign Legion post might look like without the palm trees.

For the first few days, as LeMay had predicted, there was very little to do. I milled around looking for a familiar face, while living out of a suitcase and checking bulletin boards. I was early enough to be able to select a barracks that had a latrine and was centrally located. It would eventually be designated the 367th.

Processing at Wendover was minimal. One of the suggested instructions was making out a will. I stopped by the Legal Section of Headquarters and signed the preprinted form naming my parents as beneficiaries. In the Finance Section of Headquarters, out of my monthly total pay of $187 (of which $40 went for bachelor quarters), I allotted a portion to be sent home and another amount for the purchase of War Bonds. Then I followed the odor of mothballs to the Quartermaster.

The United States Army Air Force Quartermaster Corps was the same as in any other service: pure crap!

The personnel all had voices that climbed up from their butts and escaped through their teeth in a guttural, nasal hiss. The Quartermaster Clerk would happily dismiss each item on my requisition list.

". . . don't have this . . . don't have this . . . this is back-ordered . . . hm-m, back-ordered . . . hey, we got this." I ducked as I saw the blast coming. He was going to shout it in my face: "HEY, ED, GET ME A CCNY4563897, ONE EACH GI FOR THIS GUY."

A package of twelve OD handkerchiefs came flying at me, mothball dust streaking behind it like a vapor trail. They were bound in string and tied in complex knots. The way to open them was with scissors, but there wasn't a pair on the Post. Finally, I burned one of the strings with a cigarette. The handkerchiefs were too ugly to use on my own nose, so I used them to polish the nose of the ship.

"But, this isn't my size." The protest was in vain.

"You want one? Then take it. It's as close as you'll ever get."

The same applied to the shoes. In contrast to the Marine Corps practice of fitting high-top shoes by having the recruit hold a bucket of sand in each hand while the Quartermaster Sergeant checked

the spread of the foot in the shoes, in the early days of the Army
Air Force, size was secondary to expediency.

With the other guys in the barracks, I traded and bartered the
flight boots, leather jackets and suntans, in an effort to get the
right size.

Quartermaster was an important cog in the military, a small
empire run with revenging authority. But it was a necessity we all
had to put up with.

As for my personal comfort, I was eating in a mess that was
temporarily set up in an empty barracks, buying gum and cigarettes which were all the PX had to offer and, just in case, familiar-
izing myself with the location of the bomb shelters.

The one surprise was the Skeet Shooting Range, a new sport
to me, nestled in an oasis about one mile south of runway #1. Like
a grotto, it had trees, grass and a spring of trickling well water. It
was a great way to practice marksmanship and a soothing change
from the arid landscape of the base.

The tantalizing attraction at Wendover was the Flying Fortress. I yearned to look one over, but everything was so confusing,
nothing yet assigned, that I didn't know if we were even allowed
on the flight line.

The third day, as some of us stood around Headquarters, I
thought "to hell with this" and asked if anyone wanted to go with
me to look at the Fort. A couple of us started for the flight line and
as we walked, others joined us. As we got closer, our excitement
grew to the point where we were running in a kind of all-out
"charge." When we reached the B-17, we stopped.

God, but she was big. I had never been next to anything so
big. At least four trainers would have fit, side-by-side, in her shadow.
To tell the truth, I was frightened. We all just stood there and
looked.

Cautiously, we wondered how to get inside, remembering you mount an airplane like you mount a horse, the correct way. You don't run around in front of it nor go anywhere near those damn props. You don't run into the tail surfaces and you never smoke while it's on the ground. The question was, where was the door? Well, if it wasn't on this side, it had to be on the other side. We walked around the tail, and there, behind the blister of the waist gun position, were the fixed steps of the opened door.

I wanted to look good, not overwhelmed, not embarrassed. Like, shit, I know what it's all about. So, it was with a modicum of dignity that I pushed my way in first. "Hey, hurry up." "Who's the bottleneck?" "Move on in, will ya?" "We wanna see, too." I had impressed no one but myself. I flattened to the port side as the other guys all tried to squeeze through the door at once.

"What position are you?"

"I'm a top turret gunner."

"I think that's up near the front. I've seen pictures of it."

"Hey, there's the radio operator's position."

"What's in there?"

I leaned out of the waist window. Because of the tail-wheel construction I was so close to the ground I could have jumped. We started to go forward when a blond kid in a butch came up from behind.

"I'd stand in line for tail anytime, but not in this bird. The tail back there is a belly position. That's not for me. Oh, no!"

"Sam, you'll take any damn thing they give you. Now, c'mon. Let's go up front."

I moved, we all moved, tenderly, respectfully, onto the eight-inch catwalk that spanned the bomb bay. A low whistle from some amazed throat wandered around us, over us, through the dim, cavernous ribs. To men instructed in two-engine AT-11s, we were stunned, shocked by the enormity of the B-17, its size, its space. We were Jonahs in the whale. Temerity was a whispered, "There are the bomb shackles." Boldness was, "Oh, shit!" "Hey, look up there, ahead, where the light's coming in. That must be the flight deck."

We explored the rest of the ship, totally inspired and incredibly awed by the Plexiglas turrets of gun placements, the hallowed cockpit of streamlined instruments, and the nose where you could even stand up. It was there that I lingered, that I drank it all in: the side panel of switches and indicators, the bombsight stanchions, the nuts, the bolts.

The B-17 was big and beautiful. Maybe someone in the Army Air Force, after all, knew what they were doing.

The bar & grill at Stateline was filled with the noontime crowd. I was at the lunch counter, exchanging background with a couple of other shavetails, when ol' Butterball walked up and socked me on the back.

"Hi ya, Al. You can stop worrying. Happy days are here again. Kenneth Jones has arrived."

I stood up, returned the sock on his shoulder, happy to see him. "Butter! Where ya been?"

"Alva, Oklahoma, of course, where else?"

"Alva, Oklahoma? What is that? Here," I offered him my stool at the counter, "pull up a chair and break bread."

Without protesting, Butterball sat down. "Thanks, Al. I'm really starved. I didn't have breakfast this morning."

"Help yourself, only give me my beer."

I stood waiting, nursing a bottle of Coors, while Butterball proceeded to finish my egg salad sandwich and added an order of his own.

"When you're ready, Butter, I'll take you through the hoop. We'll go down to my barracks and find you a spot. There are a lot of empties yet."

Two hamburgers, an order of a new item called "shoestring potatoes," and two Cokes later, we walked the block-and-a-half back to Headquarters. Butter picked up his assignment and his duffel bag off of HQ's porch. We headed for the barracks over the path of disconnected duck walks.

"Geez, this base looks pretty crappy to me," Kenny observed. "Is it as lousy as it looks?"

"Butter," I said, "you are now walking in the middle of mass confusion, although there *are* signs of glue around the edges, a lot more than when I got here. Still, no one really knows what's going on. Take yesterday for instance; a bunch of us went down to the flight line to look at the Fort and do you know we didn't know how to get in the damn thing? I mean, what a way to go to war!"

"Hey, a B-17? What's it like?"

"Well, it's big. I mean huge. It's hard to imagine anything that size getting off the ground. Listen, as soon as you're parked we'll go down and if the Fort is still there you can have a look for yourself."

"What about quiff? Any out here?"

"Butter, there are scads in Salt Lake City. Before I reported here I had time to take a reading and I'll tell you there is a real selection, lots of airline stewardesses stashed there."

Kenny's B-4 bag seemed to lighten. "Hell," he said, "the Fort can wait. First, let's put in for passes."

There were men, who, when they climbed into a cockpit, became a part of the airplane. They could be homely, even ugly. It didn't matter. Some men simply had instinct when piloting aircraft.

But, prior to the war and at the outset, appearances mattered very much. The candidates for flying school had to pass a rigid review board and only the beautiful young men were admitted to the inner-sanctum of pilot training. No sagging eyelids, uneven earlobes, or slumping posture were acceptable. The pilots were handsome athletes with a college background and a picture-post-card profile. They were the prototype of the All-American boy. And it was true of the pilots of the 367th, except for Oley whose qualifications had been weathered by age and experience. I had been at Wendover a week before I met my ship's CO, Capt. John Olson.

Captain Olson from Hyde Park,
Massachusetts, pilot of Snoozy II.

That morning I was outside Headquarters when I heard a plane buzzing the field. I thought it sounded like a P-38, but when I looked down towards the flight line I saw an aircraft I couldn't identify. With the wheels still folded and the wing imperceptible as it crossed in front of me, it silhouetted like a bullet, sleek and fast. Hungry for anything new, I ran to the landing strip along with the other curious of our isolated world.

The plane was a Curtis O-52. With the landing gear down it looked like a waddling duck as it tacked into a parallel park on the apron. It was pretty in its OD color with the white star insignia on the wing tips. The ship was all greenhouse and filled with camera apparatus. A dream ship for the Eagle pilot, it was the most impressive because it was the first damn piece of equipment I'd seen that looked ready to go to war.

I walked underneath the wing, admiring the projectile shape of the body and said out loud, "It's a bigger baby than I thought." A tall guy next to me agreed. "Yes, it sure fools you, doesn't it?" He turned and said, "Hi, I'm Olson," and gave me a strong "I like you" handshake.

"Glad to meet you. I'm La Chasse."

"You a bombardier?"

"Yeah."

"Hey, you're part of my crew."

I was surprised how old he looked, older than anyone I expected to fly with. His tan face accentuated the excessive laugh lines around his eyes and over his cheekbones. He was lean and except for the silver bars on his collar, he was casually put together, kind of raunchy military, in creased suntans, leather jacket, loosened tie, and a cocked garrison cap. He made me conscious of my own unpressed pants.

We had exchanged instant evaluations, but when I looked up from his shoes, which had had their last polish in cadet school, I saw that he was watching me. We broke into smiles.

"I'm from Hyde Park, Massachusetts," he said. "Where are you from?"

"California."

With a sense of anticipation, Olson asked, "You a movie star?"

"Naw. I'm not from Hollywood. I'm from Glendale, the bedroom city of Los Angeles. I haven't made my move to Hollywood yet. Lots of offers, though. Hey, tell me, what was your flight school?"

Putting his hands in his back pockets, he answered, "41-A."

"Hell. I washed out of 40-H."

In appreciation, he cracked a sly smile and said, "You're an old bird, aren't you?"

"Not as old as you look Captain, and the name is Al."

"Al, they call me Oley, or Swede, and damn it, stay respectful."

"Oley, Sir, where've you been? I've been looking for you."

"Oh, I've been here for awhile, doing a little chauffeuring of brass and some transitional training to the Fort."

That Oley had experience was evident by his rank. There weren't many captains around. I was lucky, for two reasons. I had been assigned to a guy who had background, not some giddy kid just out of West Point. More than that, he was comfortable to be with, not an iron ass who would display rank by barking orders.

"How do you like the Fort?" I asked him. "I mean the way it handles?"

"Easy. Trim her right and she'll fly herself. You'll have to fly one with me sometime."

"O.K. with me. I'd really like to try it. I've had some experience, enough to get myself a civilian license."

"Gets in your blood, doesn't it?" He took a pair of Calabar sunglasses out of his jacket and put them on. "Why didn't you go into the Canadian Air Force? That Clayton-Knight Committee was recruiting like mad. I heard about them back home."

"Believe me, Oley, when I say I tried. But the damn Marines had me by the balls."

"Who?"

"The Marines. I signed my John Doe as a Marine Reserve in college and I ended up doing eight weeks in Boot Camp at the Marine Base in San Diego. Once those gates locked behind me, the Clayton-Knight Committee dropped me like a hot potato."

"Al," Oley said, shaking his head and putting his arm around my shoulder, "you belong in *Ripley's Believe It Or Not.* Come on, let's go have a beer and you can tell me all about it."

The other pilots of the 367th gradually arrived. 1st Lt. Ralph "Bud" Gaston was Butterball's commander. Bud was a student of business administration at the University of Southern California. He had thick, black hair, which he was always combing, and dark, sparkling eyes with an engaging smile. Well-built, he personified the beautiful young men of the Air Force. Gaston had great personal charm and a professional stage presence. As a showman he could compel peals of laughter with his parodies on life. He loved good clothes and wore them to advantage. He was a skilled baseball player and skeet shooter. While Oley had graduated, Bud was the perennial collegiate. He was too versatile to specialize. In a way, he was plagued because he had so many natural abilities, but we all envied him.

There was mischief behind those blue-green eyes of 2nd Lt. John R. McKee. So much so, that he should have spoken with an Irish brogue. McKee came late to the 367th. He flew in from Hawaii where he had been sent for the Battle of Midway, which had ended three days before he arrived there. He had a wry sense of humor and referred to himself as 11/10th coward. He was tall with a good build and an all-round athlete. He loved baseball and had played center for the Calgary Canadian Professional Football Team in Alberta, Canada for $150 a game. Like Oley, he was casual and comfortable. The two were close buddies and used to take long showers at water-rationed Wendover, singing Irish songs as loud as they could in the hopes that someone would kick them off that miserable base. McKee could effect a doleful expression that would con you into anything. Before I wised up to him, he would put his arm around my shoulder and in humility say, "Albee, baby, would you do me a favor?" And, brother, I couldn't wait!

2nd Lt. George R. Buckey, on the same orders, came in from Hawaii with McKee. Buckey hailed from Trinidad, Colorado, was stocky and had a "short wheel base." Termed an A #1 guy by John McKee, George was cherubic with eyes that twinkled like Santa's.

As an athlete he played a superior game of baseball. His position as catcher was changed to first base simply because Buckey could not throw the bull (not the ball) like McKee.

1st Lt. John Ryan from New York State was tall and slender, with dark brown hair. He walked around with a pipe dangling from his mouth and he, too, had a lot of personality. He was sharp, and even things he shouldn't have done he did smartly. He executed beautiful, forbidden loops over Wendover Field. As Squadron Leader from Wendover to Westover Field on the East Coast, and with his CO, Harry Holt, on board, he led us in some low sightseeing up the Hudson River. In England, where there were no ice cubes, he took buckets of water and flew to a freezing altitude. Bringing back buckets of ice, Ryan introduced cold drinks to Thurleigh.

2nd Lt. Henry W. Terry was the Burt Lancaster of the 367th. Raw boned, tall, handsome, and ambitious, he was busy even when he was standing still. He was analytical and had a gift for making the right decision quickly. In England, when questioned by a general, Terry made suggestions about formation flying that the general adopted as his own. Lieutenant Terry became the Group Commander of the 91st Bomb Group at Bassingbourn Air Field in England and was nicknamed, "Terry and His Pirates."

2nd Lt. Don H. Eldredge was Gaston's copilot. Tall and blond, he had a wealth of intellect. He was a walking dictionary with a keen memory. Although he had an uneven voice, you could only marvel at the way he expressed himself. He would have preferred to be anywhere else than in the military, but since he was in it, the military became his total duty and he performed conscientiously. He wasn't enticed by vices, but he always stayed loose. Like his more gregarious peers, I valued his friendship.

Later arrivals rounding out the complement of the pilots of the 367th were 1st Lt. Earl Tunnell, 2nd Lt. James M. Stewart, and 2nd Lt. William L. Ely, who was the first fatality of our squadron.

My squadron's CO was Maj. Harry Holt. I met him at the second party that I attended at Stateline. The base was forming rapidly and this second party for officers showed the growing sophistication.

Along with drinks, there was a long buffet, and in comparison to the food at the base, quite sumptuous. There were delicacies like black olives, sliced rare roast beef and cakes dressed up like French pastries.

LeMay came through with his speech. He paid us all the necessary compliments, like "appreciating our patience and understanding amid the confusion and disorder . . ." The CO assured us that the line of command had been established and that orders were on their way. His words were old hat, but LeMay, intense by his very presence, had the ability to take repetition and clothe it in such sincere appeal that there wasn't one of us who didn't feel a revived determination and enthusiasm.

Among the officers introduced at that party was Harry Holt. He was about six feet tall with red hair and even redder mustache. Holt, probably more friendly with the pilots, was too remote for me to find him personable. Regardless, he faced a difficult job. With commodities like aircraft and personnel scarce, he had the responsibility to put crews together and assign aircraft; in short, to get a full squadron, not only formed, but flying. His seriousness was well founded. Ten months later, in 1943, in the April 24th issue of the *Saturday Evening Post*, an interview would be published "by cable" with Maj. Harry Holt "stationed somewhere in England." He was referred to as the Commander of the "Clay Pigeon Squadron."

Our full crew had not been assigned when Oley set up our first flight. There were other guys wanting to come along and they met us down at the flight line. I didn't see any humor in the fact that none of us remembered oxygen masks, but we sure brought parachutes!

Oley introduced some of our permanent crew: his copilot Norman Gates, navigator Bill Gise, and engineer Erwin Wissenback.

Erwin Wissenback, flight engineer and
"Top Turret" gunner on Snoozy II.

They were young, nice looking kids. It was then that I began to appreciate the lines on Oley's face.

Oley had had experience. Boy, did he. Rumor had it that he was part of the crews that were caught in the air by the Japanese the morning of December 7th while attempting to deliver B-17 Flying Fortresses to Hickam Field at Pearl Harbor. Hell, he'd already been in combat. I wanted to ask him how it felt, but since he didn't volunteer the information, I didn't ask.

I pulled myself up through the escape hatch and walked the few feet forward into the nose. Plugging my earphones into the nearest jack, I positioned myself solidly in front of the empty stanchions of the bombsight. I waited . . . in a long and "shitery" apprehension, wondering how in hell a plane so big was going to get off the ground.

An engine sputtered and coughed and the propeller launched a searing whine that sent ripples of vibration through the ship.

One after the other, the motors turned over, Oley feeding them, synchronizing the engines, until they hummed harmoniously.

We lumbered forward, taxiing down the flight line to our take-off position. The wings teetered from one side to the other, the metal skin creaked and quivered. At the end of the runway, Oley waited for the green flare. The roar was deafening as the ship revved for take-off.

Slowly we began moving, the tires rumbling over the ground, faster and faster; the outside skimmed by until it was nothing but a blur of olive drab. I held my breath, waiting for some shuddering climax when, in another instant, we were airborne. The flaps eased off and the wheels thumped into a fold somewhere underneath me.

The flight was spectacular. To the left of the Kennecott Copper Mine was the Great Salt Lake, chrome green at roadside, paling white where it lapped the sandy edge. Was it the reflection of salt water that created so much color? In the afternoon, flying west to east, the sun behind us, we were covered in a bonnet of yellow, orange and pink. Under the wing tips, shades of light blue sifted into deep purple. Ahead lay Salt Lake City with its identifying steeple of the Morman Temple and across from it, in summer canopies, the roof of the Hotel Utah. Flying over that clean, symmetrical city with the melted, mountain snow flickering along the curbs, was like getting religion. There was a feeling of well being, of protection, an assurance that no one could ever get hurt. It was our first flight. The B-17 flew with balance, smoothness, and power.

No. It soared.

The bulletin board finally announced the names of the men in the 367th Squadron and its assignment to the 306th Bomb Group.

As soon as Captain Olson received notification of his permanent crew, he pulled all of us together for an introductory briefing.

We met in one of the front rooms at Squadron Headquarters, which, like the barracks, was a tar-papered hut.

With his leather flying jacket slung over his shoulder, Oley tossed his garrison cap on the table and began.

"You guys have probably met before, but just to get us started as a group, why don't we go around the room and introduce ourselves, like, uh, your name, where you're from, your position on the ship and, uh, any personal note . . . say . . . how much time you've done in jail, your latest movie, anything of interest. Please feel free to tell us about yourselves."

Oley turned and asked, "How 'bout starting with you, Norman? Guys, meet our copilot, Norman Gates."

Composed, Gates in a quiet voice responded, "Hi, I'm Norman Gates, copilot, and I'm from San Diego, California."

"All that?" Oley teased. "Is there anymore? O.K." Clapping his hands, he pointed to Gise and said, "Next."

Bill Gise introduced himself as navigator and was as shy as Gates until, with great pride, he announced his home of Yoakum, Texas.

That was about as free as anyone got.

The guys had nice smiles and were friendly, especially Erwin Wissenback, the engineer and the ball turret, Truman Wilder. Wilder had to be the ball turret; he was so short he looked like he was sitting down when he was standing.

Tom Dynan, the radio operator, was from White Plains, New York and was as intelligent and easy to know as anyone on board. He had talent with a palette of paints and would christen our ship with a masterful Pluto and the title, Snoozy II. Bert Kaylor and Luck Talbot were waist and tail gunners. Kaylor, of a muscular build, was from Rossville, Georgia and hung a Southern accent on every word. And Luck? Well, everyone liked having a guy named Luck on board.

This was a raw, inexperienced group and we were faced with the inevitable fact that our lives would depend on each other. Standing next to these green kids, Oley must have felt, and I *know* I felt, as old as Father Time. After all, I'd been in military training for five years, longer than Oley. So when it came time for me to say my "hello," I added a little bravado, referring to myself as Official Aircraft Observer and cracked a few jokes. But it was Oley who started throwing the adhesive into the group.

"Thanks, guys. I'm glad to know you. Now that we all know each other, we can start getting the job done.

"I'm John Olson, your pilot, and I'm from Hyde Park, Massachusetts. To introduce myself to you, there's an old saying that pretty well describes me: 'I'm old enough to know better and young enough to go ahead and do it anyway.' " Over the whistles, he added, "Except . . . except when I'm flying. You can count on it.

"Please grab a chair and relax." He picked up a piece of chalk. Juggling it in his hand, he put his jacket down and settled himself on the edge of the table in front of us.

"All kidding aside, I'm glad we're finally together. Now we can get to work." He paused and then went on. "There is no question in my mind that we'll make the best team. You're here because you're good. I know that by your records. You all have the highest qualifications and I mean it when I say I'm proud to be associated with you."

Oley amazed me. He could really grab you. Boy, LeMay had nothing on this guy. Oley held us in the palm of his hand.

"Private Talbot," Oley addressed the gunner, "welcome aboard. It's good to have you as a member of the crew. Luck. I like the handle. We can all use luck. I mention this because it is important for you to remember one thing. The success of our crew depends on each of us doing our own job, the best he can, independently, but together. When we have a working team effort, everything else, including luck, is icing on the cake." He looked at us as if we were cue cards and calmly went on.

"The emphasis is on your individual effort. Hell, you can tell I'm not a stickler for Army routine. That's too GI. What you do on your own time is your business and I hope you get the most for your money. All that matters to me is that when you come on board your whole energy and responsibility is directed solely to that ship. Understood?"

"Yes, Sir," rang like a chorus.

"O.K., then we are going to start our flight training today. There is no rigid schedule at the moment, but there will be. In the meantime, we want to get in as much practice as we can. Since we don't have a ship of our own yet, we'll be taking one of the old birds down at the flight line." Taking his time, Oley looked around the room. "For some of you this may be your first flight in a Flying Fortress. I think you'll be pleasantly surprised. Everyone that has flown in one will agree, the B-17 is aptly named. It's a tough baby."

"Sir," Dynan asked, "do you know when we'll be getting our own ship?"

Oley shook his head. "I really have no idea. Believe me, there is no one who is looking forward to it more than I am. I know new ones are coming in. Slowly. The thing is, there's so much more involved than just the aircraft. There's the ground crew, the armament people, bombsight maintenance . . . besides all the Army red tape."

Oley moved towards the wall map. "Whenever it happens, it won't be too soon. Now, then, I have already filed my flight plan with the tower." He pointed at the map with a piece of chalk.

"We'll be flying over these mountains. There's a gunnery range and there's one of the bombing targets. For today and probably for the next few flights we'll be flying fuel consumption and navigational tests only."

The question was asked, "Will we be flying at altitude?"

"No, we'll be flying around seven-thousand feet. But whether we fly at altitude or not, from today on you are to bring all of your flight gear with you. Is that clear?"

"Yes, Sir."

"Any more questions? No? Then we'll meet at the flight line in twenty minutes. O.K. Let's do it."

Training at Wendover began.

"And don't shoot off the ass end of the ship," Oley cautioned. He was referring not just to our aircraft, but to the Douglas B-23 that was pulling the tow target, the big white sleeve with a "SCREW YOU," the familiar center finger and red and black swastika painted on it.

Pilots lagged nickels at the flight line, hoping for accuracy and opting *not* to fly the 1939-built modified B-18A. The guys who came up with the duty had a right to be nervous.

The men behind the guns were untrained for they had had little or no air-to-air gunnery practice. They did not know how to compensate for speed, wind or drift. They did not understand air conditions or how to lead a target. The tracers, those missiles that fired every fifth shell, were not so directional as they were distracting to the novice gunners.

John McKee and his crew were next in line to practice air-to-air gunnery when the crew in front of them shot and damaged the engine of the plane pulling the tow target. Lt. John Ryan and copilot Gaston, who were flying the twin-engine B-23, made a forced landing on the Bonneville Salt Flats. The subsequent air-to-air gunnery practice for McKee's crew would come in a battle with Focke-Wulfs on their first mission over Lille, France.

Gise and I had our own problems.

It was unbelievable, the lack of weaponry in the nose. There was one machine gun positioned on the port side, near Gise's station. It rotated in a tight circle and the higher the sighting, the lower the gunner had to get to the floor. If the projection was up, the sighting was made on hands and knees, and past a certain point there was nothing being taken but a "pot shot." There was also a frailty in the mounting. A burst from the gun jarred the surrounding glass to such an extreme vibration that at any moment it seemed the gun would kick right out of the wall and back into the compartment.

There were sockets, one in front of the nose and one on the starboard side. These provided versatility for gun placement. But what was command thinking? "Pass the pot-holder?" The gun, though only thirty-caliber and ineffective at a distance, was a heavy bastard and when fired, became very hot. To move the gun to a different position was difficult, but in combat with enemy aircraft attacking, it was impossible. We might as well have crapped in our pants and used Colt .45s.

The gun positions on the rest of the ship were far more effective.

The tremendous winds that sucked into each side of the waist did not affect the fifty-caliber weapons. Secured in metal sockets, they were supported by movable arms that allowed an effective sighting radius. Stops were provided, eliminating the chance of shooting off the wings.

Many gunners learned the hard way, through black eyes and bruised faces, that the kick from the firing gun was instant and forceful and the hot, spitting shell casings could burn.

The difference between the two calibers was enormous, not only in the size of the ammunition, but in the confidence that the twin fifty-caliber was properly engineered and with them you had a chance to defend yourself and the ship.

The top turret also had twin fifty-caliber and was the best gunnery position in the ship. It had a superior view and there was no better way to go to war than standing up.

The tail position was not as easy. The gunner lay on his belly facing the tail of the ship in close and confined quarters.

But the guys who deserved the accolades were the ball turrets—people who *could* work that position and who *would* work it.

The turret on the belly of the ship was very small and the gunner had to assume a fetal position to fit inside. Once in place, he could rotate the compartment to face any direction independently of the ship. In doing so, he locked himself in. The only way out was to bring the unit back to its original position, the hatch level with the floor of the ship. If the gears stuck, or one of the teeth broke, or the electrical circuits malfunctioned, the gunner was dependent on an awkward manual system that in an emergency "MAYDAY" most certainly would seal his doom.

Truman Wilder, the ball turret on our crew, besides having the guts, had a happy nature. Proud of his job and with a big smile, he insisted that everyone try his position, myself included.

For one flight I flew the ball turret. After having removed my wallet so that I could squeeze into the seat, the door bolted down above me. With the air hissing through the seams, I looked down through the transparent bubble at the earth moving below and felt that I would fall out, that I would eject momentarily. With that sensation gnawing at me, I fought a panic of claustrophobia for the remainder of the trip. Just to think of that ride makes me sweat. I have nothing but great admiration for Wilder and all the ball-turret gunners like him.

For each bombing practice, I, as bombardier, would check out the secret weapon of the U.S. Air Force, the instrument that would make daylight bombing possible: the Nordon bombsight. They were kept in a storage shelter that was half buried underground at the flight line and guarded twenty-four hours a day. The sight, weighing about forty-five pounds and carried in a heavy canvas bag, was released along with a companion Colt .45 automatic on presentation of ID and signature. At the end of the bombing practice, the sophisticated weapon (over two thousand working parts) had to be returned immediately and signed in.

The bomb runs were relatively easy in that the targets were so well defined in isolated areas. They were shacks built into the ground, made of large wooden slats and painted white.

They were marked like a bull's-eye, the white circles expanding outward from the center. In contrast to combat bombing where smoke and shadows blurred the objective, these were clearly visible. It was simple to score a direct hit, especially from the

Fortress, which sat out like a table compared to the small, fluttering AT-11s I had trained in.

Besides Utah and Nevada, we made bombing runs over targets in Arizona, New Mexico, and California. It was on one of the practice runs in California that we got lost.

Flying over the Mojave Desert, over an expanse of sand and Joshua trees, we lost radio contact. Oley produced a roadmap that Gise and I studied, endeavoring to pick up some ground point of identification. We located a main highway. At an altitude of four hundred feet, we followed it north until we picked up a homing signal that brought us back into Utah.

Every flight had a training purpose. If for no other reason, it was flown for a fuel consumption test. That's the way we filed it when we flew to the Air Force base at Ogden, Utah for two dozen apple pies.

When the squadrons formed, they eventually got their own mess. So did the 367th. Through no fault of his own, the mess officer assigned to our squadron was a highly qualified aeronautical engineer who was not rated to fly and who knew nothing about food. His philosophy was to buy the most for the least amount of money. For days at a time we would have potatoes, then meat without potatoes and always there was macaroni. Our mess purchased so much pasta that it became stale, and before we left Wendover, the macaroni we were eating had turned to lavender.

One day, on orders, we flew a training mission to Ogden AFB where I ate lunch with some of the men stationed there. They complained about Utah being a dry state and envied Wendover's location, so close to Nevada and those alcoholic beverages. I envied their quality of food, especially their fresh-baked dessert.

"We have the liquor, all right," I agreed, "but our food is lousy. Unless you like pasta and potatoes and milk that comes out of a box. Anyway, I have a proposition. I'll trade you booze for some of your apple pies. Whadd'ya say?"

One of the lieutenants answered, "Wait a minute. I'll get the mess sergeant. He's the one to talk to." A rotund, burly guy came out. He reminded me of my Marine instructor, Corporal Gemoets. He got right to the point.

"How many fifths per pie?"

"How many pies per fifth?"

"Name your price."

"Say, ah, six?"

"Go tell that one to Sweeney. That's a lot of pie dough for a bottle of hooch."

"Not at all. It may be easy to buy the stuff but it's gonna be harder than hell to hide it on the ship. How 'bout five?"

"How 'bout three?"

"Deal me four."

"O.K. Deal."

At the base, five of us put together the bourbon, gin and scotch that Honest John and I carried on our "fuel consumption test" to Ogden AFB. Completing the exchange and with the precious cargo of pastry stacked in boxes in the radio compartment, I flew copilot back over the Great Salt Lake. Turning the ship over to me, McKee said in typical observation, "O.K. Albee, just keep it at 240° at four thousand feet. I don't think the waves will hit us here." At the base we carefully proportioned the pieces of pie to each man of the 367th, including the ground crew and Headquarters.

That was the beginning of many trades I made with my collected bank of booze for desserts and for #10 tins of fruits and puddings. It was fun duty, augmenting our diet of macaroni and distributing the apple pies. I remember it as one of life's more illustrative moments and probably one of my better contributions to the war effort.

The base expanded rapidly. I never heard them come in, but each morning there were two or three new aircraft parked at the flight line. The motor pool swelled every day. New buildings were constructed. The sounds of sawing and hammering were constant. Military personnel, including regular Army officers, arrived daily. But Wendover didn't really begin to function as a working post until the base echelon started to form. The echelon, composed mainly of civilian military reserves, were the people that put the operation together. For all the pomp allotted the career men—the West Point graduates—it was the brain power of the civilians that implemented a working structure that would eventually get the job done.

Within a week there was a noticeable tightening of organization. Bulletins were being issued with regularity. Instructional films and specialty meetings were scheduled in an ongoing educational program about the new and improved equipment and procedures.

That Wendover was fast approaching a full-fledged military establishment was evidenced by the emerging RHIP—Rank Has Its Privilege. A lot of pleasures I had enjoyed earlier were phased out. There were sheets of waiting lists for the Skeet Shooting Range. I stopped going because of the officers and political brass. There were no more cars to town, only trucks. The Chevy and Plymouth sedans were used by the brass. Separate johns were reserved for the field-grade officers and so was central seating in the post theater. Ranking personnel participated less and less in group activities and in town they would disappear into private homes and parties.

Relaxed, without other pressures, the crews were spending their full time doing their job, which was getting ready to go to war. The new squadrons were doing well in a sloppy way; the embryonic air echelon was beginning to make progress.

Then, along with the necessary ground support people, came the savvy officers, the "paddlefeet" pushing the C.S.—"chicken shit."

The reserves, pouring in, were mostly officers. They had trouble staying out of each other's way. With not enough ground troops to work with, how to keep busy? More important, how to *look* busy. The answer was the Army Instruction Manual. Officers could employ unnecessary training discipline with no fear of disapproval from senior officers.

While the Table of Organization was being structured—the ratio of colonels to majors, of majors to captains, etc.—the officers implemented the marching, the daily inspections, the daily drills, the protocol such as starched shirts, when to wear ties, when to salute. Air training was desperately needed and marching was as important as tits on a rain barrel. The "paddlefeet" were, in effect, concentrating on putting a wartime Army together with a peace-time manual, the one I had trained with at the Presidio in 1938.

For play, it was baseball by day and poker by night.

Softball, like the base, started out loosely. It was initiated by Col. Bill Langford, who began the game with grammar school work-up. As the Post organized, so did softball. After work-up, it was crew vs. crew, the losing outfit providing the winners with a steak dinner or a drunken brawl, whichever was preferred. With the completion of assignments, the competition moved from single planes to full squadrons. Winning at that point was more impor-tant than eating or drinking. It meant superiority of a whole unit. When the game was between the air echelon and the base echelon, that's when the stakes were the highest.

It was hot in July and the players showed up in anything that was cool. Boxer underwear, bloomer pajama bottoms, GI long socks, whatever was on hand was the uniform of the day. One guy wore long johns that were minus buttons from the waist down. There was nothing left to the imagination as he spread his legs on a leadoff from first to steal second. The underwear and bloomers hung just as loosely. Who cared? Out there in the barren solitude, the breezier the better. Even when the blue-draped Florence Nightingales walked down from the infirmary to watch the game, the only gear that was banned was the flying boots. They were too bulky, and therefore, too slow.

I retired early from the competition, my ability leveling off when the rivalry was between crews. When it became inter-squadron, I joined the ranks of spectator. But others in my barracks stayed for the whole show.

Honest John McKee was a catcher of real talent. No one would know it by his appearance as he stood behind home plate. Wearing next to nothing, his hairy legs extended beyond the chest protector and disappeared in socks that folded over worn-out sneakers. His face hidden in a catcher's mask, he chewed on a cigar and looked the most improbable of athletes, though hardly a stinging foul tip escaped his mitt.

Bud Gaston, on the pitcher's mound, went into a windmill wind-up that sent the ball zinging in an underhand toss for a strike. Surrounded by a sea of underwear, Bud was immaculately dressed in clothes of cardinal and gold, initialed with the letters USC.

The playing field was an area cleared of aircraft at the flight line. The baselines were drawn with flour, each mess sent a coffee urn filled with lemonade, and everyone whistled and yelled, "give it a nickel for car fare" as the ball sailed over runway #2 for a home run.

"Pick a spot, win a lot," "play a hunch, winna bunch," "dig deep, sweep the street," "You wanna play some Blackjack?"

"All right, you guys, get your money down," ordered John McKee. He was the dealer in the 367th barracks and came by his name Honest John because he was so swift with the cards no one could question him. At night, huddled in the middle of the room, a light hand-clamped onto a metal bed frame spotlighting the circle on the floor, McKee dealt the rounds of twenty-one. Rolling a cigar around in his mouth, he gruffly announced the rules, the same as in Vegas; dealer hits 16, split the paint cards, 1-1 odds on splits, 2-1 on blackjack. And, like Las Vegas, the house, McKee, inevitably won.

Between baseball and poker the real get-a-way was the Hotel Utah. Located in Salt Lake City about 130 miles east of Wendover, it was the center for good food, dancing and, most important, it was a layover for commercial airline personnel. As a sense of urgency permeated the base and the rumors of training accidents increased, we felt a growing compulsion to live life to its fullest. On open-post weekends or whenever possible, we hitched a plane ride or drove by private car into downtown Salt Lake. It was a town full of greenery, with clean streets, fresh, cool air and cold, snow water in the drinking fountains. The Hotel Utah offered all the amenities for pleasurable living. Part of that living was eating good food, and the hotel had it, including Maine lobster.

Five of us were beginning a weekend pass, having dinner together in the Empire Room at the hotel. Honest John, Oley, John Ryan and myself were on our third setup, while Butterball was still playing with his first, a Manhattan; he would have preferred a Coke.

"Get a load of the broad with Wilson," Butterball said, "she looks like she's smuggling cantaloupes. Boy, I hope she sits down soon so she can rest them on the table."

I agreed. "She isn't from any Teeny Weenie airline, that's for sure."

"I don't think I'm hungry for food anymore," Ryan whistled under his breath.

"Hey, John," Oley said, nudging him, "you've got all weekend to shop. There's more where she came from, though . . . maybe not bigger, I'll have to admit."

"Oh, hell, who cares about knockers," McKee countered. "I'm a leg man myself."

"Aw, c'mon, you mean to say, honestly, John," teased Ryan, "you'd reject that equipment?"

"Well." McKee shrugged.

A young shavetail stopped by our table and asked, "Hey, are you La Chasse? I hear you're from California."

"Yeah."

"My name's Horton and I'm from Cherry Hill, Pennsylvania. Glad to meet you."

"Likewise." We shook hands.

"Hey, I've got a cousin in Visalia. Do you know anyone from there?"

"Gee, no, but I know some people from Glendale."

"Glendale? Where's that?"

"It's a long way from Visalia."

"Yeah, well, see ya around some time." Disinterested, he hurried off.

"Cripes, what is it about California? I mean you're supposed to know everyone in the whole state?"

"Aw, sit back and enjoy it, Albee," McKee urged, as he snuffed his cigar in the ashtray.

"Hey, is that . . . Hmm-m, I wonder. Butter, move your head." I stretched as I watched the man walk across the room to the other side of the restaurant. "Hey, everyone, see that tall, gray-haired guy carrying the homburg? I think he's Charlie Howard."

"Who the hell is Charlie who?" inquired Ryan.

"Charles S. Howard? You mean the guy who owns the thoroughbred stable?" The horse-loving McKee craned his neck to get a look.

"Yep," I affirmed. "Charlie Howard, who bailed General Motors out of financial difficulty and now gets a royalty on every Buick that's sold west of the Mississippi. He owns Sea Biscuit, a Santa Anita Handicap winner."

"Sea Biscuit? No kidding?" Oley perked up.

"What a beautiful horse," McKee said wistfully. "He's small for a thoroughbred, but beautiful. They describe him as a 'blocky little bay.' Did you ever see him run, Albee?"

"Sure I did. I saw him win the Handicap. I bet ten dollars on him, ten whole bucks that I had been saving especially for that race. Charlie Howard had one entry of two horses, Sea Biscuit and Kayak II. He declared to win with Sea Biscuit."

"Whadd'ya mean, declared to win?" Butterball asked. "Doesn't the horse that crosses the finish line first always win?"

"As I understood it, between the two horses, if both were winning, the jockey on Kayak would hold up and let Sea Biscuit win."

"Is that what happened?"

"Well, Butter, no one can prove that the jockey, Ralph Neves, held up on Kayak. He denied it, so who was to know? But, the horses ran one, two. Just between us, if they had run another quarter of a mile, Kayak would have won it. It was a beautiful race to see."

"How come you're so hep on racing, Al? You a gambler?" Ryan raised an eyebrow.

"For two winter seasons I worked at the Santa Anita Racetrack as a box usher."

"Did you lose money?" McKee wondered.

"Who me? I banked every paycheck and lived on 'tout' winnings. By the time I'd worked my way to the finish-line boxes, I was a proficient tout."

"What is a tout?" Oley questioned.

"Well, in a six-horse race I would tout six winners. Someone in my section would ask, 'Who do you like in this race?' And I'd say, 'At lunch in the jockeys' cafeteria, the word out there is bet number six. Get yourself ten on the nose and two for me.' And they'd bet the money for me because I gave them the tip. Then as I walked down the aisle I'd answer the same question with horse number five and then number four and so on until I had two dollars on each horse in the race."

"Where did *you* run after the race?" Oley inquired.

"Good question. I took a twenty-minute leak in the girls' room. Naw, there were lots of excuses, like the horse had the wrong jock, too much weight, wrong post position, the distance was wrong . . ."

"Izzat legal?" Butter looked at me, wide-eyed.

Winking at him, I said, "That the name of a horse? Then get ten for yourself and two for me."

"Anybody want another drink?" I asked, pouring myself a little more scotch that was going down smoother all the time.

"Later for me," Oley declined, picking up the menu in front of him. "I'm going to find myself some chow."

"Butter," I insisted, "you've loved that drink to death. Don't you even want a little more ice?"

"I'm fine, Al. I didn't care too much for this drink. I think next time I'll try a whiskey sour. I've heard that's really good."

"I'll buy you the setup, Butter. I just hope you find something you like. Geez, you're an officer now, and you're supposed to be able to drink. You don't want to be a disgrace to the Air Force, do you?"

"O.K., O.K. But after dinner?" Butterball disappeared behind a menu.

"What I want to know, Butter," I pushed, "how's the patchwork coming? Have you finally decided on the insignia for the mighty 367th?"

Putting the menu down, he enthusiastically answered, "Yeah, I sure have. You know the sign they put on poison, the skull and crossbones?"

We nodded, afraid of what was coming.

"Well, we'll use the same thing, only ours will be in a helmet and goggles."

"Really?" asked Oley, looking over the top of his menu.

"That'll scare the Axis to death." Ryan shook his head.

"Butter, ol' boy," I kidded him, "I'm afraid all your taste is in your mouth."

"Don't let these guys intimidate, you, Jones," Honest John said, as he stood up. "The other squadrons are going to be damn jealous. Now, is there a navigator in the place? I gotta go to the crapper."

Ryan directed him. "Just follow your nose, McKee, to the end of the room and turn left. It says 'GENTLEMEN' on the door, but go in anyway."

"You're a pal, John," McKee muttered as he moved off into the room.

"There are only two choices as I see it," Oley said, putting down his menu.

"What are they?" Ryan asked.

Oley managed a thoughtful look. "Either we go to the ETO or the PTO."

Ryan slumped back in his seat. "That's pretty smart of you, Oley. Did you just figure that out?"

"Yep. Just now."

"If you had your choice, where would you go?" asked Butter-ball.

"Hell," Oley swore, "if I had my choice, I'd be an Eagle pilot. I'd much rather be a P-shooter than a truck driver."

"I'll drink to that," Ryan agreed.

"I'll tell you right now, Oley," I said, "I don't want any part of the Pacific Theater. When I read about the atrocities that the Japs commit against our captured guys, like bamboo shoots under the fingernails . . . I scream if I get a splinter. And to think I might be over there now on Corregidor with the Marines. I get nervous just thinking about it. Let's face it. I am a coward."

"Gee, Al," Butter murmured, "I'm with you."

"All of us feel fear," Oley reflected into his drink.

A silence hung over the table.

"Hey," Oley looked up and hustled an impish grin. "Come on guys, let's not get sticky. I'm sorry I brought the whole thing up. When I talked about two choices I was really talking about the menu. Either it's steak or lobster, and as far as I'm concerned, the lobster has it."

McKee, seating himself, grumbled, "None of that Friday fish eating for me. Pretend it's Thursday. I want a porterhouse, medium rare, with lots of onions."

"You can order for me any day, Oley," Ryan said, "There's nothing in the world like Maine lobster. How about you, La Chasse?"

"O.K. by me."

"Make it four," added Butterball.

After ordering, McKee leaned forward. "Wait until you see the doll Bill Casey's with." Shaking his head, he remarked, "Way too much for a little guy like that. She must be his cousin."

"John," Oley laughed, "you're forgetting the guy's Irish. That makes all the difference. You should know that."

McKee took out a fresh cigar. "Yeah, that makes a difference. Just the same, I ought to offer my services. A friend in need, you know." Honest John lit his cigar with a lighter that flamed like a torch, commenting, "Best damn Zippo I ever had."

"That ball of fire you call a cigarette lighter reminds me of when I was in flight training," Oley began, settling back against the smooth leather of the booth. "It was my first night flight. I was about to fly light lines, like they do in the flat lands of Texas. Well, there I was, all tucked in behind the instructor, who, well, he was all right as far as instructors go. By any ordinary standards, he'd just as soon wash me out as the next guy. Anyway, we had climbed into one of those AT-6 Trainers and I was feeling pretty confident about the whole thing. Then, the engine turned over." Gesturing, Oley described, "This long blue flame choked out of the exhaust right by me, licked up my sleeve and, I'm not kidding you, singed my left eyebrow."

We were all smiles as he went on.

"I jerked back in my seat and kind of folded up tight, as tight as I could. I thought Keee . . . rist, if this is the way you learn to fly, I mean, trial by fire? Of course, the instructor didn't see me. Hell, for all I know he was looking through the rearview mirror, testing me. Come to think of it, he probably was. But, damn, I was startled enough to take a get-out discharge right then."

McKee winked. "Did you jump in the front seat with the big man to protect you, Swede?"

Oley winked back. "I didn't have time, McKee. We were taxiing down the runway before I could unfasten my seat belt."

Our dinner started with a green salad and hot, homemade bread. I would have been content to eat bread and butter for the rest of the evening, but then the waiter came. He was carrying a large platter. Red pincers, hanging from the sides, lobbed up and down with each step he took. He set a lobster down in front of me, cracked off the claws and laid them to the sides. I was then tied up in a big, white linen bib and handed an ornately scrolled shell cracker. I had never had lobster in my life, and the ritual left me feeling quite helpless. Ryan and Oley were already into the body of the shellfish before I, with regret, began to crack the shell. I had difficulty pulling away the meat and used my fingers as well as my fish fork. I was surprised by the taste, not fishy, but rich in a bland sort of way. I felt very messy and noticed the bowl of yellow liquid that the waiter had set in front of me. I'd heard all about finger bowls, and, if, by an Act of Congress I was declared an officer, thereby a gentleman, then, by damn, I could act like one. I took my napkin and dipped a corner of it into the bowl and rubbed it over my fingers. I did it a second time. My situation was definitely not improving. I sneaked a look over to Butterball who was spooning his bowl of liquid out like a soup! It was then that I noticed Oley and Ryan were using it as a sauce for the meat. What a difference in the lobster! Even my fingers tasted good.

The evening wore on. The music began. The lights dimmed and floods spotted the dance floor. The crowd of people increased and so did a feeling of well-being. The finger bowls were finally brought and taken away, as was coffee and dessert. Feeling mellowed and content, we lingered over the last of the bourbon and scotch. It was when the band asked for requests that Oley jumped up and asked for one of his favorite Irish songs. The bandleader shook his head.

"I'll sing you the tune, then," Oley answered, sprinting to the stage. Taking the microphone, he commenced:

> McCarty had a party at his house the other night
> And everyone invited brought along his appetite,
> The best of folks were there; it was a grand affair,
> The police were not invited but later they got there,
> But nobody knows what happened to McCarty
> For he kept disappearin' all the time.

The band picked up the melody and to whistles and applause, Oley, now completely confident, continued to sing:

> First a brick came through the air
> And it landed on O'Hare
> But nobody knows what happened to McCarty
> For McCarty simply wasn't anywhere.

Repeating the tune, the band played on as Oley put his hands into his pockets and, lifting his pants a couple of inches higher from the floor, shuffled through a soft-shoe routine. McKee joined in, throwing in a few Irish kicks and finally, even Ryan, awkward but gregarious, completed the trio. They were happy, handsome young men, and everyone loved it. They could have packaged it and sold it to the USO, if they hadn't already been under contract to Uncle Sam.

The hotel offered other pleasures. To a young kid like myself, coming from a home that was furnished in the Depression, and to the guys just off the farm and from small towns, the hotel was especially luxurious. Marble columns, two stories high, lined the perimeter of the lobby, alluding to its massiveness and solid structure. There was an opulence in the furnishings, ample couches and chairs, leather, fine fabrics and fresh bouquets of flowers. The polished tables and writing desks mirrored the huge crystal chandelier that shimmered like a crown from the ceiling. The service in the hotel was just as impeccable, its staff attired in subdued uniforms. I saluted the doorman more than once.

It was the perfect setting for a "ready situation,"—wartime, good-looking women of the airlines with good-looking men in uniform. An invitation to "let's have a drink" implied "let's go to bed." And it wasn't only the men that were eager.

Housing at the hotel was not a problem, *if* you knew the right people. There were a couple of them stationed at Wendover. Just as my specialty was getting fruits and desserts from Ogden AFB for which I made an appropriate trade from my bank of booze, and as Butterball made it his business to create an insignia for our squadron, so there were two guys whose talents were setting up rooms and reservations. Both were from wealthy families and had traveled extensively. Whether they dropped names or money, I did not know. They never failed to have waiting accommodations at the hotel, including a salesman's room, a large room with one bed and space to display merchandise. In the event a group of us were on orders for training or on a pick-up of incoming supplies at one of the military installations that bordered Salt Lake City, we could stay overnight at the hotel. We would simply call and order enough beds rolled into the large room to accommodate all of us. Who wanted to stay at a base, if you could have comfort like that? It was because of this availability that the game "Red-Dog" evolved.

One evening, one of the officers got together with a willing female and, time being short, they didn't shop for a private room. He took her upstairs to the reserved "salesman's" room. The men coming back for the night found the scene sensual and stimulating and many hurried back downstairs to the lobby to find someone so that they, too, could join the fun. Cohabitation became commonplace and then, eventually, so did Red-Dog, an exchange of partners. In a room full of bedded couples, someone new wanting to participate or someone wanting to go on to another experience would yell "Red-Dog," and all the guys who were willing would move one bed to their right. The rules were loose. If you were sleepy or just in love, you played it to your own comfort.

Red-Dog was an institution forever associated with Wendover and so was Torchy.

The elevators opened. "Going up?"

"Yeah." We all were. The operator would toss back her flaming red hair and her boobs would bounce. She was 5-feet, 3-inches of provocation, of seduction, of lust, of advanced technology: two huge gyros and a bombsight.

"What floor do you boys want? The mezzanine?"

"Gee, I didn't know this hotel had a mezzanine."

"It doesn't!" Her false eyelashes tangled as she winked. Torchy's ability to 'give you a job between floors' was never disputed. Her reputation proceeded all the way to Germany, where the interrogators asked, "Kenne-sie Torchy vom Hotel Utah?"

In July of 1942, each of us searched for fulfillment. For some, it was a game called Red-Dog or a redhead named Torchy. Or it was drinking booze smuggled into the room from the state-operated liquor store. Others enjoyed a private room, either for romance or quiet conversation. Still, for some of us it was a song and soft-shoe routine and the appreciation of a close and possibly final friendship.

The Hotel Utah, haughty and sedate, and the people of that Mormon city, smiled on us young romantics as we indulged our whims under an umbrella of innocence. They were all too few, those moments suspended in a time of fateful and uncertain tomorrows.

It was the last week in July. S-2 held a series of mandatory intelligence briefings. There were to be no more communications home. We filled out a kit of cards that would be used by the base personnel to inform our kin that we were no longer at Wendover. We were instructed to stay close to our squadron. There were no leaves, and passes were canceled. We were ordered to the post theater to meet the base commander, Col. Charles B. Overacker. I had seen the Colonel before at the base and at Stateline. I had no idea who he was. Like all top brass, he was a pontifical figure, surrounded by aides, unapproachable and observed only at a distance. Up to that point I didn't give a damn. But when he was introduced as our Group Commander, I cared a whole lot. His appearance was disappointing. He was small, a peanut of a guy with big ears. He was a long way from the dashing figure that I pictured as an Air Force Command Pilot. His serial number, 0-17007, indicated he had been around for a long time. He stuttered, with a voice that began shaky and got worse. I thought he must be a hell of a pilot, because as a leader he seemed like a cream puff. I felt sorry for the guy, but I couldn't afford him as my problem and dismissed him from my mind, resolving that he couldn't hurt my crew's efficiency. I was wrong. He did.

Movement orders were imminent. I returned all that I could of the base-owned equipment to the Quartermaster. I collected my clean laundry. No matter whose clothes came back under my name, if they fit, I packed them. I gave what was left of my booze to the ground crew, a kind of thank-you for the work they did at the flight line. Besides, they could carry more than I could; they were going by train. In a flurry of last minute details, I purchased those important incidentals—cigarettes, chewing gum, razor blades—just in case we ended up in North Africa.

The ship we were assigned for our "movement" was a 1941 B-17E. It carried no bombsight. The obsolete armor plating that had backed the bombardiers' and pilots' seats and collectively weighed close to one thousand pounds, had been removed. The guns in the nose had been upgraded to two thirty-caliber and were moveable between *five* positions. Our flying gear was stored in the respective compartments, checked and ready to go.

On July 31st, Field Operations Order Number 5 was cut, ordering the movement of the 306th Combat Group (Heavy). On August 1, 1942, the 306th took off from Wendover. It was the first bomb group to depart that field. The lead ship of the thirty-eight B-17s, designated Group Airplane #1 of the Air Echelon, was piloted by Col. C.B. Overacker. The four squadrons comprising the 306th were the 423rd, the 367th, the 368th, and the 369th. Each squadron consisted of nine aircraft with crews. One additional aircraft flew with the 369th. Piloted by Maj. William H. Cleveland, it carried S-2 officers and ground crew personnel.

From the air, I took a last look at the Post where I had trained for less than six weeks. When LeMay said they were going to put something together there, it was hard to imagine that those scraggly beginnings could mushroom into such a thriving military operation.

I felt apprehensive that I didn't get it all—all the necessary training—because of the lack of early organization. But, someone, somewhere, said we were ready and I had no choice but to buy it.

With little experience in formation flying, we flew, one after the other, in line of stern behind our Squadron Leader, Lt. John Ryan. Our course was due east. Our destination, unknown.

7

PATHÉ SOUND NEWS

Thunderheads choked the air lanes into East St. Louis. We flew around the storm, choosing to land at an alternative destination in Illinois—Chanute Airfield.

Few fields could readily accommodate the giant B-17s, and Chanute wasn't one of them. The Fortresses had to fly in low over the mess hall to utilize as much of the runway as possible; so low that a couple of smoke vents were knocked off the mess hall's roof.

On arriving at any base, the first duty was to check the HQ roster listing permanent party, for any old buddies that might be stationed there. After that, there was nothing to do but to ignore the hot, muggy weather by drinking cold beer in the canteen bar. For our overnight, each man had the luxury of sleeping in a bed with metal springs, no small accomplishment for four squadrons of men.

The next day, the 368th and 369th flew to Westover Air Base in Massachusetts. My Squadron, the 367th, and the 423rd flew to Washington, D.C.

Our flight into Washington was an unrehearsed commercial for the war effort. We were eighteen tangibles, a vanguard of the fleet to come, rallying the American people to the "cause."

Into an overpopulated District of Columbia audience, the Fortresses zoomed, one after the other, into the restricted air space. Clipping close to the Washington Monument, coming in east of the Capitol Building and on a downwind, south heading, they made their approach into Bolling Field.

By the time Oley brought us within range of the Washington Monument, P-40s and P-36s were zipping through the air, nervously eyeballing the aircraft that were flying into their protection assignment, the nation's capitol.

Like Chanute, Bolling was not yet equipped with long runways, and the B-17s dragged in low with lots of flap, stalling to waste air speed. A plane in back of us wasn't making it, so he bounced over the chain link fence that bordered the runway and then bounced back again, an intricate maneuver that cost speed enough so that he was able to pull to a stop at the end of the runway.

After a briefing outside our plane, we went to the Officers' Club for lunch.

The large rooms of the club were jammed with people, but we were standouts in our baggy ODs.

Most of the casual uniforms were suntans, crisply starched. Many of the officers wore their "pinks," the jackets splashed with medals, ribbons and stripes. Buckled in Sam Brown belts, the men postured smartly, reflecting the importance now relegated to the Air Arm, formerly enjoyed exclusively by the Navy.

There were as many women civilians in the club as officers. Over drinks, they laughed and flirted, vying for attention. Attired in soft frilly dresses, some wore small, veiled hats; others wore their "pageboy" hairdos wrapped in snoods. They all showed their legs to the best advantage in skirts, seamed silk stockings and high-heeled shoes.

The field-grade officers crowded around us, wanting to hear about our crews and the B-17s. They didn't know our life and we sure didn't know theirs. Were these people in the same war?

"What are you guys doing here? On your way to Europe? North Africa?"

"Now, Major, you really don't want an answer, do you?" Oley's tone was friendly.

"Ah, c'mon Captain, relax. Have a drink. Where ya from?"

"The Northeast."

The Major's girlfriend wiggled up to Oley. "I'm from Florida. Do you like Florida?"

"Sure." Oley liked her.

A Marine lieutenant greeted us. "Hi, fellas. I'm stationed at Quantico. Welcome to D.C. Nice to have you guys here. What kind of aircraft you flying?"

An ensign answered, "Those are B-17s. Big aren't they?"

"Damn big. Especially in the air. Hi, the name's Harrison." He shook hands all around. "It was my outfit that welcomed you out there this morning. We didn't even know you were coming."

"The B-17, huh?" an Army lieutenant mused. "Mmm . . . is that what they call the Flying Fortress? What a wonderful name."

"It should be," McKee tossed. "It's a military secret."

"You're a big group. Eighteen, twenty planes. Big movement," Captain Harrison observed. "Makes me proud to be a part of the Army Air Force. Hey, why don't you men put on some Class A uniforms and come to this evening's dinner dance? We'll provide the lovely ladies, there'll be good food and one of the university bands will play your favorites."

"Thanks, but our Class A's are packed."

"Hey, Freddie, this a Sunday night dance?"

"Yes."

"Then you guys come as you are. There won't be any generals tonight."

The lifestyle at Bolling Field was conveyed to me by a cadet classmate of mine who was stationed there. Bob's name had fallen alphabetically into a slot assigning him as an aide to a general. We had been out of Cadet School just six weeks and he was already a 1st Lieutenant. That Bob was extremely handsome was no deterrent. It was a shame he had so much. As an aide, he accompanied the general everywhere. He had already flown all over the country. He shot skeet and played golf. He attended parties and receptions and was an escort for officers' daughters. His eight-hour-a-day job was a piece of cake layered in protocol.

I admired his moxie—his ability to handle the politics involved. He understood the campaigns men waged and how they took advantage of the war's early confusion and others' mistakes to elevate themselves, no matter how many people they climbed over or stepped on. He recognized the competition and demands of the social structure between officers, and more ostentatiously, between the officers' wives who wore their husbands' rank as if it was their own.

Bob had to move fast, use the right propaganda, know what was going on around him and be resourceful. He proved the latter by coming up with a military limo—with gas—and taking me and some buddies into downtown Washington.

The city was drowning in people. There were lines for everything. A stool at a lunch counter became a combat zone. The parks were littered with people sitting on the grass eating brown-bag lunches. The hotels were filled to capacity, their lobbies congested with the hopeful, waiting for a cancellation. Even the Statler Hotel, under construction, with prices of $3.85 a night, single, and $5.50 a night, double, would not absorb the overflow. Amid rippling flags and multicolored defense posters, white-gloved traffic cops struggled to unsnarl traffic and corral the crush of pedestrians. We crawled up Pennsylvania Avenue, nudging bumpers with other OD staff cars; many marked by one to three stars on the car's red ID license plate. One blink at the Central Railroad Station and I counted my blessings that I was leaving Washington by air.

On Monday, August 3rd, we left Washington. There at Bolling Field in the nation's capitol, the war provided an opportunity for rank, status and recognition. The people based there were in the same war, all right. The difference was they were planning the war, the one *we* were going to fight.

We were a live Pathé Newsreel as we flew from Bolling Field to Westover Field in Massachusetts. The 367th Squadron's John Ryan led us sightseeing up the East Coast, his home territory. Manhattan looked like a big hot dog, split in the middle. There were lines of cars winding along Riverside Drive, their windshields reflecting the sun. Flying directly toward the big, gray Statue of Liberty, close to the tip of her crown, there at the mouth of the Hudson, we made an oblique left turn and flew up the river. We were "beating up the deck" we dropped so low, flying between two hundred and three hundred feet above the water.

We skimmed over rooftops of sunbathers and brightly colored umbrellas. Everyone looked up at us, waving their towels in greetings. They sheltered their eyes from the sun as they gawked at the spectacle of the big four-engine bombers with red, white and blue roundels of dot, star and ring. We passed over barges and tugboats and over military docks—fingers that bridged the river's muddy edges, linking depots of men and machines.

Ossining, New York was our departure point from the Hudson. At the corner of Sing Sing's yard, Captain Ryan expertly wrapped his craft around the prison's tall smokestack, and, using it as a pylon, he turned northeast. It was a performance the other pilots competitively followed. Oley, not to be outdone, stood us on a wing, low enough in our turn that we could have caught a baseball from the inmates playing below, who waved and cheered. We hedge-hopped over New England. The green, grassy hills climbed to meet us and, with trees still reaching up, dropped back down, only to rise and fall again. We cruised over white-steeple churches and clustered tents of summer camps. On every lake, on every spot of water that nestled in the rolling slopes, white sails of sloops leaned in the wind. Like starched, three-cornered handkerchiefs, they were the signature of summer.

Entering the traffic pattern of Westover, our reckless, carefree flight changed to one of regimented military bearing. This was a disciplined base, run by an iron ass, strongly flavored with an omen to behave yourselves. It was a warning I did not heed.

8

WESTOVER

Westover was a big, beautiful field, located between Holyoke and Springfield. It was the staging area for the ETO, the European Theater of Operations. Now we knew where we were going.

While we waited for our equipment to arrive, we made navigational and fuel tests by flying sub patrol over the Atlantic Seaboard.

We were briefed for these patrols in a "War Ready" room, aptly named for its basement location and gray, dank atmosphere. The walls were covered with maps. In the center of the room was a large fish bowl nearly filled with dimes. The liberty-head coins were contributions from the personnel at each briefing and were designated as a prize for the crew who sank a sub. While sightings of subs were reported, none were sunk during the time the 306th was at Westover.

Even our crew made such a sighting.

It was a murky day, the type of protective weather in which subs would surface to recharge batteries and replenish their fresh air supply. We were patrolling our sector of the ocean that was within fifty miles of landfall—the Atlantic City Boardwalk. As we passed into a clearing in the fog, the waist gunner called to Oley, "Right waist to Pilot. Looks like a sub floating at 2 o'clock."

Oley immediately dipped the right wing and we all looked out to see a clear slash in the water, a swell that could only be attributed to a diving sub. We made a pylon right there. By the time we had completed the 360° turn, all traces of the inland wake had dissipated.

The subs had the advantage. It took time for the aircraft to make its reconnaissance between clouds, and the sound of an approaching plane re-echoed in the fog like a magnified warning.

We sighted, in the same area, a gray naval-type tug with no visible identification and a civilian single engine aircraft flying about five hundred feet above the water. The grouping seemed more than coincidental. According to the morning's briefing, no craft or boat was known to be in the area. It was specified as our airway and ours alone.

Back at the base we made our report at the debriefing. Surprisingly, our findings received little reaction and no explanation. But, what seemed so possible as espionage could have been simply the lack of communication due to rivalry between the Services.

Early in the war, the Services, to a large extent, acted independently of each other. They competed for appropriations and authority. The Navy was the most abrasive in that it considered itself superior. So first-class, in fact, that it was said, "Had they been in the trenches, they would have had knives and forks, not to mention monogrammed napkin rings."

An example of self-serving interest was the Army and the Navy's opposition to the Air Force procurement of the B-17.

As General LeMay put it:

> It could be observed readily that in our attempt to demonstrate that multi-engined bombers could seek out, discover and sink a battleship approaching our United States coast, we were faced not only with congenital resentment of the Naval Brass . . . We were faced with the jealousy and suspicion of the Army itself.[3]

General LeMay based his conclusions:

. . . from historical cognizance that the entrenched military hierarchy—military or naval, it matters not—has always disputed the power of a weapon which was not a part of their traditional arsenal.[4]

Commander of the Army Air Force, Gen. H.H. Arnold, wrote:

Realizing this soon (that the Flying Fortresses could cover in an hour more distance than a fast enemy ship could be expected to cover in a night) . . . The Navy raised hell like a country gentleman finding poachers on his property.[5]

To the crews who flew the patrols, the effectiveness of the aircraft was obvious. On one patrol we would spot a convoy moving out to sea. Two days later on our next patrol we would see the same convoy, their rate of speed as fast as their slowest ship.

This competition between Services and the lack of cooperation, created problems for Intelligence and for the whole war effort.

We were so short of supplies that nothing was expendable. If a crew dropped a depth charge and didn't get a sub, they had to pay the cost of the lost explosive. The same was true for a pilot. If he blew a tire or damaged the landing wheel assembly because of an improper landing, he was docked the cost of the damaged parts. It seemed ridiculous. Lost ammunition should have been part of our paid expense account.

But materials were scarce. It served as a reasonable pressure to keep us from screwing around with the equipment we did have. And it was precisely because of the lack of equipment that our movement into the ETO stalled at Westover. It must have been abysmal frustration for General Arnold when he inspected the naval operations in the Pacific.

The General began his tour the next month on September 20th and twelve days later would make his evaluation:

"There were numerous things throughout the Pacific the Army did not like. One was the apparent fact that the Navy would do anything to keep control. They used higher-ranking officers than we had, and so normally retained command . . . The Navy did not understand the technique of ground operations, nor the technique of our air operations. They did not plan logistics in supplying troops . . ."[6]

Having returned to Washington, he explained the problems as he saw them:

". . . the lack of unity of command; the concentration of ships in the harbors when there was such a shortage of ships on the other side of the world; the stacking of airplanes, with the planes and crews in reserve, unused, when everybody was yelling for airplanes. . . ."[7]

President Roosevelt; Secretary of War, Stimson; Chief of Staff, Marshal; and Undersecretary of the Navy, Forrestal, listened with interest. But not Secretary of the Navy, Frank Knox. The Secretary stopped Arnold in the middle of his account and as Arnold quoted Knox, ". . . He did not care to have me criticize the Navy! That ended our interview."

General Arnold further observed:

". . . the Marines on Guadalcanal wanted to know when the Army was going to relieve them. The Marines had understood they were to be there for a few days only, and then were to be relieved. Where was the Army? Naturally, as this whole area was a Navy Command, that was their business, not ours."[8]

It wasn't until the 15th of August that we received our first B-17Fs. The equipment was flown into Westover where it was to be inspected and made ready for the recently pioneered, nonstop flight across the Atlantic.

With our ground crews in transit, awaiting embarkation on the liner, the Queen Mary out of New York, the pilots assumed the responsibilities for the aircraft. Except for the adjustment of the rocker boxes (cylinder heads) on the engines and some leaky thermos jugs, the uncomplicated Forts checked out quickly.

For all the objections, doubts and criticism that had shadowed the acquisition of the B-17s, the Fort proved to be the one piece of equipment, the one absolute, in our inadequately trained and supplied Group Movement. There wasn't a man in the crew of the Flying Fortress who didn't love her.

Among the first of the individual gear to be distributed was the Colt .45s. The pistols were packed in large boxes and were handed out still covered in Cosmoline, a lubricant that looked like dark red jam.

The holsters that followed were immediately recalled. They looked to be of Civil War vintage, made for the Cavalry. The holster, properly buckled around the waist, hung over the left hip. They were deep, designed for a .38 revolver. In order to draw the 45-caliber weapon from that holster, you'd have to reach behind your back, and then, as you pulled it from the holster, you'd probably shoot yourself through the left armpit. The proper replacement, the shoulder holster, was not available through the Quartermaster and had to be located and purchased through a private, local distributor.

The early issues were of the finest quality. The flight helmets were of soft, seamed leather with U.S. Air Corps stamped in the lining. The heavy winter flying suits were made of leather as smooth as kid and lined in curly, white sheep's wool.

But no matter what the quality, there were always screw-ups.

In the flying suits, it was not unusual to have teeth missing in one of the arm or leg zippers.

Some of the guns issued were without hammers or trigger guards.

Navigational hack watches that were distributed in envelopes would come with half a wristband or none at all.

The flight goggles came in batches and were issued to each man, regardless of size. One guy had two pair issued to him, both too small for his head. In protest, looking like a four-eyed elephant, he wore one on each thigh to the shower.

A set of U.S. flag insignias was made backward: if sewn on properly, with the colored side outward, they would be upside down in the form of a distress signal.

The binoculars, manufactured by Nash Kelvinator, were an example of the problematic transition of rushing from peacetime to wartime production. One kid in our barracks stuck his fingers through the ends of his pair; they had no magnifying lenses. Others could not focus theirs. Lacking threads, the glasses were freewheeling. Although they represented the small percentage of mistakes that could be expected from the assembly line, yet they were no less deadly if taken into battle.

There were no gloves issued. I still had mine from Ellington. Heavy underwear was also not available. I had purchased two pair in Albuquerque and from my experience with them, I found that civilian merchandise was also subject to defects. Both sets of long johns were the same size and manufactured by the same company. After washing both pair in the same laundry, one fit perfectly but the other had shrunk to one-half the size.

At the base, while we waited for the arrival of equipment, we went on sub patrol. Downtown it was skirt patrol.

It was our first Open Post weekend at Westover. A fellow bombardier, Jim Kissberth, and I stepped off the bus in downtown Holyoke.

"Hey Jimmy, look at that," I pointed, "that candy store. What's it called? Fanny Farmer's Candy? Damn, if that doesn't look exactly like the See's Candy stores back home. All white-and-black trim and so clean. And all those jars of jelly beans in the windows. Let's go in and buy some."

"I'll get some fudge."

"Suit yourself. That is one line I won't mind standing in. What a cute brunette behind the counter!"

"The blond one isn't bad either."

"Good. You wait for the blond and I'll try to get a date with that brunette. What a dish. Looks like a combination Betty Boop and Betty Grable. Oh, that's the best I've seen since Rheva back in L.A."

It was sinful: chocolate, butter, caramel, nuts, and the Fanny Farmer candy girl. A line never moved so fast. When I finally stood in front of her, facing her gamin brown eyes, I went blank.

"May I help you?"

"Yeah," I stared, as her mouth opened over beautiful white teeth and curved into a dimpled smile. The red, cupid bow lips parted, moist and succulent.

"What would you like?"

"You gotta be kidding," I said under by breath. "Uh, . . . oh, yes. I would like a pound of jelly beans."

She leaned towards me, reaching over the bonbons and salt-water taffy, the opened ruffled collar of the smock framing her face and figure.

"Is there anything else?" she asked, her animation dancing across the glass.

"I'll have a pound of that, too." I pointed toward the next counter.

"The peanut brittle?"

"Fine." I didn't give a damn. I just wanted to see her as she walked between the candy cases. She had shapely legs and her bottom, wrapped in a black gingham apron, was roundly enticing.

"That will be eighty-five cents, please."

"O.K." I fooled around finding the change in my pocket, deliberately bringing out a few coins and then reaching for some more. "Oh, gosh, this isn't enough. Wait, I'll find it. By the way, I, uh, I know this is short notice, but I'm new here in town, and well, maybe you'd consider showing me around. Maybe, ah, have dinner with me tonight?"

She took the four quarters I handed her and without a word walked to the cash register.

"Ninety-five and one dollar." She counted slowly and then looked up at me. In a hushed voice she answered, "I'm off at five. I live just a short way from here. It won't take long for me to change."

"I'm sorry, Al, we had to wait so long for a table," the Fanny Farmer candy girl apologized. "I can't seem to get used to the crowds that come in on the weekends."

"Who cares? Being with you, Rita, is what matters. We'd better make these drinks last, though. I don't think that waitress will be back for a while." Rita took a sip of beer and with determination, swallowed it.

The Italian restaurant was small. The tables were pushed together to allow a space for dancing. The corner jukebox, the only source of music, bellowed joyful Italian songs. Strung around the room on a flimsy, latticework frame were bunches of dusty, artificial grapes and empty Chianti wine bottles. The lights were central and bright and they glared off of yellow-enameled walls. In Hollywood, the place would have been considered a joint, but, to the servicemen, it was a restaurant full of candlelight and romance.

"This sure is a pretty town," I broke the silence. "I have it in my mind that this is the way Harvard looks. In fact, this is the way I picture all the big Eastern schools—mossy buildings, big trees, lots of green." Rita didn't say anything but she paid me attention with her eyes. "Not like California. Have you ever been to California?"

"No."

"Have you ever been out of Massachusetts?" I leaned forward. "Out of Holyoke?"

"I've been to Boston many times."

"I was teasing. Tell me about Boston. I want to go there, if I can get a pass. I want to visit the Christian Science Church."

"There's a lot to tell, I guess, but at the moment I can't think of anything interesting."

"Yeah? Well, I can think of lots of interesting things to tell you about California, but let's not waste time. Do you want to dance?"

"Sure."

Confined to a tiny spot on the crowded dance floor, her body scented of roses, she felt as good as she looked. Rita was curvaceous and soft in my arms. Holding her close, I thought I could feel her heart beat through the crush of firm breasts. I didn't want to let go. I wanted to hold on and on.

"Now, Al," Rita took my wandering hand and held it firmly around her waist. "Did you like the spaghetti? Didn't you think it was good?"

"Yes. So much better than the stuff they served at my last base. We used to have pasta all the time."

"Oh, dear. We could have gone to a Chinese restaurant."

"Not at all. I loved it. This pasta had sauce."

It was only five minutes before the cab pulled up in front of her house. She kissed me quickly on the lips and whispered, "I hope we see each other again."

And we did see each other, as often as possible. When I returned from patrols, I called her. If I couldn't leave the base, she made arrangements to come out. We would go to the Officers' Club or walk in the woods that fringed Westover. On Sunday, I went to Mass with her. In town we window-shopped and went to dinner. We didn't go to the movies. They took up too much time. Occasionally we sat in the wooden swing on the front porch of her wood-framed, two-story house. I never met her family. They must have regarded me, a serviceman, like her New England neighbors who gave me disapproving glances. We talked incessantly, yet said nothing. We didn't need each other's history in our pursuit of the moment. Rita and I pleasured each other's senses. Away from her, I couldn't get her out of my mind. To think about her brought a surge in my groin. I liked her Eastern softness, more feminine than the girls exposed to California's year-round sun. The closer it came for me to leave, the more involved I became, the more I depended on being with her. My defenses let down. My attitude softened. I wanted the luxury of a one-to-one relationship. She became an anchor, a life raft. I seriously considered marriage. I rationalized—I must be grown up enough to know what I want. Look at what I was being asked to do. I *must* be a man.

"Thanks for coming out this morning, Rita."

"Lucky I had the day off. And I really enjoy the bus ride, Al."

"I'm glad. I wanted to talk to you."

We walked unhurried. The woods were quiet, very quiet and peaceful. I was not. I held her hand tightly as if everything I wanted to say would be transmitted through clasped fingers.

"You're leaving soon, aren't you?" She gazed up at me with a melting sweetness.

"Soon. Yes. But, we haven't gotten our orders yet."

"Then . . .?"

"You can feel it, the tightening of security, the restrictions. It's the suspense. The air is heavy with it. From day to day, you never know. But," I shrugged, "there's nothing I, nothing anyone can do about it."

Rita looked straight ahead, posture erect, her steps in cadence to mine. There was a small crease in her forehead beneath a pompadour of auburn-gold.

"I love you, Rita. Do you love me?"

"Yes, Al. With all my heart."

Emotionally strained, I squeezed her hand but somehow managed to speak deliberately, to sound as if, in my mind at least, it was already resolved. "I want you, Rita, all of you."

"I know," she responded quietly.

In a grove of sycamores, we stopped. I turned to her and put my hands on her shoulders, explaining, "I've got a pass, a twenty-four hour pass starting at four this afternoon. I made a room reservation at the Hotel Essex. Well, Rita, shall we?" She took my hands and wrapped them around her neck. We kissed.

Dinner had been romantic, particularly meaningful in anticipation of the evening to come. We arrived at the hotel at eight. As we walked across the lobby, holding hands and high on sexual energy, we passed a buddy of mine from the base.

"Hey, Al, ol' friend. Why don'tcha bring your gal and come up to my room for a drink?"

"O.K. with you, Rita? Sounds like fun." Rita nodded. After all, we had all night.

"That's great," I agreed. "Wait for me at the elevator. I gotta get my key."

Entranced by her brown eyes, I was slow to become aware of the commotion in the lobby. I looked up with wonder as the registration clerk came charging through the front desk's swinging doors. With my friend following solicitously, the clerk walked over to us. The man appeared to be flustered.

Wrinkling his brow, squinting his skimpy eyes, he waved his finger at me and said, "You can't take girls up to our rooms."

"What?" I asked in disbelief.

His veins pulsated into engorged lumps and then disappeared under slicked, black hair as he warned, "You can't use our rooms for immoral purposes!" Self righteously, he threw his arms across the elevator doors.

I was so surprised I couldn't speak. Involuntarily, I reached for him. He slipped under my extended arms and ran back behind the front desk. Slamming books closed and banging the desk bell, he summoned attention.

An older man in glasses emerged from one of the front offices. "What's going on here?" he demanded.

The desk clerk gibbered like a bird protecting its nest.

The senior gentleman approached us. "Now," he said, "we don't want any trouble, but we simply cannot allow you to come here and use our rooms. We have a high set of standards at this hotel. We must maintain our reputation."

"What are you talking about?" I asked, astonished. "What the hell business is it of yours?"

Ignoring me, he looked at Rita. "You will create problems if you bring men in here and use our rooms."

"Who do you think you're talking to?" I asked angrily. "Why, she might be my wife."

"I know her," he said defensively. "She works across the street in the candy store. I don't want any of this nonsense starting in *my* hotel!"

That did it. I threw a right punch. Lowering it a fraction to miss his glasses, my hand landed on the cheekbone and slid off into his nose. His spectacles flew off, as his head jerked from the blow. Stunned, he staggered backward into the revolving front door. As he started to fall, the door swung around and hit him on his ass. He fell forward, sprawling at my feet.

The lobby was full of GIs and they cheered. "Hey, Lieutenant, you want us to clean the place out?"

Geez, what had I done? I grabbed Rita, and, hailing a cab, I took her home. She was disappointed and so was I. But, more than that, I was mad. My hand hurt. I had nothing left. With a tired, "I love you," I walked her to the door and went back to the base.

For the next few days I basked in praise and admiration. The guys in my squadron loved it. "Hey, Al, that was great. Those mean civilians out there; you whipped them. Sticking up for a girl's reputation, getting involved, that's the way we of the Air Force are: HONORABLE."

Rita called me from work. "Gee, Al, I can't understand Mr. Kelly. He's always so polite and pleasant. I thought he really liked me. He comes into the candy store all the time. It just isn't like him. He must still be upset by what happened the week before."

"What happened?"

"Well, the American Legion held a convention at the hotel. Those WW I guys got pretty rambunctious. I heard some of them were drunk the whole weekend. At their party on Saturday night, some of them rolled a piano out of the third-story window." Rita giggled. "Some of the ivory keys are still scattered in the alley."

"Now you tell me," I moaned.

"Oh, but Al, I thought you were marvelous. You were so protective. I love you, Al."

No wonder the guy was so P.O.'d. Still, he got what he deserved. I felt pretty good about the whole thing *until* the following Tuesday morning when I was paged over the loudspeaker to report to the office in the Officers' Mess. A uniformed Holyoke policeman, holding a stack of subpoenas, greeted me.

"Sure sorry about this, Lieutenant," he said as he handed me one off the top.

~~~~~~

COMMONWEALTH OF MASSACHUSETTS
HAMPDEN, s.s.

To <u>Lieut. A.W. La Chasse, Westover Field</u>, in the County of Hampden.

YOU ARE HEREBY SUMMONED IN THE NAME OF THE COMMONWEALTH OF MASSACHUSETTS to appear before the District Court of Holyoke, to be holden at the District Court Room, in said Holyoke, on the <u>first</u> day of <u>September</u> in the year of our Lord one thousand nine hundred and <u>forty-two</u> at nine o'clock in the forenoon, then and there in said Court to <u>show cause why a complaint should not issue against</u> <u>you for assault and battery on James P. Kelly, Mgr.</u> Of Essex Hotel <u>and breach of peace</u>

at said Holyoke,
        HEREOF FAIL NOT
            Witness, EUGENCE A. LYNCH, Esquire at Holyoke, aforesaid this 27<u>th</u> day of <u>August</u> in the year one thousand nine hundred and <u>forty-two</u>.

(Gregory J. Scanlon)
CLERK OF SAID DISTRICT COURT

~~~~~~

"Oh, no!" Commander Holt shook his head. "I told you guys to be careful. The base commander is death on this type of thing. He's had nothing but trouble here with these guys about to ship out. You know yourself, the MPs and SPs are all over the place trying to maintain order."

"I know, Major," I implored. "I was just defending her honor, you know? Like a gentleman of the Air Force?"

"Sure, Al, I know, I know." Holt, sustaining his seriousness, thought a moment. "The important thing is to keep this within the squadron. We can't let the Old Man know. I'll get in touch with our Intelligence Officer, Phil Haberman. We'll let him handle it."

I was worried. I could just hear the base commander: "Throw the guy out. Give him to the town. Let's make *him* a peace offering." There was nothing honorable about going to jail.

We were put on notice that week, confined to the base. There were no passes. It was just as well. I wasn't worth much. My drives were greatly diminished. I didn't eat and couldn't sleep. I loved Rita, but I *needed* Haberman. The Intelligence Officer was in Richmond with the ground echelon. He would travel to Holyoke to defend me if my case went to trial. If it did, he was going to bring a civil action for slander. Meanwhile, Haberman coached me by telephone on how to conduct myself in court.

I had just finished a conversation with Captain Haberman and was walking back to the barracks, when I heard the sound of bullets ricocheting. The twang of the shells grazing off rocks came from behind my barracks. I couldn't believe it. The officers had been issued live ammunition without formal training. I was shocked!

I learned in the Marines to have great respect for weapons. We were taught first how to handle guns, and then, only on the firing range under the supervision of the Range Master, were we given live ammunition and directed, step-by-step, how to "squeeze" the trigger as we aimed at the target butts.

These guys were acting like children with a new toy. It was a miracle that no one was killed. Some men had shot holes in their mattresses. They were fascinated by the tiny hole on top of the material and the gaping tear underneath where the bullet had emerged, leaving a pile of stuffing. But, on the second floor?

Oley, sitting on his bunk, called to me as I walked in. "Hey, Al, how do you fire one of these things?"

Sitting down next to him, I explained in proper nomenclature the use of the weapon. He had put the ammunition clip into the bottom of the handle. I instructed him how to pull back the slide, which, after letting it go, would arm the chamber with a bullet. I was about to describe the safety features of the gun, and how, only after they were both depressed, the weapon would fire. But Oley already had a death grip on the whole handle and trigger, so that when he let the slide go, the pistol automatically discharged. The bullet passed between my feet, blowing out the underpinnings of the building beneath us. I looked down at the hole and then at Oley. The look on his face could have only been matched by my own. We were both shitty scared.

"Oh, Al. What have I done?" Oley gasped.

"Oley, give me that." With my hand flatly extended, I pushed the barrel so that it pointed to the wall and took the gun, as if it were a carton of eggs. With extreme care, I laid it on the pillow.

"Leave it there, Oley, and find someplace to hide. We've got to get these guys out on a firing range."

In Headquarters, I talked to the officer of the day and told him that there was promiscuous shooting going on and, unless he organized something quick, very few of us would make it into battle.

Monday, September 1st, on a special pass, I went to the court hearing. It took place in the District Court in Holyoke, a big wooden building that looked old and smelled old. We were seated around a long conference table in one of the courtrooms, the judge in a black robe at one end, myself at the other, with three people on either side. Mr. Kelly, as plaintiff, sat to my left. He had a large, gray swelling of discolored flesh under his left eye. He sat there looking victimized, not saying a word.

"Tell us, Lieutenant, why did you hit Mr. Kelly?"

"Well," I began, "He said . . ."

"But why did you hit him?"

"I'm trying to tell you." I began again.

"You are a disgrace to your uniform. And to your country. And to the flag. And to the Air Force."

I politely interrupted. "I'm supposed to be out on sub patrol right now, protecting *you* . . ."

"There was no reason to hit him."

They were not about to listen to anything I had to say. They were going to make me a beautiful example to the base and all its personnel. They already had made up their minds they were going to have my ass. Trial was set for the following Monday.

After the hearing, I stopped by the candy store to lick my wounds. Rita said all the right things. I was her hero; her knight in shining armor. Refreshed by her bouncy smile and another bag of jellybeans, I went back to Westover feeling satisfied I had acted as only a gentleman could.

It was true that my future was clouded with ifs. What if Haberman couldn't get me off? What if I had to go to jail? What if Rita and I got married?

They were questions that would not be answered. That very afternoon on September 1st, we received our orders. By September 7th, the date set for my trial, I, along with the 367th Squadron, was already in Scotland.

9

OVER THERE

After a twenty-four hour layover in Gander Bay, Newfoundland and an unromantic last American Air Force dinner of liver and onions, the first of the thirty-five B-17 aircraft, on a 52° latitude, began the Great Circle Route to Europe. The Flying Fortresses, gloved in the blackness of night, flew on a bold and recently activated flight plan, a 2,119 mile nonstop crossing over the Atlantic.

We were on our way. They termed us "complete combat crews." The word "ready" was rightfully omitted. The thirty-caliber guns in the nose were as effective as sling shots. Some of our crews had no practice in aerial gunnery. We had no training in combat-type formation flying. We were not trained nor equipped to fly in weather. Not until September 1943, would the 8th Air Force Training Command, established July 4th, 1942, be activated in the European Theater. We had made no provision for communications people or meteorologists. They were services we would beg and be greatly thankful for from the RAF, their lingo and codes another language to learn. Because the English used the metric system, they could not help us in servicing aircraft. Finally, as perfect as the B-17 was, its maximum speed was overrated, its range not proven, and . . . it was not a fortress.

Yet, we accepted the equipment and the organization of our advancing movement. We were trusting and naïve. We did not even put on our parachutes for the flight. We would have, had we known that 150 miles out from Gander Bay, 423rd Squadron's 1st Lt. John Leahy's B-17 exploded, leaving no trace of plane or crew.

A mile and one-half above the ocean's icy eternity, in seventy-five feet of gauges and bulkheads, we relaxed in our ignorance. In the brand new aircraft, wind noises, peculiar to every ship, had staked their territories, whining and huffing through sliver-wide trenches in the joints and seams. Machine guns rattled on the supporting linkage. In the cabinets, tools glided in place. Metal lids trembled over first-aid kits. Across from the bomb bay gas tank that provided the extra, necessary fuel, solemnly humped the olive green B-4 duffel bags.

The fishbowl turrets were empty. The waist windows, in a struggling effort, had been pulled closed. The gunners leaned back on the inside panels between the ribs of the ship, cozy in their heavy winter flight suits. Smoking, napping, with voices overwhelmed by the drone of engines, each contemplated the same wonder. Would he make the trip back home?

In the nose, comfortably propped on an arrangement of the crew's parachutes, I looked into the nocturnal sky and felt relief to be away from the jurisdiction of that Holyoke Court and all those self-righteous bastards. Rita and I, well, we'd make up for lost time, doubly make up for it, after the war.

Gise worked at his table. The pale light from his desk lamp slipped into the compartment. Between smokes, I dozed.

In the early morning hours I ate one of the brown-bag lunches that had been packed for us at Gander Bay and stored in the nose. Trading sandwiches with the bombsight maintenance officer, 1st Lt. Percy Vincent, I gave him half of my soggy tuna for half of his soggy egg salad. The paper wrapping the food, though heavily waxed, would not stem the saturation of the vinegary mayonnaise or the smells of the menu. Fumes from the dill pickles mixed in equal potency with the smoke from my Camel cigarettes.

Thermoses of water, coffee and hot cocoa were stored in the aft bomb bay bulkhead. Stretching my legs, I walked through the ship, over the bomb bay catwalk, to get a drink. A ribbon of water from the thermos' spigot expanded the small envelope paper cup. In the turbulent-free flight I carried it back with me, being careful not to step on bodies of the sleeping crew. As I passed the flight deck, I stopped to talk with Oley and Gates, but they were busy comparing notes and making calculations. They were working through the night, keeping a watchful eye over the instrument panel of green lights. The bank-and-turn indicator was absolutely straight. Oley, as usual, had melted the ship into a perfect trim. Ahead, far ahead, where it looked like the world dropped off, was a white sheet of morning. The tips of the wings had picked up its light. I went back to the nose.

One-half pack of Camels later, the dawn broke over the ship and a short time after, a big, white sun edged up directly in front of us.

As we neared the end of the ten-hour flight, we tightened up, dropping altitude to less than several thousand feet. I put on my earphones and ate a chocolate bar for breakfast.

"Well, whadd'ya know, we've bumped into Europe," Oley announced in a calm, but pleased voice.

The coast of North Ireland was as craggy as the voice of its people.

It was at that moment, while we made our landfall over the tip of the North Irish Coast, that it hit me, that grip in the gut. We were approaching the Theater of War. War! WAR!

There we were with our tokus hanging out, with no place to go, no place to hide, no trench, no building. War in the air was always a major engagement.

"Get to your stations," Oley ordered. "Try your guns but don't lay on the heat. Just make sure they're working."

Oley, along with the rest of us, didn't know if there were any enemy fighters around. How far west was the open door to war?

In its approach to the same landfall, the Fortress of Capt. W.C. Melton of the 368th Squadron, out of gas, crash-landed in the Irish Sea. For all the crew's wishful thinking and hoping, they couldn't get the aircraft to the sandy shore. Air Sea Rescue saved the crew, but the ship was lost. They were lucky. The beach was heavily mined.

Past the lacy outer islands, the view became obscured in clouds. Through a blue sky and warm sun we flew above the lumpy cotton blanket of cumulus. No other aircraft was visible.

In the flight cabin, Oley picked up a radio signal. He turned the radio down to its weakest volume and began a right turn with the dial. The signal faded. He moved it to the left and the signal returned, becoming louder. Hmm, hmm, hmm, in a northerly direction, Oley homed in on the Prestwick Air Tower. Dropping into the soup, we sliced through the clouds, dispersing the flimsy white masses that solidified behind us. Lower and lower, abruptly the clouds broke. Opening up below, was a large bowl of landing strips. It was as if God had pulled up the curtain and said, "Let these kids in, they've come a long way."

Oley, circling the huge base, waited for his landing assignment. Cleared to land, we completed the approach. The tires buffered the runway. We taxied across the field and stacked neatly beside the other B-17s that had already made it. The landing was as sleek as the flight.

Three months earlier in June, the first contingent of American bomb groups, the 97th had arrived. The 92nd and the 301st followed. We were the fourth Bomb Group (H) to reach Scotland.

Prestwick was a bustling air center, inordinately large and crowded with aircraft. There were American ships, some under repair. Other planes of various types lined the aprons. Most of them had the red, white and blue roundel of the RAF on the wing with identifying insignia of the pilot's country printed on the tail: Polish, Free French, Argentine and Australian. All of the aircraft looked awkward compared to the graceful, sleek-lined B-17.

Oley was still in the cockpit with Gates, logging his notes on a clipboard, while the rest of us had eased ourselves out of the escape hatch and were shaking off the wrinkles from the long crossing. Another B-17 thumped onto the ground. Trailing a thread of blue smoke, the tires squealed as they made contact.

Oley, with Gates following, opened the side door and crunched down the stairs. The Captain stretched his arms above his head, releasing his body from the cramped flight.

We all praised the two pilots for the smooth flying.

"Thanks," Oley said. With his thumb pointing over his shoulder to the aircraft behind him, he explained, "It's this baby. She's perfect. Now, then, who's got a nickel and where's the Coke machine?"

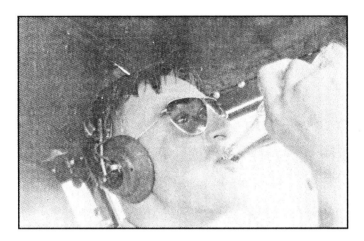

Captain Olson in the cockpit.

Copilot Norman Gates in the cockpit.

We stood around the aircraft, waiting for some instructions. The airport had socked in again before a truck was dispatched that picked us up and took us to the Headquarters building. In the converted terminal, filled with desks, phones and both American and RAF permanent party, we smoked and waited and bitched and waited some more. Straggling around in the lengthy confusion was a letdown. It created doubt in our minds. Did anyone know what the hell they were doing?

"Hey, 367th," Gates called, "Captain Olson's crew. Jump on that truck out in front. It's here for us. It's going to take us to our quarters."

The crew, billeted together, was dropped off at a white, stone hewn, thatched roof building that edged the west side of the field. Gise and I shared a room on the second floor. It was large enough for two thin, slat-board beds and one shuttered window. The room, like the rest of the building's interior, was clammy and damp and smelled of wet cement. There was no suggestion of heat and electricity barely eked from several central light bulbs. Our bathroom was downstairs. Except for the pull-cord toilet, there was no running water. The tub was fashioned out of rock and the marble basin, supported on a pedestal, had no faucets. Water came in pitchers.

The rough stucco walls, maze of small rooms and corridors may have suggested warm accommodations to Prince Valiant, but they left me bone cold. I hurried back to Headquarters.

Lunch was being served in the mess hall, a converted hangar around the corner. All of us were starved. We hadn't had food for hours.

I ate every bit of the oat-flour bread and meat-roll filling that was smothered in chutney, the fresh tomatoes and flat, sweet biscuit that crumbled like cornbread. I wasn't particularly fond of the condiments, but if that was English food, I was determined to like it, even the tea.

Uck, plain tea tasted like varnish to me. Then I found out
what the English meant when they said "a spot of tea." That's all it
was. The rest was milk and sugar, rationed to one cube during
wartime.

The luxury of lunch did not escape me. How could it? It was
dressed up like a birthday present. It was a peach, meticulously
wrapped in cardboard and tissue.

As we finished lunch with cigarettes, a ruddy-faced man in a
tan uniform and the collar of the ministry came over and set two
bottles of scotch on the table. The Canadian priest, who they called
"Padre," poured us a round of whisky and, in a thick English accent, toasted our health. He invited us to a party that had been
arranged for the next afternoon.

A party? Yes, I wanted to go. I was anxious to see Scotland.
There was certainly nothing uncommon about Prestwick Air Base,
except perhaps for its size. It looked the same as any other base. I
hadn't heard bagpipes or seen men in kilts. And where in hell were
the fair "lassies"?

I looked forward to the opportunity to sample any flavor that
was Scotland. Was a party here so different from a party in California? If I had known, I would not have been able to sleep that
night.

10

"GOODBYE, YUNK"

When we climbed aboard the bus that would drive us into Glasgow for the evening's affair, visibility was no more than half a mile. The afternoon sky was an oppressive gray, like dying twilight. All of us wanted to ride upstairs on the double-decker bus. Major Holt was escorted to a front seat but the rest of us had to stand while waiting for seats to empty.

The civilians were dressed in dark, heavy overcoats. The women wore scarves over their heads and nearly all the men smoked pipes. The people had a healthy, clear skin and for all the years of rationing, a cheerful demeanor. They were quiet, overly polite. When I asked what a scone was, I received nineteen different answers.

You could see in their faces the genuine esteem they held for us. We were young men—their protectors. We were joining the team and, being among the first overseas, still unique. The children, especially, clung to us in worshipful admiration.

"Hallo, Yunk. Di'ye come in one o' thim big aroplanes, yisterdy? Ye must ha' beene guid and scared."

Who could resist the youngster in his knickers, high-top shoes and peak cap, when he asked, "Dinna ye have iny ghum in yer pohckets . . . perrhaps a wee cahndy barr?"

Traveling on the road were pedestrians, cyclists and a few cabs. Patches of sheep roamed the fields close to the sides of the road.

We had all managed to sit down when Major Holt yelled in a shaken voice, "There's tanks coming—we're getting near the front."

Treaded machines spooked through the mist; clumsy boxes of an antique vintage. A Scotsman on the bus laughed and explained their value was only in training maneuvers.

The stores were closing when we reached Glasgow. Some of the commercial buildings had their windows boarded over. In the display cases of the stores remaining open were household items, rationed and expensive.

A tobacconist carried an extensive supply of goods, more than any other shop. Inside the store, smelling sweet and aromatic, were pipes, tobaccos and a large assortment of cigarettes—Canadian Sweet Caporals, English Ovals, Players, Navy Cuts, and French and Turkish brands. And, while the windows displayed cardboard ads of American cigarettes, there were none.

Another shop down the street was still open and it also had an aroma. It stunk like hell. Women stood in line waiting to buy a piece of fish.

As he walked up one of the streets that curved like a canyon between the tall buildings, a guide cautioned, "Look out for beans." Sheep strayed ahead of us.

The dusky weather closed over the town. Austere light from the old, moss-covered lampposts added loneliness to the district and to its inhabitants, who, wrapped in woolens, walked hurriedly to their homes or to a night shift. For the promise of gaiety, we followed our guides into a building to its upstairs party.

The walls of the dance hall were filled with war posters. Ugly-looking Germans, brandishing swastikas, hovered over British ships; evil Japanese bathed in flags of the Rising Sun; and Mickey Mouse, with one ear enlarged with radio antenna, warned that the "walls have ears." Leftover crepe decorations from a previous party straggled from the high ceiling. Some RAF officers were already there and a group of young women sat together at the end of the room.

A waitress in a white apron brought me the gin and tonic I had ordered. It was gin and bitters. There were no ice cubes. The only drink worse than warm gin was sloe gin. I sipped the medicinal liquor and took large inhales on the cigarettes. While sauntering around, I evaluated the girls. They were young and attractive and their cotton stocking seams were straight.

Finding myself in a new country and feeling unsophisticated, I didn't rush to become acquainted. Trying to look casual, I remained an observer to the early evening's proceedings.

For dinner we were served slices of fresh pot roast, potatoes in a milk sauce, fried tomatoes, and one lump of sugar with tea. The dinner was enjoyable. The evening had so far been pleasant and genially uneventful. In California, I would have termed it dull. But, over there in that misty North of the British Empire, I felt a simmering excitement. The double-decker bus, the Scottish brogue, the argyle socks, the shrouded buildings, the skimpy staircase to the private club, the black-market beef—all of it was fascinating.

And so were the women. They remained reserved and quiet as they sat apart from the men through dinner. Then, when the band gathered and the music began, the girls became lively and gay. They could jitterbug better than most GIs. It was a grab for a moment's happiness; for that, too, seemed rationed.

"My name's Al," I introduced myself, as I led her onto the dance floor.

"All," she pronounced it in a soft, bell-like voice. "My name is Elly."

Her face was thin and fragile, her nose unusual, flattening at the tip, then rounding nicely around the nostrils. Swinging to the rhythm of a Benny Goodman tune, her dark eyes picked up luster and vivaciousness replaced the drawn, war-weary expression.

We spoke little. Our commentaries about our lives, mine from California and hers, about the Red Cross work, were simple. The flowing conversation was between our bodies. Hers was nicely arranged. It fit mine. In a slow fox trot, with her arm wrapped around my neck and her head on my shoulder, she made love.

We had only two dances when the band broke up. Though the evening was young, the party was officially over. Disappointed, I took her back to her table. What appeared to be the beginning of a warm and expanding friendship was cut short. Oh, I knew I hadn't swept her off her feet, but it did have possibilities.

Everyone waved goodbye as we all made an exit at once. I wondered how to kill the next hours. I didn't want to go back to the humdrum of the base, but I didn't know where else to go. As I started down the stairs, a small hand took mine.

"All," Elly said, "I'll go with you."

Delicious questions ran through my brain as we were pushed along with the crowd through the double doors of the building's entrance. Outside, we jumped onto some type of tram, a conveyance that was noiseless except for the ring of a bell when it started moving. It resembled a San Francisco cable car. In the ceiling's central row of sockets, two electric bulbs cast a diluted light over the interior, enough so that I could see the whole trolley was jammed with passengers.

Squashed against her body, I felt an exhilaration. Where was she taking me? I didn't know. I was too heady with intoxicating ideas to give a thought to danger. As long as she was happy, I was happy. Whatever she had planned was all right with me. I nuzzled the cords in the back of her neck, and, turning her head around, I planted a kiss on her lips.

A few blocks and she said, "Here we are. Shall we?"

She pulled me by the hand, off the tram, across the stone-faced street and to one of the three-story buildings that were adjacent to and part of each other. She unlocked a tall, oyster-colored door that was encased in leaded glass and started up the stairs. I closed the door and turned around to find her climbing the broad, wooden stairs, two at a time and already halfway to the top. Leaping three at once, I chased after her. I sure didn't want to lose her now.

The brass coving glimmered in the weak light on the second-story landing. At the top of the stairs, I followed her into a high-ceilinged, wood room that smelled like trees after a rain. She kicked off her sturdy, sling-back pumps. One went flying through the air like a punted football. Stifling a laugh at the sight, I veered to the left to avoid stepping on the other shoe.

Elly had unbuttoned her blue suit jacket and was working on the zipper of her skirt when she moved behind a partition next to a corner kitchen. As I threw my jacket on the chair, the other door to the room opened. An older woman, with a man standing behind her, peered in at me. She smiled a toothy grin and made a salutary greeting. Then she closed the door.

Who was that? Her mother? Her sister? Her friend? Whoever they were, they seemed pleased to see me. Man, this was another country. Over here anything goes! I didn't know what to expect next, but I kept hoping.

Predominate in the room was a big, high bed. With my back to it, I jumped up and, landing on top—pooff—sank back towards the floor. The bed and its covering were made of down; unbelievably soft. I took off my belt, marveling at the way the comforter billowed around me. It was like lolling in soft whipped cream, in forty-two square feet of air bubbles. I had never experienced anything like it.

I pushed off shoes with my toes and lay back. Snaking out of my trousers, I felt the material hug me. It swirled about me like a waterfall. I glided out of my shirt. Lying there, I was tantalized by the enclosing cloud. It was enough sex just to lie on the damn thing.

Bare feet pitty-patted across the linoleum floor. I wanted to see what was happening, but I couldn't lift my head beyond the banks of the comforter.

Jesus Christ! Suddenly, there was Elly in flight above me. With her legs separated, her black snatch like an airborne bat, her firm breasts thrusting forward, she was like a B-25 with the landing gears down. It was a hell of a jump. She must have been on some Olympic team.

I was paralyzed. In her acceleration, was she going to crash through the wall? Were we going to bash heads? How *was* she going to land?

Expertly.

One hand landed above my right shoulder, the other next to my left arm. Her knees settled over my left leg. In another instant, her legs straddled mine as she sat herself down right on top of my erect cock which had pulsated out of my undershorts.

I could feel the cold skin of her feet next to my legs as she rocked back and forth, smiling in her sensation. Her intensity worried me. I wiggled down, trying to be more accommodating, but her motion was all-consuming. I became frightened she might break it off.

When she saw my lack of enjoyment, more like anguished pain, she stopped. Laying her body down on mine, without separating, we rolled over. The foreplay of anticipation culminated quickly. Her passage gripped me tightly as I thrust against the elastic, milking walls once, twice, the penetration so pronounced my resistance shattered into a wave of explosions. Gurgling noises climbed from her throat as we swooned together, down, down, into wet exhaustion.

We lay together without moving, Elly beside me, silent as a breath. Her hand rested on the bed like a pale kid glove against the white covering. The fingers were long and sensitive with short, trimmed nails. I took the delicate hand in mine.

For a moment I rolled away from her, and, while repelling the comforter's fluidity, I pulled off my shorts and T-shirt. Reaching under her waist, I pulled her close. As I looked at her, I thought, how lovely, how absolutely lovely. Her body was like a vanilla confection. I was flushed with affection for her.

Briefly, we slept. The second time I mounted her, I had to fight the foamy intrusions of the quilt and my dog tags poked her in the breastbone, but they were only momentary distractions; our appetite, our eagerness, ultimately convulsing and satiating.

Yet a third time? So soon? I feigned sleep. But strong fingers fondled me. Elly leaned over, kissed my closed eyes and rubbed her tongue around the ridge of my nose. Opening my mouth with hers, she nibbled my lips. She washed my face with small kisses and blew softly into my ear. Lowering her head to my chest, she ran probing fingers over my body. I was completely at her mercy.

I was ready for sleep when the door opened and the man I had seen earlier, announced, "You'll want to leave now. It's time to go." Respectful of future engagements, I didn't want to overstay my welcome. Pulling my shirt from beneath her small shoulders, I quickly got up. Elly stayed on the bed. Every few minutes, as I dressed, I leaned over and kissed her. I took my time, hoping she would say something, perhaps of another meeting. She made no sound.

It was hard to leave. I opened the door, winked and said, "So long for now."

From the bed, Elly sing-songed, "Goodbye, Yunk."

Down the stairs and out into the wet night, I saw a tram. The front of it had vanished in a heavy fog. It was like a fantasy. I rode back to the building where we had attended the party. From there, along with other military people, I boarded the bus for Prestwick.

Gise was snoring loudly when I fell on my bed. Compared to Elly's, it was like a slab. My exerted body welcomed it. The evening, like the tram, seemed a dream. I was too tired to recount the order of events.

What an initiation to the British Isles! With lassies like that, who needed bagpipes or kilts? Imagining the Allies ahead of me, I fell asleep.

11

"INTENSIVE TRAINING COMPLETED"

The tarmack was barely dry when we flew from Prestwick into Thurleigh on September 8th. The 97th, the 301st and the 93rd (the latter's Liberators landed at Alconbury the day before) were in such close proximity that the tower at Thurleigh broke radio silence to aid us in identification. "Attention, American aircraft. This is your field. You are free to land." From the air, Thurleigh looked starkly bare. Like Wendover, it was undergoing the rites of expansion. But the base, rented from the English under lend-lease, was far different in that a green border of forests and farmlands surrounded it.

The RAF officers greeted us with friendly enthusiasm. They hadn't seen many Yanks. As the first squadron to land there, in numbers alone, our presence was impressive. After introductions and handshakes, we were driven by American and English jeeps to one of the gray-green hangars. In a side room of the building, they were preparing tea, a social ceremony that was conducted, regardless of war, morning and afternoon. We helped ourselves to the jams, cheeses, crackers, tea and coffee and exchanged cigarettes— Camels, Lucky Strikes and Chesterfields, for Canadian Sweet Caporels (Caps) and English Ovals.

The English officers were dapper, both in their carriage and dress. Their durable uniforms were trim. The trousers were sharply pleated and their blue shirts were pressed and knotted with black ties. Some of the men had their pants tucked in around boots and nearly all the RAF had carefully primped mustaches. They carried leather gloves and while suavely smoking cigarettes, punctuated conversation by slapping their gloves from one hand into the other. The higher-ranking officers carried swagger sticks. One had in attendance a "bat-man," a lackey to aid him as a valet and chauffeur. In comparison to the gentlemen of the British Empire, we Yankee colonists appeared happy-go-lucky slouches with our shirts opened at the throat, no ties and some very wrinkled suntans.

After tea, we were driven around the perimeter of the base. Civilians, happy to see us, waved from the fields outside the protective fencing. "Down the road a bit," at the south end of the field, we "popped" into a local pub.

The pub was right out of English folklore:

> "In merry England in the time of old, when good King
> Henry II ruled the land, there lived within the green glades
> of Sherwood Forest, near Nottingham Town, a famous
> outlaw . . ."

The Falcon Inn, with thatched roof, polished tree-stump table tops, small benches, a man playing a tiny hand-accordion and warm beer, was as authentically English as I had ever imagined. I couldn't wait to see London. Intrigued, I watched the bartender in his blousing shirt and suspenders pull the long handles that dispensed the dark and light beers. In this quaint, romantic room I expected Robin Hood himself, to come bounding through the door. I felt like a bard, a rogue. As I began to drink my beer, I flamboyantly swept my foot onto the table and leaned dashingly forward.

Out of the shadows of the room, a barmaid, like a magpie, hurried toward me. Flailing her arms against her long, white skirts, the housemaid cap corking her bounce, she proceeded to give me a piece of brittle English temper. "Yank!" she addressed me in a shrill voice. "These are *my* tables. I work hard. I slave to keep them clean. They are for *my* customers. You, Yank, better bloody well learn not to put your foot on *my* table! We're civilized here. In this country we don't tolerate manners like yours. Hmmmf!" And taking her skirt, she wiped off the table.

So much for the male ego. Somehow, after that, as a mere shadow of my former swashbuckling self, I never felt quite as romantic or merry in that little old pub at the tip of the base, called the Falcon Inn. Robin Hood or no Robin Hood.

On the 8th of September, 1942, we arrived at Thurleigh and on the 8th of September, 1942, we were welcomed to Thurleigh by the infamous British voice from Nazi Germany, Lord Haw Haw. We were eating dinner in the Officers' Mess when the BBC picked up the Oberkommando radio broadcast. In a refined and friendly voice, Lord Haw Haw said, ". . . and I would like to welcome to England, and to its new base in Bedford, the American 306th Bomb Group."

Uncanny and unnerving. Our movement was top secret. Even *we* didn't know where we were going. The first day, and German Intelligence knew we were there. As a further cause of anxiety, the same night a German observation ship dropped flares in the shape of a Christmas tree as it took film of our ships on the field. We learned later that a Spitfire had shot down the enemy aircraft, but that didn't help the sprouting neuroses.

We were green American kids. We had barely made it there, due to, among other reasons, inter-Service rivalry. There we were with the war in our laps, Johnnys-on-the-spot, attempting what the Germans and English considered suicidal, daylight precision bombing. When the RAF chap said to me, as we walked across the field to our temporary tents that night, "Don't light your cigarette. Jerry will see it," another fear was added to the ones I already had. It was a hopeless feeling.

> "We were a pretty sorry lot in 1942. Many people didn't live long enough to learn much."[9]
>
> Gen. Curtis LeMay

Learn what? Command really didn't know . . . enough. We were occupied with RAF jargon and aircraft identification. We attended specialty meetings. If these were instructive, they gave us no training experience. Because of a varied schedule of meetings, we flew most of our flights with a decimated crew. The gunners were practicing gunnery in the pits, not in the air, and the radiomen were still learning Morse code.

We made practice bomb runs, dropping baby-blue one hundred-pound bombs over that big hunk of missing land, an empty inlet from the channel called the Wash. The assignments for the practice runs were made on an irregular and arbitrary basis; a loose, unorganized schedule that concerned flight personnel, who queried, "When are we going to get some real training?" The bombing practice, normally made by not more than several aircraft at a time and at relatively low altitudes, was insignificant in contrast to large-formation bombing at high altitudes. The thinner atmosphere significantly increased the reaction of the aircraft and the difficulty of maintaining a stable platform. High-altitude combat bombing would quickly distinguish the better pilots.

To help fill the gap in an empty training schedule, Command required that pilots and copilots train in blind-flying Link Trainers, a move that, if it was necessary, was made too late. And, a paradoxical one, considering that the role of the Eighth Air Force Bomber Command was to prove heavy bombardment, high-altitude, precision daylight bombing.

In riveted attention, we listened to the men who had already flown missions. One of the men, Bombardier Robert Scheible (an early recipient of the Distinguished Flying Cross) related how a plug of tobacco rubbed on glass could prevent icing on the windows and how certain lubricants used on bomb bay doors would freeze.

But the most impressive information relayed to us by Scheible and the men who had "been there" was the enlarged scope of possible dangers including the imperfection of machines: a catch in the linkage of a machine gun demanded instant correction by the gunner (some, forgetting the altitude, removed their gloves and their hands froze to the metal); blacking out due to oxygen failure; the limited firing range if a turret stuck; the freezing of guns at altitude if not cleaned of excess oil; the nonexistent room for error while firing guns in combat formation; the erratic reaction of the compasses because of the proximity to and vibrations from machine gun fire; the malfunctions of bomb shackles which had forced some bombardiers to release their bombs with screwdrivers; the inability to control the leakage of shell-perforated gas tanks, even though they were supposed to be constructed with self-sealing interlinings; the loss of ship-to-ship, station-to-station communication if the radio was hit. And the standing joke continued to be the thirty-caliber machine guns in the nose. For men nagged by doubts about their own training, it was difficult, at best, to tolerate the understanding that their lives would depend not just on human reflexes, but on an increasing span of circumstances over which no one had control.

Though hardly applicable to the B-17, the RAF described tactical maneuvers they employed in combat. A Spitfire pilot being chased by a German fighter would begin trimming his plane while still in the dive. With the elevators trimmed, at the precise moment the RAF pilot would let go of the controls, the Spitfire would nose into a beautiful climb. The German pilot, still battling manual controls, would continue the dive and over-fly his target. The RAF pilots would feign damage by letting oil run along the stacks. They knew the markings of the German fighter outfits, where each was stationed and what range they had. Recognizing a German squadron's insignia and knowing when they had reached a point of no return, the English could write the danger off.

We flew practice missions, several across the Channel, as diversionary actions, dropping propaganda leaflets over the French coast. We familiarized ourselves with the English IDs and with flying conditions. One of those flying conditions was fog.

On a solo navigational test to the Isle of Man in the Irish Sea, we became engulfed in fog. It became thicker and thicker, until visibility was about fifty feet. I happened to look into the soup that afternoon from the nose at just the right moment. I saw we were skimming treetops. We were brushing along the side of Scafell Pike, the highest elevation in England at 3,210 feet.

"Oley," I called over the intercom, "pull up. We're on the deck."

Throwing the coals to it, the ship groaned as Oley pushed the throttle forward and pulled back on the wheel. The Captain had responded quickly, but carefully. In the fog, it was as if Oley had drawn the mountain in his mind, for he alternately leveled off and then pulled up so that the ship climbed without stalling. After dropping the craft into a hole of sunshine over the water, Oley found his altimeter was more than three hundred feet off!

Back at the base, Wilder, the ball turret, pulled off some branches that had been caught on the underside of the ship. He asked one of the RAF ground crew what the name of the shrub was.

"That's English heather," he replied.

"How tall does it grow?"

"Oh, about ten feet."

John Olson was too smart a pilot to make an error like that. There were Irish laborers working at Thurleigh who were unsympathetic to England, but capable of espionage? The ships were guarded twenty-four hours a day. Still, espionage had been suspected when Leahy's plane was lost outside of Gander Bay. Oh! Another layer of fear to add to those I already had.

Despite the effort on our behalf, in the gestating Eighth Air Force our ETO training was expeditiously thin. The hurry was to get a large bomber force assembled and over enemy territory. The U.S. had opted for the B-17 and its capability for heavy daylight bombardment. The moment had come to sell it to the world. Militarily and politically, time was the priority.

If some of our pilots were well trained because of pre-war competition and that era's extensive discipline, the rest of the crew was not. How could it be? At Wendover, I knew of only one plane with a tow target, our sole object with which to practice aerial gunnery.

One plane for a whole group! Our crew had a turn at shooting at the flapping third finger, two, or at the most, three times. It was a slow, level, parallel shoot, absolutely nothing like firing in combat. The ammunition was scarce but even if it were supplied, how long would a plane have to stand in line, or hang out in its airspace for the arrival of that flying sleeve with a swastika on it? Command would order crews to shoot so many rounds of ammunition, but there were occasions when logistics did not make it possible. Men would grow tired, weary, frustrated, waiting especially in rain and approaching darkness. Eventually, to satisfy orders that so many shells be used, they tossed the canisters of ammunition overboard. Bomb-run orders were just as hypothetical. No sheet of paper could produce what was not delivered. One half dozen or so bomb runs were flown with between three to ten explosives and when we were not supplied with enough gas to complete a bomb run, we listed the flight as a "fuel consumption" test.

But even the necessary equipment and materials could not solve the problem that shadowed the crews and Command alike: simply, that *no one had the experience.* We were the crews that would provide the experience. We were the baby being slapped on the butt for the first time; the test group that would fly a force of B-17s in combat. With us would come the experience. With the experience would come the training. Hero or victim? Alive or dead? In the lurking possibilities we celebrated life with an increasing fervor.

"O.K., guys. Put on the after-shave. Let's thumb a ride to town!"

A dirt road led into Bedford. Past the outlying cottages, it became cobblestone. At the edge of town the road hyphened into a wooden bridge that spanned the Ouse River and then, as summer dust or winter slush, it curled off into the distant farmlands.

The town of Bedford was my home for an unknown time and I embraced it, reveled in it: the petrol station with its three taxis, the bicycle repair shop, the business houses dabbed in lion heads and iron grill-work, the pubs, those dark, mythical closets that apportioned large mugs of beer for threepence, the idyllic tree-lined paths along the river, the postman on his bicycle and the constable with the black-and-white checkered band around his hat, the window flower tubs, the chimneys' tiny roofs; all of it was to me a piece of blimey, jolly well, "Long Live the King" tea cake.

And for military comradeship, there was the Key Club. A ten-shilling note bought a key—a pass—to the private club. Through a narrow entrance and up a stairway was the room where we crowded together for Bully Beef—canned corned beef from Argentina—a chicken sandwich (pigeon), fresh beef (black-market meat), lots of booze, no ice, rumors, talk of hometowns and women.

Give a guy just enough nourishment and, more than any other comfort, more than cigarettes, toilet paper, jellybeans or Coke, quiff topped life's necessities. More than airplanes or folks back home; the talk of conquests, possibilities, new faces, knockers and swinging hips headlined the conversations. Bedford offered plenty of pulchritude for discussions; good-looking gals who would gladly join in a chorus of a favorite Dominion song:

> Roll me over, in the clover
> Roll me over, lay me down and do it again.
>
> Oh, this is number one, and it's only done in fun
> Roll me over, lay me down and do it again.

Nice gals, lots of them, but none like Elly. She happened once. I didn't meet her again. After that night, we were restricted to Prestwick Base on Standing Movement Orders, on one hour's notice. I didn't realize it then, but she would be my last erotic fling for years. Sure, I was looking, but there were only a few short weeks left in our training schedule. Most of the women I met at

Thurleigh were officers, knowledgeable and aristocratic. And *none* of them were going to give it away. God knows I did my best to persuade them.

One evening I met this nifty little brunette at the Key Club. We played a game of darts. She beat me handily. We bought each other a short snorter drink. She ordered a Pimms and I had a beer. Then we signed our names on paper money and exchanged it. The practice of short snorters had begun for me back in Gander Bay, Newfoundland. I was well on my way to collecting a wallet full of money autographed by the RAF. We sat at one of the small tables and ordered supper from a very good-looking barmaid. The evening, I thought, was progressing well. She liked me. Did she like me!

Twenty-pound cans of Spam were making regular Atlantic crossings from the U.S. to the U.K. Pink slices of the ham loaf arrived at our table with greens and home-fried potatoes. Along with the food came the inevitable tray of condiments: mustard, curry, chutney and horseradish.

The RAF officer helped herself to every one of them. She arrayed them around her plate like a palette of paints. Holding her fork prongs down, she dipped every bite of food in each of the seasonings until a mound layered the silverware. She never dropped a crumb.

We finished the supper with a cup of tea and then, holding hands, we walked through the town to the banks of the river. As it became darker, we walked above the paths. The stars came out. A distance away from other couples, we sat down and threw pebbles into the water. We lay down on the grassy slope. I lit two cigarettes and gave her one. We talked about the flickering searchlights in the distance and the beams they projected on the clouds.

I felt the time was right. I reached over to touch her body.

I couldn't find it. There was too much uniform. I loosened her necktie and unbuttoned several of the buttons around her throat. They were stiff and I had difficulty dislodging them. Slow progress until the lapel buttons. They were impossible. It was the belt that was locking up the blouse-works. Kissing her lips, I groped for the buckle, a peculiar piece of metal stabbed in place. It was a lock I could not decipher and the belt had no end. On top of that, she had a handbag strapped across her shoulder. When was she going to help?

She had not moved. Her contribution had been to make small moans. Oh, hell. This was dumb. But I had the throbbies. I was drooling in my pants. I pulled up her skirt. She giggled and smoothed it back down. I pulled it up again, higher. Before she could protest, I reached under her skirt. Her stockings were like leather. I ran my hand up her legs, which she held together in bonded union, and discovered garters like mousetraps. Over the garters were pants and over her pants was the damnedest rubber device I had ever felt. I poked the outer garment. Not a chance.

Shit on this. Oh, oh. What was that? Ah, a bit of petticoat had hiked to her waist. It was the thinnest encounter so far. It provoked me into having one more go at it. With my lips dried to hers, I grappled with one of the garters. With one hand I tried to push the small button out of the metal clasp. Attempting to force the hook apart, my little finger became pinched in the damn thing. I muffled a scream from the pain that was radiating from my blood-swollen fingertip. The small digit was now my sole throbbing member. Wiggling it brought no release. No other way but to yank it out. "Ouch!"

That was it. I was through. There was just so much a man could take. It was like trying to pry a lid off a can of paint. My knuckles were sore from so much bending. The prick teaser, she lay in the dark like a mannequin. At the finish, like at the start, she was all wrapped up, like a piece of meat ready for shipping. She was like the RAF Wellington bomber, of competent and sturdy geodetic construction, tightly knitted and impregnable.

My shirt was wet from sweat and my trousers were stained from the grass. I was so pissed off, if she had gotten up and done a naked belly dance I wouldn't have cared. I pulled her up by her hand. Without saying a word, we walked back to town. It was more than annoying when I realized that she was as relieved to end the evening as I was.

Sgt. Tom Dynan painted the name and the figure
of Pluto on his crew's B-17.

Before a week had passed at Thurleigh, Sgt. Tom Dynan had taken paint and brush to our B-17 and christened it Snoozy II with a drawing of Pluto beside it. It was rumored that Snoozy II was the nickname of Captain Olson's girlfriend. "Tad" Dynan did a hell of a piece of artwork. He was proud of it, proud of the aircraft, proud of the crew. He referred to us as the "best doggone crew in the entire Air Force." He had three brothers who would serve, along with himself, in WW II—one in the infantry in the Philippines, one with the Marines in Okinawa, and the youngest would enlist in the Navy in 1945, on his seventeenth birthday.

During the month of September, feelings ran high. Like Dynan, we felt we had the best people. More and more, the indications were that the Fortress was all that it was promised to be. The missions that were flown had had few fatalities. They had demonstrated that the B-17 could take a beating. The returning men from those missions were proof of our rosy future.

And how we admired them. Meeting those guys was a big thrill. When bombardiers from the 97th who had been in combat came to Thurleigh for meetings, we held them in adulation. I was happy just to use the same john they did. Geez, that guy had been up there! The enemy had thrown hot lead at him. He'd been there and had come back. Look at that guy! He can talk! How come he just doesn't fall apart?

The crews were elated by those first successful encounters. Our crew landed at Grafton Underwood on a training flight and watched a B-17 from the 92nd come down, scrape the deck and execute a semi-chandelle—an abrupt climbing turn. The aerobatics were done with permission. It was an exclamation over the crew's successfully completed mission. They were being sent home to spread the word, to advertise their accomplishment. And the press, hot for propaganda, would report their every word.

The biggest story circulating at Thurleigh and probably every other base, and the most appreciated by bombardiers, was the heroic action of a washed-out pilot, Bombardier 2nd Lt. E.T. Sconiers. On the 21st of August, with the copilot dead and the pilot's hands burned, Sconiers took over the controls of the damaged ship, Johnny Reb, and flew it from the Dutch coast back to England.

The fallacy of those baby missions was that the Forts hadn't mixed it up that much. There weren't many German daylight fighters in the ETO. There was no reason to have them there. Because of the devastating losses suffered by both the English and the Germans, daylight bombing had been shelved. Respect for the Abbyville Kids, that elite group of fighters held over from the WW I outfit of Von Richthofen, was yet to come. And so was proficient formation flying.

We practiced formation flying according to established procedures. Combat techniques were not yet known.

After one day's practice of formation flying over the Wash, I saw my first generals. As I stood at attention in the middle of a row, all I could see were two hats walking down the center aisle. One was carried high and forward. The other was on a shorter man and set far back on the head. Together, they couldn't have looked more like a joke if they had tried. The tallest man took over the meeting.

He chastised us for our performance. He called us "sloppy," "ragged," "uneven." We had been there "long enough" and had made "little progress." We should be "doing better." The General paraded up to the large board in front of the assembly and drew two positions of one squadron, not very instructive for a whole group. One showed a squadron in a V shape, the second a head-on view with the elements of the squadron staggered. It was a simple formula, but tight and compact. A beautiful arrangement for planes to fly over the grandstands of the aeronautical show. Fine for peacetime newsreels, but how protective was it with fighters poking around?

The General moved closer to his audience. Stern-faced and strutting importance, he said, "This has been the standard procedure formation. Why can't you do it?" He turned to 367th Capt. H.W. Terry, who was standing close to him, and said, "You're a pilot. You were flying. Why can't *you* fly this formation?"

"I have no excuse, Sir." Terry gave the standard subservient response.

"Well, why not? Do you have a better way?"

"Sir, since you've asked my opinion, I think we've been fortunate in the missions we've flown so far. And, Sir, I think, in combat where the consideration is for defense, which will assure a successful mission, in my view, the essential formation is one of flexibility."

"All right, Captain, why don't you go to the board and give us an example."

"Yes, Sir." Terry walked to the board and drew a squadron in a flat V; the head-on view showed the aircraft staggered, but in a broad spectrum. "The relaxed position," Terry explained, "allows for that flexibility. An example: if necessary, in a turn, the squadron can form a slanted angle. The inside element, cutting back on power and dropping altitude, would allow the accelerating outside element to dive, resuming close formation."

"Splendid, Captain," the General complimented Terry. "We'll recommend that to the staff for their opinion and judgment."

It was obvious to us that the General was going to make the suggestion and use it to his own political advantage.

On September 28th, the report was filed: "Intensive familiarization training to acquaint personnel with operational methods in European Theater completed and 306th Bomb Group (H) reported as ready to conduct operational flights."

On October 2nd, while flying an early evening's practice mission over the Wash, a waist gunner in 367th Lieutenant Ely's plane suffered oxygen failure and blacked out.

Over the intercom in Snoozy II one of our crew called, "Captain Olson, Sir, Sir . . . on our left, Sir . . ."

On my knees, I inched over to the window near Gise and saw a plane in a perilous dive. The pilot was attempting a safer oxygen level.

"O.K., O.K., take it easy." Oley reminded us, "We've got a job to do, a mission to complete."

I watched the plane, a plane from our squadron, in its dive for descent. I turned away. I felt guilty watching it. Reproving myself, that I had better get tough, had better harden, I turned back to look. Ely was still diving, and then—he pulled up, too fast. The right wing broke at the root and snapped back into the right side of the fuselage. Penetrating through the weak apertures at the back of the ship, the wing severed the tail from the body. The trunk of the plane, with one wing surface, was sucked like a roller coaster as it accelerated down out of sight. The tail, buoyant with air surfaces, circled down, in a slow spiral, until it, too, disappeared.

We completed our mission.

There was a hush over the base that night. In the Officers' Club, the RAF tried to ease the calamity: ". . . these things happen. Lots of accidents in training." The pilots, each assuming the cause of the plane's failure, conjectured opinions and discussed what actions they would have taken. Two of Ely's crew had parachuted, including the tail gunner. The rest had been killed. It was a ghastly feeling, those deaths. They were guys in our own squadron, who had started with us in the sticks of Wendover. It was our first shock. The ultimate had happened. Our guys were dead.

Mingled with the horror was the warm and comforting feeling I had for Oley. He knew his job and he could do it. From the first flight at Wendover, I knew he was capable. At Chanute when we approached the runway, and the ship, caught in a down thermal, had mushed, Oley blasted it with enough power to bring us down to an A-1 landing. The flight over the Atlantic was a daring feat. When I saw the map at Prestwick and was asked by a doubting voice, "Did you fly all that way?" it was the first time I realized the distance and wondered if we had a life raft on board. But Oley knew, and how calm he was, how poised. On the navigational test to the Isle of Man, on the deck of the Scafell Pike, Oley responded with a veteran's skill. And then, out there with Ely in a death dive, in the face of panic and tragedy, Oley cooled us with his dispassionate direction to duty. Now, I allowed myself that full measure of confidence. Without hesitation, I knew Captain Olson was a Commander, the best in the air.

12

V-MAIL

Oct. 6, 1942

Dear Latch,

Hot Damn—I was sure glad to find out where you're stationed. I've been asking everyone I've met who might know you to look you up for me. No one had come forth with any information to date.

Unless I hear from you immediately, I will assume that there is a field that I can land on, and Hively and I will be over next Tuesday for lunch. Unless something big prevents us, look for us to come in around 11:30 o'clock.

I guess you know by now that the Eagles transferred to the U.S. Army Air Force, so I'm now a 2nd Looey in Uncle Sammy's outfit.

Hey, I had a forced landing the other day and was commended by the CO for excellent flying ability and saving the aircraft (ahem)—wish the guy that washed me out in Santa Maria could have heard it.

I'm still looking for Jimmy, but have heard nothing of him. One of the cameramen that came up for our big ceremony the other day knew Jake Mackenzie and thinks he's back in the States now.

Look for the old wings on a Spittie Tuesday. If you're not on an airdrome, write me immediately and tell me where there is one we can use—it's gotta be damn close though, cause I hate walking . . .

Love and kisses,

Pappy

Oct. 8, 1942

Dear Pappy,

You ol' peashooter, you. Thanks for your first letter to me on His Majesty's shores.

Well, here I am with my 306th Bomb Group (H), ready (?) to meet the "HUN-IN-THE-SUN" on DAYLIGHTS. I'm in the 367th Squadron.

If your navigation is what it should be you will have no trouble landing at Thurleigh Base, my new home. It's just north of Bedford in the Midlands.

If you can't land a Spitfire on a B-17 Flying Fortress base, then you better have someone fly you over and you can "bail out."

I must warn you that we are on RAF rations. No great American food yet, but you must be used to RAF food. Have you lost weight? You were sort of pudgy when I last saw you.

Have you located Pat Carey over here yet? Hank Rogers has your picture hanging on the wall at the "Arsenal" just behind the organ. He is still singing "For That Old Gang of Mine."

The Clayton-Knight Committee never did get me out of the Marine Corps. I finally got an "On Base" discharge that they say is impossible to arrange.

Have you got any quiff lined up? Have I got a story for you! See you Tuesday.

As always, Al

"Hey, Al, you wanna' play some blackjack?"
"Sure. Why not?" I slid the letter into my back pocket. "I'll mail this later."

13

FRIDAY, OCTOBER 9TH

"All right, you guys, drop your cocks and grab your socks."

On went the lights. Our alarm clock that morning was a little guy named Hanson, who relished his job. After shouting the greeting, he beat against the door with a long stick. Then, in fiendish encore, he banged against the coal-burning metal stove, our central heating system. The reverberations from that black iron tube could kill you if you had a hangover, and, if you didn't, by the time the gong evaporated, you thought you did.

"Get the hell out of here." "Crissake, it's the middle of the night." "Is this the way you get your jollies?"

"Shit," Hansen retorted, "you guys have it too easy. I've been up all night." Opening the door, he tossed us a loud announcement. "I know something's on today."

Silence layered the room. Everyone turned to look at him. There had been rumors of a big DO, but there had been rumors before.

"What?" "What's on?" "What do *you* know?"

Hanson, enjoying his moment of glory, replied, "There will be American doughnuts this afternoon." Vocal applause followed him out of the door.

Doughnuts, I thought. God, something American. It's about time.

Someone turned on the small radio, the Nissen hut's single source of broadcasting. Static and music beamed though the room. Some guys reached for a cigarette. Others kept their eyes tightly shut, trying to close out the inevitable. Not me. I hated waiting in lines. I kicked out of my sleeping bag and, still in skivvies, grabbed my shaving kit and headed for the latrine. As I walked to the other end of the room, I passed Oley, who was still prone and trying to get one eye opened. Too bad there wasn't some way for him to start the day without having to get up.

"You got any toothpaste?" "Who took my bar of soap?" "Hey, would ya mind movin' over . . . I'd like to take a piss." "Spread your legs so I can go, too."

By the time the latrine became crowded, I was getting dressed. I put on my suntans I had worn the day before. Anxious to know what, if anything, was scheduled, I decided not to wait around for company, but to go by myself to Headquarters.

"Hey, Butter, see you at mess."

"O.K., Al. I'll be there in a couple of minutes."

Outside, the early morning was still dark, but high above, the sky already reflecting the sun had turned a deep aquamarine blue. The air was cool and unusually crisp. There was no mist, no fog, no threat of rain and most of all, there was no mildew dampness that was so natural to that midland area of England. As I walked towards Headquarters, I noticed the buildings on the field silhouetted black against luminous hangars. Something was on. The ground crews were already working. No assignment was posted at Headquarters so I went on to the mess hall.

That Thurleigh was still RAF was characterized by the morning's breakfast. It was the English version of the American GI mess, shit-on-a-shingle, this one without the shingle, the layer of bread. My plate was ladled with a generous portion of brown, lumpy sauce. The orderly added a plate of sliced tomatoes and a crumpet to the tray. I took a seat at one of the long tables and helped myself to the coffee that was conveniently placed on it.

The chopped giblets that floated in the greasy mire were not exactly appetizing, but the Depression had taught me to appreciate food and I always ate everything that was on my plate. The meat dish was considered fuel food, and they weren't kidding when they said it stuck to the ribs. I had to eat it quickly, while it was still hot, because if a giblet cooled on your fork it would glom to it like an all-day sucker.

"Hi, Al." Butter greeted me as he lifted his portly figure across the bench and sat down.

"Welcome to breakfast and pancakes dripping in butter and maple syrup, and these spicy pig sausages," I said with a sigh as I ate another bite.

"Shut up, Al. It's hard enough to eat this crap without being reminded of real food. Pass the milk, will ya?"

Handing him the pitcher of lukewarm milk, I reminded him, "That's what we're getting this afternoon, real food. Doughnuts! I can hardly wait."

Butter nodded. "Neither can I."

"You want some coffee, Butter?" I poured myself a refill.

"Thanks."

"Looks like it's going to be sunny and clear today. If a mission is on, one thing's for sure. They won't be scrubbing it because of weather."

"On, off, on, off, they flip missions on and off like a light switch," Butter bitched, studying the meat on his fork. "I guess they have their reasons, but it sure gets to be a pain."

"At least you don't have to get yourself up for any on or off this morning," I reminded him. "Generous of you guys to give us your expander tube."

"C'mon Al, it wasn't generosity. It was the flip of a coin. Otherwise your crew would have given us one of your turbo super-charges." Spreading a coat of marmalade over his crumpet, Butter added, "What an organization, having no spares around. Unbelievable, having to use parts of another plane."

"You're in a cruddy mood this morning. What's bothering you?"

"No, I'm really not." He winked. "Just horny as usual."

Finished with the last slice of tomato, I peeled away the tinfoil from a fresh pack of Lucky Strikes.

"But Al, you know as well as I do that somebody out there hasn't planned the damn thing. Imagine, no wing jack in all of England?"

Inhaling the first drag of the after-breakfast cigarette, I agreed. "Yeah, I know. But it was kind of fun, standing on the wing with all those guys rocking that plane back and forth so they could prop it up and change the wheel. You were there, weren't you?"

"Yep." Leaning on an elbow, Butter declared, "A $238,000 teeter-totter. I do believe that's the most expensive one I've ever been on. Speaking of equipment, did you figure out what was wrong with your bicycle?"

"Yes. It was a bad valve that was causing all those flats. But I got a new one and now I have a bicycle where everything works AND fits. Gise should be so lucky. He hasn't been able to find one that does either. It's just too damn bad that the Brass' bikes are so identifiable. I've seen a couple of them that look like they'd be the right size for him."

"They are different," Butter agreed, taking another crumpet, "but Al, at least the Brass has the same problem we do. Just like us they have to sit on that ridiculous narrow seat." Butter bounced me on the shoulder, "Hardly wide enough to get your crack over."

"True. Whoever designed them must have liked being goosed all the time."

Butter laughed. "Does that happen to you, too?"

"Of course. It happens to everyone. Is there any GI around here who doesn't have his bike diapered? All I can think is that the English must have smaller asses."

"Hi. Is there room for me?" Gise asked.

"Sure. Here, I'll move over. Butter and I were just talking about you and your luck with a bicycle."

"I don't have any," Gise confirmed. "I can barely reach the pedals on the one I've got. By the way, the 'poop from the group' is that we've got a mission on for today. Have you heard anything?"

"Nope."

Gise picked at the meat. "Jeepers, I hate this stuff. What I wouldn't give for one of those doughnuts right now."

"Or a hamburger," Butter daydreamed.

"Al," Gise asked, "if we go today, are you going to wear that electric suit that we got last week?"

"You mean those blue BVDs with the conduits? Shit no! Somebody's cousin thought that thing up. If a circuit's knocked out or if it malfunctioned, you'd freeze to death. Remember, Gise, when the juice supply conked out in one of the legs of mine? Between the asbestos and cotton, it smelled like burning feathers. I almost choked to death. Didn't you?"

"It was terrible."

"And they're always doing that," joined Butter. "I heard one guy's suit smoked so badly he started to bail out. He thought his plane was on fire."

"Better to stick with the heavy flight gear. At least it's predict-able."

"My sentiments, exactly," Gise nodded, pushing his half-eaten plate away.

Butter stood up. "Everybody finished? Then let's drag our asses over to the briefing. It must be about ready to get under way."

We followed the crowd to the Post Theater. As we neared the entrance, a funnel of human beings sucked us into the room and spit us out on a wooden bench. The theater, a combination Nissen and hangar, was the only room large enough to handle all of the flight personnel. The benches and metal-backed chairs faced an elevated platform that held a large, draped bulletin board sup-ported by a tripod. The officers sat towards the front, the enlisted men in the rear. I saw McKee and Oley seated off to the side. Oley was wearing his leather cap with the wool flaps turned up. We had all hurried like hell so we could sit there and wait. Sleepy and full, we wondered what Pinetree had scheduled today, only to cancel.

"TEN-SHUN!"

We stood up as the commanding officer, Col. Charles Overacker, walked down the center aisle from behind us and onto the stage. "At ease, Gentlemen," he said, motioning for us to sit down. Chip Overacker was a diminutive man with ears too big and a mustache too small. Without projecting poise or conviction, he hardly seemed to be a commander of men. His reputation as a brilliant pilot preceded him. Still, every time I heard him speak, I asked myself, "This is the man who's going to lead us into battle?"

He spoke, somewhat nervously, relaying a message that you felt he'd rehearsed all night. "Well, we are finally involved in a big mission . . . and . . . it looks like it will go. The weather is good and the equipment is ready, and . . . ah . . . I know you are ready." He showed relief as he motioned for his executive officer to take over.

It really didn't matter if Overacker had presence or not, because his exec, Col. Delmar Wilson, could sell any mission with his generous energy and personable voice.

"All right, guys. Pinetree has a big DO for us today. If this one really goes, it will be the largest effort in the ETO by the American Eighth Army Air Force to date. O.K., pull the drapes."

With a pointer, he motioned to his aide to pull the curtains. They parted to reveal an oversized sectional map of Europe, from the British Isles up to the North Sea over the old WW I borders of the Alsace-Lorraine area and as far south as the Brest Peninsula. Different colored strings tacked at Thurleigh spun off to form varying arcs and return corridors that converged on Lille in northern France. One glance and the target jumped out like a neon sign. The "oh's" and "ah's" sounded in concert. Only about eighty kilometers inside of France, it would soon become a "milk run," but on that first mission any target inside the German-held West Wall seemed formidable.

Colonel Wilson slapped the board with the stick and said, "Our mission today is to attack the marshaling yards and locomotive works and the attending buildings here at Lille. The locomotive works is a large plant that repairs trains and other vehicles, such as wagons and trucks. You can understand the importance of this mission. An effective strike will hurt the transportation system so acutely needed by the enemy. You get the picture?"

Everyone nodded.

"For those of you who experience problems, the secondary target is the aerodrome of Courtrai/Wevelghem, and the last-resort target is the aerodrome of St. Omer/Longuenesse.

"The assignment proceeds as follows: we will climb to 23,000 feet, our cruising altitude. Pathfinders will establish the points where you turn to make your bombing runs. Your heading will be 170º with the ETA over target at 0927 hours. After the bombing run, we will make a 360º turn to the east, and then home."

The last announcement ushered in whistles and groans.

Executive Officer Wilson turned and faced us. He announced reassuringly, "You are lucky today, guys, because you are going to have lots of company in this DO; the 301st, the 92nd, the 93rd and the 97th. You will form up over Felixstow at 0857 hours and then proceed five miles east of Dunkirk where you will rendezvous with Spitfires and, believe it or not, American P-38s! Thirty-six of them!"

Wow. P-38s. The mission was sounding better all the time. I remembered them making practice runs over my home in California at speeds that seemed incredibly fast. I would hear cracks of thunder and look up into the blue sky only to see, miles ahead of the sound, splinters of silver twin booms disappear into the sunlight.

The Colonel cuddled us some more.

"There will be diversionary efforts by the RAF over the Dunkirk, Ypres, St. Omer regions and over the Schouwen/Walcheren area. Part of the 92nd Group will join the RAF in a diversionary sweep over Abbyville, Yvetot and Fecamp areas. Five RAF squadrons and the three P-38 squadrons will provide cover and rear support."

Colonel Wilson pointed to a board resting against one of the map stand's tripod legs. "These are your squadron assignments."

Four encircled numbers lined up towards the target. The 367th was last.

"I will simply mention that the weather looks good. You will get your accurate weather from the meteorologist at your specialty meetings. We will have a question and answer period after the S-2 reports." Colonel Wilson stood aside as Intelligence took the stage.

Air Corps Capt. John A. Bairnsfather began slowly, "Remember, men," and everyone knew the next five words, "flak is only a deterrent." He wanted a laugh and he got it. "Some, of course, as we all know, is portable. Indications are, from the latest reconnaissance flights as of 1500 hours yesterday, there will be some concentrations over St. Omer, Dunkirk, Halluin, Cassel and between Ypres and Roulers and at Roubaix. Yes, you have a question?"

A hand was raised in the back of the room. You couldn't see the guy. He must have been a ball turret. "Can we anticipate *heavy* flak, Sir?"

Bairnsfather replied, "Everyone laugh like hell."

S-2 Officer Capt. Phil Haberman was on next. "With all the protection you're getting, you probably won't need this info, but, just in case you find yourself walking around France this afternoon, look for a clothesline; don't laugh, guys, a clothesline that has a pair of pants hanging between two blue things. That will be the signal of your underground contact. Handle it smartly."

"Now, for reminders. If captured, give only your name, rank and serial number. Do not agree to broadcast back to the States. You will be making a recording. Do not talk to yourself or among yourselves. Walls have ears. Make good use of the phrase '. . . according to the Geneva Convention.' Finally, take nothing with you but your dog tags, your escape picture and your escape kit. Pick up your kit on the way out. Good luck."

Most of us listened to Haberman like a recording we'd heard over and over. At that point it was conceivable only that you would either complete your mission or get killed. Becoming a prisoner was unthinkable.

The Executive Officer came forward and asked, "O.K. guys, any questions?"

Someone behind responded weakly, "Yeah, I have a question, Captain Phil. Was it something blue between two pairs of pants or the other way around?"

The S-2 officer stood up and repeated, "One blue, one pants, one blue. Don't forget it."

A voice asked, "Is it pukka, doughnuts this afternoon?"

"Guaranteed."

Amid whistles of appreciation, the sky pilots stood up and announced the locations for their individual morning services.

Colonel Wilson concluded the briefing. "Fellas, you finally have a chance to have a go at it. Make it count. See you at debriefing."

We filed out of the theater and into the early sunshine of the morning. The macadam walks that threaded the base were narrow and the crowd of men spilled onto the surrounding dirt, their oversized flying boots trampling the last remaining splotches of RAF grass. The beginning of the day was unusually warm. By noon, the black walks would reflect the heat and the field would be dusty. Better that than rain and the infinite mud.

I went to the bombardiers' meeting where Butterball left for the mess hall and more crumpets. As I entered the room, I was handed a mission kit that had Snoozy II's numbers on it, AC# 41-24510. With the maps and photographs contained in the prepared folder, I followed Intelligence as he explained the target area and ID points to those of us in the 367th Squadron. The pictures and maps were stacked in the order of use: the regular maps of the Channel and Channel cities on top, with the largest and closest blow-up of the target, circled in white, on the bottom.

S-2 described the site: "Your job is to center between the smokestacks where the rails narrow. It is a bottleneck of tracks and it should be easy to tie into, once you have spotted the smokestacks, the largest of which is on the right of your target. Be sure that the table of altitude, time and speed, etc. is enclosed in your folder."

Bombsight Maintenance Officer Percy Vincent spoke briefly. He was followed by the weather report.

The RAF meteorologist proudly, like he had it made to order, gave the forecast for the beautiful October morning: "Bases: $2/10^{ths}$ or less stratocumulus becoming $3-5/10^{ths}$ over the Channel. Visibility 6 miles but reduced to 3 miles in industrial areas. Target: Clear to scattered clouds, total coverage $2/10^{ths}$ or less. Visibility 6 miles or better."

S-2 ended our meeting tersely. "Remember this. More than thirty tons of airplane, equipment and men are going to hang out there for you, I repeat for *you*, the bombardier, to deliver. Have a good mission."

I made it to the 367th Squadron Headquarters just as Major Holt, who walked in with Ryan, arrived from the pilots' meeting.

Drinking a cup of coffee and without a formal introduction, the Major gave his personal introduction to the mission. "I guess we're going to carry the big package today. We're trained for it . . . I think we're ready."

Yes, it was becoming more and more apparent that this one wasn't going to be scrubbed. The authenticity of the fact showed in Holt's face. "Hope I can sell it" was the look in his eyes. I was old enough to feel for him. My own mind was already entertaining flutters of trepidation. This was awful. Really? Tons of explosives? Oh, how I loved those little blue jobs. Why not another practice run over the Wash?

"Being the last squadron in the group," Holt intoned, "we have a big protection job, more than the other guys. Let's stay tucked in . . ."

Holt treated the subject like a hot potato. He didn't want to do anything wrong and he couldn't, under the circumstances, do everything right. He knew he would be held responsible for losses, including human life. It would be lights out for the people who screwed up. Like most of the other commanders, he was feeling his way along.

There were commanders, like LeMay, Armstrong, Ryan and Terry, who held strong convictions and followed them through, but they were exceptions.

"If we hold formation," Holt explained, "we should be accurate over the target. Dress the way it's comfortable for you . . . be sensible, stay warm. If you become a casualty and can't hang in formation, hit the deck and go home.

"Gunners, I realize you could have used more, but this is the experience by which you can gauge future missions. Are there any questions?"

"Why, Sir, are we going back over the target?"

"Don't worry about it. We've got the P-38s today and remember, there's protection in the formation. Keep tight. Anything else? O.K. Good luck."

The men left to get their gear. I waited for Oley. The Captain, sunk in a chair, had his hands clasped behind his neck. Suddenly, aware that I was present, he looked at me. Valleys of dimples creased his face as a sarcastic smile bridged the big ears.

"Well, Al, guess what? Command has chosen us as the hotshots. We have been assigned as the ass-end airplane of the ass-end squadron. In other words, we are ass-end Charlie. That makes *you* the fire control officer. So, buddy, you watch for the Jerrys when they try to peel us off the edge . . . and I'll do the fancy flying."

Oley, slowly, got up from the chair. As we walked out the door, he said, more to himself, "We'll celebrate this afternoon, Al, and the drinks will be on me."

Al's crew on bicycles at Thurleigh, England.

14

SO LONG, BUTTER

'Twas the night before Christmas and all through the group
The "big wheels" and "wigs" were grinding out "poop"
The bombers were parked on their hardstands with care
Waiting for ammunition soon to be there
The flyers were nestled all snug in their beds
While visions of "milk runs" danced in their heads
When out of the darkness there came quite a knock
We cursed the OD and looked at the clock
Briefing will be in two hours he said
And if you're late you'll wish you were dead
Time marches on and the minutes fly by
So it's out of our beds get ready to fly
We rushed to the mess hall quick as a flash
And ate cold powdered eggs with hideous hash
Then a long bumpy ride to the group briefing room
Where the "big wigs" preside and dish out our doom
The target is told and the first six rows faint
For lo and behold Berlin—it ain't
The "brains" had slipped up—oh my poor aching back
We're bombing a place that throws up no flak
So it's back to the truck and off to the line
The road is now smooth and the weather is fine
The crew is at stations—the checklist is run
The engines run smooth as we give 'em the gun
Then suddenly the pilot wails in despair

"Look at the tower they just shot a flare"
We dash to the window with a heart full of dread
The pilot was right—the darn thing is RED
So it's back to the sack as we sweat out our fate
For there's a practice formation at a quarter past eight.

Anonymous

Back in the Nissen, after a routine trip to the latrine, I straightened my corner of our quarters. With the ends of the sleeping bag pulled together, I smoothed the wrinkles to the side and put my shaving kit away in the footlocker. I arranged it with the other padding of towels and socks around the box that contained the silver tea service that I had bought to send my mother for Christmas. It was such a novel gift with its condiment pots and it cost only fifteen pounds, too inexpensive to pass up.

Over the suntans, I put on a pair of flight coveralls. From a second pair of ODs that hung on a wall hook and served as my chest of drawers, I took gum, a fresh pack of cigarettes and sunglasses.

"God is here, God is there, God is everywhere," I repeated my own personal prayer. With a last caress, I aligned Mary Baker Eddy's *Science and Health* over the bible. The two books, the sliced piston I used for an ashtray, and a handful of American and English coins covered my bedside table—a metal crate that had been used for shipping fifty-caliber shells.

Let's see, do I have everything? My escape picture, wrapped in toilet paper, was in the front pocket of my suntans. I shook my front shirts together to hear the jangle of dog tags and patted the outer pockets in a recount—lighter, cigarettes, gum, glasses, the escape kit buttoned in the pant leg. Yeah, guess I'm ready. With the bombardier kit hooked over the handlebars, I climbed on my bike and pedaled out to the revetment.

There was excitement at the flight line. Real bombs were being readied for loading. They were of various colors—black, silver, yellow—and some had accumulated rust from storage. Recalling classroom color charts, I determined we were going to carry ten heavy demolition, plus incendiary canisters.

White paint had been brought out to the pad by the ground crew and everyone, including Gaston's crew, were christening the five hundred-pound explosives.

I parked my bike inside the ground crew's tent and freed myself of the bombardier kit by pushing it up into the escape hatch and letting it slide towards the nose. Grabbing a brush, I rendered on one side of a silver egg, GREETINGS FROM HHHS, GLENDALE, CALIF.

"There's only two H's in Hi Ho Silver," Butter yelled at me as he lowered the stand on his bicycle.

"That's awful, Butter. This, my friend, is hello from Herbert Hoover High School."

"Oh, hell, I can do better than that." Taking the brush from me, he dipped it in the paint and printed, "HERE'S AN APPLE FROM ALVA."

We stood back in admiration, elated, as if someone was actually going to read the damn things. Everyone took a turn. Gise lettered "FROM DEEP IN THE HEART OF TEXAS." Oley outlined a four-leaf clover.

Snoozy II had been hooked up to the gas-powered generator, the small ground unit affectionately called a "put-put" by the pilots.

"I'm going to get set up, Butter," I announced. "I'll be back in a few minutes and we can make plans for tonight."

"O.K., Al."

Near the escape hatch I saw Gates making his pre-flight inspection with customary efficiency. I joined him as he walked around the ship. Giving him lots of room, I teased, "What kind of sandwiches did you bring today, Lieutenant?"

Slapping a clipboard against his thigh, the 6-foot, 1-inch copilot opened his eyes in a puzzled expression. Finally he answered, "The drive-in's don't open this early."

"Hey, that's all right, Lieutenant. Everything checking out?" Gates ran his hand along the trim tabs on the tail control surfaces. "Looks good," he confirmed. "Oh, Luck Talbot is in the infirmary. He has an ear infection or a cold or something. Anyway, his replacement came out of the flight personnel pool, a Staff Sergeant Nicholson."

"Talbot sure picked a time to be sick. He can get a suntan today."

"Nice weather, all right," Gates agreed. We had circled back to the open door of the plane. "I'd better check in with the Captain. See you later, Al."

In the nose, I folded the sight's cover. Putting it to the side of the tray, next to my gloves, I flipped on the automatic pilot master switch. While waiting for the power to warm up, I propped the bombardier kit in the lower right-hand corner at the base of the stabilizer. Then I arranged the tables, grids, information sheets and photos in the order I was going to use them. After the five-minute warm-up, the gyros were humming with full power. The sight was ready for pre-flight completion. I centered the turn control, turned and tested adjusting knobs, turned on the servo pilot directional indicator, disengaged the bombsight clutch . . .

Gise had come on board and was unzipping his kit. I turned off the master switch and threw him a bone. "I think we're really gonna do this one, Billy. Looks like no stand-down today."

"It sure looks that way," Gise concurred as I left the nose.

Throughout the ship, preparations were being made for the mission. Gates and Oley were in the flight deck. The gunners, pulling the arms backward and forward, adjusted the linkage on the gun carriers. A hoist had muscled in over the dolly of bombs and had begun lifting the explosives into the shackles of the bomb bay. The tail gunner was lining up ammunition trays.

Outside, Butter was rolling a silver dollar over his knuckles and catching it. It was a trick I could never master. Not that I let Butter know.

"What are the plans, Al?"

"You make them. Check out what's going on at the Officers' Club and then weigh that with what's going on at the Key Club. You could call Sarah. You know, Sarah, the gal who lives over the bakery? Maybe you could arrange a double date. Her phone number's listed in the Bedford Central Directory under Goode."

"She's not bad," Kenny mirrored my suggestion.

"So anyway, Butter, I'll take care of the war and you figure out a program for tonight. And while I'm at the Front will you do me a favor? Will you pick up my laundry when you pick up yours? Let me think. How much do I owe Mrs. Eddington? Uh, half a crown? Isn't that about fifty cents?"

"Sounds reasonable. I hope I can get away from the base. I bet they've set us up with half-assed duties all day long."

"Butterball, I've told you. Stick a manila folder under your arm and you'll look like you're too busy for any assignment."

"Shit, Al, you're the only guy I know who can get away with that. But I'll try. Where do I get the folder?"

"In my footlocker."

Gaston stepped down out of Snoozy II. Smiling a million-dollar smile, he said, "I've just warned your pilot, Swede, not to swing any loops over the target. I don't want him to risk losing my expander tube. I want it back for my ship." Gaston's ship, silent with inactivity, was parked directly across from us. "Keep an eye on him," he added. Running a comb through his hair, he half apologized, "Sure sorry we're not going with you today."

"Why don't you come along as a gunner?" I offered.

"I just remembered I'm on duty as latrine officer."

Gaston really meant it when he said he was sorry he wasn't coming along. It was what we had been trained for, why we were there. We all wanted to get on with the job. Sure, we felt the suspense, but there was no feeling of panic. None of us had been exposed to the dangers. Like a jolt to the body from an injured nerve, it was pain that could not be imagined before it was experienced. In the weeks that we had been stationed at Thurleigh we had flown only five missions of the many that had been assigned.

Those were diversionary or "nickel runs," dropping leaflets. The other missions had been weathered out or commanded out. We had encountered no Jerrys and the little flak we saw was always in the distance.

Personally, I was cocky and secure. It would be a short trip, a sweep. There was no doubt in my mind that I would score over the target at Lille. I never dreamed I would be firing the guns in the nose, those thirty-caliber that were one war too late. There just wouldn't be any German Fighters in a head-on attack. They didn't know what kind of weapons we had. Besides, Oley would take evasive action before he'd let us do that. We'd show the Huns. Today's mission, if we didn't abort, would be a good one.

There was a thundering roar as ships from another field mounted formation. At the other end of our field, engines were cranking up. Members of my crew, who, like myself, had been standing around kibitzing, climbed back into the ship.

"Well, it sounds like we're going. Guess I'd better get on board."

"Here, Al, take a piece of Juicy Fruit. Chew it for good luck."

"Thanks, Butter. Don't forget the manila folder and the laundry. Be sure there's no starch in my shorts."

"I'll see you at doughnuts," Butter called after me.

Gaston and the others on the pad yelled, "So long. Good hunting."

On the way to the nose, I checked the bomb bay. The morning had been my first opportunity to observe armament doing its job. The last of the bombs had been shackled in and one of the armament people was fusing them. The explosives were angled on the banks of the bomb bay for easy access. Three bombs on my lower left still bore the unarmed ID tags so I depressed the springs and pulled out the pins, arming them.

The bomb pins and the unopened pack of Lucky Strikes shared the tray on my desk with pencils, the Colt .45 and a magnesium stick. Every time I looked at that six inches of incendiary, I thought, how stupid. Its purpose, in case we had to land inside German territory, was to scrape off the top and set it on a metal surface, where it would ignite and burn up the ship. But what if a piece of flak hit it and started it burning? With nothing to stop it, we would all go up in smoke.

The oxygen mask dangled to one side as I pulled on the leather helmet. With the earphones and throat mike in place, I tied into the ship's radio. Leaving the shoulder holster and heavy winter flying pants hanging on the bulkhead, I put on the heavy jacket. I preferred not to wear the gun because it was a heavy bastard and when I leaned over, it would fall forward. I was afraid it might hit the sight. And the pants, well, they made too much bulk. Over the flight jacket I buckled my harness. The words from one of the briefings carried back to me in capitals: "DON'T SIT ON YOUR PARACHUTE TODAY. PUT IT ON." Eyeing it in a corner of the nose, I resolved that I would if the mission was on. The ground crew had delivered to each position a walk-around oxygen bottle, a portable unit that I placed in the lower left pant pocket. And last, I pulled out an OD handkerchief and dusted the compartment's surfaces, including the guns. Gise and I were tidy as houseladies, keeping everything in the nose immaculate. We were forever wiping off lubricants that seeped from the ship's seams and the Cosmoline from the weapons.

"Gise," I commented, "it's too bad they don't give medals for neatness. You and I would have gongs all over us."

"Yep," Gise agreed, "generals of good housekeeping. My mother wouldn't believe it."

"Have you got a fix yet? What are the heavenly signs?"

"Clear and warmer."

"Clear and what? And *you're* the navigator? Hell, I'd better get out my E-6B computer."

A cloud of gray-white smoke dusted the air as engine #1 turned over. After a momentary stutter, the motor grabbed again and caught power. The blasts of engines #2, #3 and #4 followed. Oley throttled them into a simultaneous pulse. There was no border-line mechanical, no comma of hesitation. The motors on Snoozy II synchronized like clockwork.

The big aircraft began moving, taxiing the mile of runway. It was the kick-off. The game was on. I put on my parachute and settled on the metal box I used for a seat. As we bumped over the uneven asphalt, I watched the tacking aircraft in front of us as its pilot tested the ailerons and tail controls. At the end of the flight line we waited, idling power; one thousand-one, one thousand-two, one thousand-three, in a carefully timed pattern, the varied pistol (different colors) shot a flare. Oley, right with it, released the ship for its takeoff run.

Twenty to thirty feet in the air, on the last revetment apron, I saw Butterball astride his red-and-green bike, the front whitewall tire turned in. He swung his garrison cap, like a pendulum, back and forth. There was a smile in his wave.

Oley, as flight leader, led the last ship to take off from the field, Rose O'Day, in a loose half turn over the base. Staying low, gathering power, we curved northeast. Below, I could see Butter still straddling his bike, holding his cap in a salute after us. As the ship nosed upward, he disappeared behind the tail.

Kenneth Jones, with thumbs up, his blond hair blowing in the wind, that Oklahoma grin sprawled across his face. I really loved that guy. I never saw him again.

15

FLIGHT

It was shortly after 0830 hours when Snoozy II took off. Throwing full power, the ship pulled hard in a grinding effort to reach the squadrons already forming. Beneath the Curtis-Wright radial engines and gray circle of their spinning props, the countryside appeared peaceful and orderly. Symmetrical fields in variegated browns and lush greens, interlacing hedgerows, wandering rivulets, small towns of clean white buildings, the many aerodromes; like English "high tea" at four in the afternoon, everything was in its place. There were herds of horses and cows, some cyclists, and the sun was high enough that camouflaged convoys spilled identifying shadows.

"Hey, Gise," I yelled, pointing down through the windows, "admit it. Yoakum, Texas doesn't look anything like that!"

Gise took a quick glance over his shoulder and looked back at me with a smirk.

That kid! He knows there isn't any place in Texas that looks like that, but tease him about Yoakum and it's an attack on his honor. It's funny, but he really bristles. All Texans are alike. Then there's Butterball. He's nuts about Alva, Oklahoma. What a bunch of bananas.

From airfields all over England, the American bomb groups—the 301st from Chelveston, the 92nd from Bovington, the 93rd from Alconbury, the 97th from Polebrook, along with the 306th from Thurleigh—set their course for France. It was the American Air Force's first major assault in the European Theater of Operations.

'A

"The first climax of the VIII Bomber Command's offensive against Nazi-dominated Europe came on October 9 when 108 heavy bombers—including for the first time, the slab sided Liberators—were dispatched against the steelworks and locomotive factories in the great French industrial city of Lille."[10]

". . . for the next six mortal months, the Lille mission was to remain the high-water mark, in terms of numbers, of the daylight bombing offensive."[11]

Shouldering the heavy load of bombs, the motors throbbed rhythmically in a laboring climb. Air whistled through loosely riveted seams and part of the Plexiglas flapped freely.

As I chewed a second piece of gum to reduce the pressure in my ears, I wondered what kind of doughnuts would be waiting for us that afternoon. Chocolate? Crumb? Jelly? I didn't care. I just wanted some American chow.

"Bombardier to Pilot."

"Pilot to Bombardier. Go ahead."

"Altimeter reads 5,000 feet. Check?"

"Check."

We made it into formation. Leveling into a slower climb, I could feel the ship straying slightly away and back to center in a controlled "hunt." I lit a cigarette. Ahead, I could see the clusters of planes, jockeying back and forth, as they stacked to our left and, in a last glance at England, a haze that was gathering as the Island's edges steamed in the warming sunshine.

The 367th was all tucked in as it rendezvoused over Felixstow and headed out over the Channel. We flew in elements of three, in undulating Vs, weaving in and out in loose-to-snug Ss, as we continued the climb to altitude.

I felt some anticipation; the need to get on with it, to do our job. But there in the friendly skies, the war seemed far away and I relaxed and enjoyed the scenic morning.

Wispy clouds dallied in the blue sky. The North Sea glittered. There was traffic all over the Channel. The business of war was going on as usual.

Irrelevant to our Group, there were formations of English and American aircraft moving towards their individual objectives on separate headings and radio frequencies. Some planes, having completed their missions of Reconnaissance, Search and Destroy, Espionage and Pathfinding, headed home.

There were Spitfires, like kites; bulky Hurricanes; high-tailed light Mosquitoes; obsolete Douglas A-20s and Boston bombers.

More streamlined and graceful than any other aircraft, the Fortresses paraded across the Channel. Some of the lead elements were already turning inland, specks in the distance.

The Channel's green waters were choppy and washed with westerly caps of white foam. Small vessels, including the white Air-Sea Rescue boats, bobbed resiliently, buoys in the water.

On a course set at a north-northeast heading, the sun followed us on the ship's starboard side. It was a full, warm sun, the kind that hung over a Southern California Indian summer.

It was the type of weather that made me want to jump into my '28 Chrysler roadster and head for Castle Rock State Beach, which bordered Roosevelt Highway (California's Hwy. #101), or Santa Monica, the beach north of Castle Rock, better known as "Muscle Beach." There we bodysurfed, played volleyball and watched girls in the new two-piece swimsuits covered by a fringe skirt and matching neckband. The beach of Santa Monica was synonymous with screeching bodies riding the pier's roller coaster and ten-cent hot dogs smothered in onions and mustard.

When was I last there? With Rheva? Yeah, it was Rheva. What a body! I had her picture in my footlocker. It was inscribed: "Dearest Al, to know you is to love you. Rheva." I wondered what she was doing, probably in bed, asleep. Ah, to be there with her . . .

The cigarette that I had butted out into the empty sardine can was still smoking. I squashed it and lit another. Feeling lonely,

I moved the radio bands around. On every channel was the familiar crackle and Morse code. I would have enjoyed some music.

I swept a look around the nose. Gise was talking on the intercom. It was 0907 hours. My watch checked exactly with the clock on the nose tray. I sure liked that Gruen Sportsman. It was always accurate. It cost a lot of dough, thirty-two bucks, but it was worth it.

"Oley to crew. Clear guns at will. Short bursts. Make'em count." The weapons specific to each position trembled and clattered around the ship.

Walking on my knees to the starboard side and picking a safe field of fire, I gave the gun a few bursts. A reflection high above caught my attention.

The sun glanced off the silver skin of aircraft. I'd recognize those big twin booms anywhere. There were gaggles of P-38s!

"Gise," I shouted, "look up, about two o'clock. Aren't they beautiful?"

Gise spotted them through his astrodome and whistled. He climbed down and came over to my position to get my view. We relished the sight. We couldn't get enough of them. "Oh, man," Gise exclaimed, "with all that protection this is one trip we don't have to worry about. We're damn lucky."

"They're the ones that are lucky, Gise. They can get the hell out of here."

Those silver angels, three dozen of them. So reassuring. At 30,000 feet, they flew like the song, "Off we go, into the wild blue yonder . . ." I started to hum the melody.

Heat filtered through my glove, reminding me of the cigarette I was holding. I went back to the sardine can and put it out. Gise went back to his station. The P-38s might as well have gone back to England.

"Pilot to crew. Approaching 10,000 feet. Prepare to go on oxygen."

"Bombardier, roger."

"Navigator, roger."

"Radio . . ." All stations checked in. Oxygen O.K.

From the nose I could see the leading edges of our wings, masked in splotchy colors like the rest of the ship. And on the rims, the black de-icing boots. The outboard motors were visibly purring.

I leaned back against the bulkhead.

October 9th. What was it going to be like out there? I began to feel anxious. Where was I this time last year? Oh, no. I was in the Marines. I could still be with them. Nah, more likely dead on Guadalcanal. What if I hadn't signed up at all? I'd be playing football in the Los Angeles Coliseum. Or Monday morning quarterbacking. This was perfect weather for football . . . or even baseball. I wonder if the St. Louis Cardinals made it into the World Series?

"Pilot to radio. All channels in working order?"

"Radio in order, Sir."

"Pilot to Wilder. Everything working down there? Swing the ball around and check back."

"O.K., Captain."

I had to take a leak. I pulled the tube from my oxygen station and stuck it into my walk-around bottle.

Gise was working at his desk. I leaned over his shoulder and asked, "How many minutes till landfall?"

Checking his times, he raised eight fingers. I had time.

As I walked back to the relief tube on the aft bomb bay bulkhead, I could see the waist gunners leaning on their weapons. No one was talking. I stood there. I couldn't go. It was a dry run.

Still fading north, we made our landfall over the coast of Belgium. We were taking the most evasive route possible, as much as our fuel would allow, in the attempt to confuse the German Fighter Command. Lille, France was about eight kilometers inland, just south of the Belgian border.

Officially, I was fire observer for my Squadron, for that matter for the entire Group. But over land we all knew we could expect fighters at any time and everyone was "observing."

THEY COULD APPEAR AT ANY TIME, from any direction. Now I was nervous. The butterflies had hatched, but it was too cold to sweat, even in my heavy winter flying jacket.

I turned on the bombsight juice, then watched and waited. Peripherally, I caught glimpses of John McKee's wing tip floating in and out of the nose windows as his plane flanked us on our left. On our right was no one but God.

The land was pitted, pockmarked by bomb craters. Smoke curled from the chimneys of scattered farmhouses. Sporadically, black flak belched below us.

We had reached our altitude of 23,400 feet.

Wads of smoke dangled ahead. They were smoke bombs dropped by our navigational pathfinders, signaling our turning point towards the target.

We began our turn over the Continent, a sweeping starboard arc that would straighten into a southwest approach over Lille.

I put on my sunglasses and rechecked the target's diagram. I noticed a floppy shoelace and reached to retie it. The spit-and-polished leather reflected my face. Corporal Gemoets, from my Marine days, would have appreciated that shine. He also would have had a few swear words about my high-top GI shoes. I laced them only to the ankles so I could bend easily. They were an unorthodox choice, but where were a pair of flight boots that fit?

From the end of our turn to the conclusion of the bomb run would take no more than five minutes. Our course set, suddenly the ship was rocked by flak, bursting puffs of smoke in fanciful hues—blue, gray, mustard, pea-green and dusty-pink. For a few moments, I was captivated. No one told me flak came in colors. I wondered which one was the worst.

The anti-aircraft guns must have been reloading, for the sky around us quieted.

I waited.

My maps waited. The tables of information had long since been fed into the bombsight. The 30-caliber guns were positioned in the right and left sockets, the clips to the ammunition belts inserted, ready for firing. The armament people did a good job. The guns had been serviced, the canister trays in place, the windows cleaned. Yes, they always did a good job.

I took off my left glove and wiped the eyepiece with the knitted wristband. Seeing my Air Force graduation ring, I automatically pulled it from my finger, blew on it and polished it across my pant leg. The ring, mail-ordered, was the only one I had ever owned. Crested on the garnet was my class number, 42-8. Sliding it back on, I moved my finger so that it sparkled in the light. I should have given it to Rita. I had seriously considered it. Gee, it was good to get her Western Union Telegram: "DEAR AL THREE LETTERS ON WAY LET ME KNOW HOW YOU ARE ALL MY LOVE= RITA." Maybe they'll be in today's mail.

"What the hell are *they* doing there?"

I heard it over the intercom before I saw them. I looked up. Out of the east came a cloud of B-24 Liberators. Like boxcars, they lumbered toward us. Heading west, they would cross directly below us.

Through the radio, I heard my thoughts expressed around the ship. "Whose snafu was that?" "I don't believe it." "Pinetree's lost its needles." "Grab that." "What a screw up."

It was a problem, but it was their problem. I had no time to think. We were approaching the bomb run. I threw both gloves up on the tray, stuck my gum wad on the hinge and folded myself over the sight.

There were concussions from flak that began, again, to explode around us.

I scanned for the target outline. As we moved closer, I peeled off the corresponding maps, tossing them over my shoulder.

There it was, on the right, a forty-foot smokestack. It stood out prominently amid the rising dust and smoke. I dropped the bomb bay doors.

"Bombardier to Pilot. Bomb bay doors open. I'm lined up."

"Roger, Bombardier. I'll give it a last trim." Oley switched the ship over to automatic flight control equipment. "O.K., Al. It's all yours."

I could feel the bombsight snap in as I took control. The indicators moved slightly as they adapted to the fix set by Oley. I turned the knobs, adjusting for wind and drift. I had to crab hard to the west to compensate for the winds aloft.

There was a THUD. The ship winced. It had been hit by flak.

"This is top turret. Inboard engine on fire and trailing smoke."

Momentarily knocked off course, the Norden sight regained position immediately.

I continued to crank in the visual information. Looking through my eyepiece, I lined up the crosshairs, centering just to the left of the smokestack. The bombsight, computing air speed and altitude, joined indices at exactly the right moment, releasing the bombs.

"Bombs away."

Lightened by the discharge of explosives, the plane lifted.

There was no sign of the B-24s.

It was 0942. For Snoozy II, the war was about to begin and . . . end.

16

DEATH ON BOARD

With one engine feathered, Oley quickly took control of the ship and began a left turn back over the target. Purpose? To draw up and engage enemy aircraft. Where were the P-38s?

Off to my right, at three o'clock, just out of range, about 1,000 yards, appeared a line of German Messerschmitts. They stalked us with such expertise, they could have been on a Sunday stroll. In fact, we were like ducks in a shooting gallery.

"This is top turret. Jerrys climbing into the sun."

Red lights flashed on my instrument panel. Four bombs had not released. I *had* to bring up the bomb bay doors. They were dragging us, slowing our speed by fifteen miles an hour or more. But I couldn't bring them up with bombs still inside the ship. An armor-piercing bullet in the right spot on the bomb and we'd all go to pieces.

"Rat-a-tat, rat-a-tat." Sounding like typewriting on loose paper, bullets strafed the ship.

Everyone spoke over the intercom at once. "Bandits at three o'clock." "I see 'em, I see 'em." "God, look at them come." "Where are the goddamn P-38s?"

We were still in a left turn. With one engine gone, Snoozy II started to lag.

Commander Overacker had set the pace. He made a "needle point" turn back over the target. The truth was, in our position high and on the outside, even with six engines, there was no way Oley could keep us in formation.

I had to get rid of the bombs. With the ship canted to the left, I braced myself by holding the bombsight, gingerly, between my legs. Clutching the gun handle with one hand, with the other I reached for the toggle switch on the instrument panel. At nine o'clock, I spotted another group of Focke-Wulfs and Messerschmitts.

Tracers zigzagged in all directions. Cannon detonated in loud BOOMS. Vibrations from our gunners' firing positions stuttered through the aircraft.

My heart was pounding. How to toggle armed bombs? CARE-FULLY. This was not light skip-bombing that we did during cadet training. Because of the position of the ship, I couldn't use the toggle switch. I reached for the salvo switch.

The salvo switch was housed in a red metal box covered with the warning "DO NOT USE UNLESS IN CASE OF EXTREME EMERGENCY." Shit! Typical military procedure. With whatever arm you have left *and* after waiting for an Act of Congress . . . I tore off the lid and pulled down the handle, dropping bombs, shackles and all. As I did, I almost wet my pants. Still slanted in the turn, the rolling bombs could hit the ship and explode. We must have righted in time. The red lights stopped flashing. The bombs were gone. I pulled the lever to shut the bomb bay doors. The servomotors rumbled as the doors closed and locked.

We had completed our turn. Oley had trimmed the ship and headed back to England, but we had fallen way back of formation.

"Tail to crew, tail to crew. Jerrys at six o'clock."

The fighters had climbed into the sun, hanging onto a skyhook until they were formed, and then as we headed west, they swooped down to attack us from the rear, where we were most vulnerable.

Bullets continued to rake our metal surfaces, some penetrating the compartment, whining as they passed close to my body. Every thump from piercing cannon knocked the wind out of the ship and me.

Where were the P-38s?

I looked up and there they were, still flying at 30,000 feet. Someone had made the decision that the P-38 Lightnings would not engage that day.

In the 423rd Squadron, Bombardier Frank Yaussi, flipping radio bands, heard a familiar voice. It was John Olson, singing "How ya gonna keep 'em down on the farm, after they've seen Paree . . ."

Ahead, I saw tracers aimed at us from John McKee's plane. Trying to protect us, he had dropped back and they were shooting at the attacking enemy fighters.

"Germans at nine o'clock."

I could feel the ball turret's guns firing as we picked up a belly attack.

From nowhere, a gray-white blur streaked with oil, a German fighter, flew right by me. It had a yellow belly and nose; the prop spinner was painted in white-and-black circles, like a top.

I watched, cross-eyed, as the nose turned like a screw. I stood there just looking at that cocky son-of-a-bitch, admiring his flying ability as he engineered a victory roll above me.

I grabbed the gun with both hands, squeezing off some bursts, hoping to lead the fighter that must be coming up behind him. The pilot of the second plane could have grabbed those thirty-caliber in his teeth, but someone with a fifty-caliber got him. He pulled up above the nose. There was a thundering CRACK . . . CRUMP . . . DA . . . DAA. The fighter exploded into confetti. I worried about the falling metal.

From behind came a succession of muffled noises, ripping, tearing, and culminating into an enormous THUMP. We had taken another blast of cannon. The ship yawed, pitched and rolled. It was crazy.

I touched the silent throat mike for clear broadcasting. "Bombardier to . . ." No sound. I traced each station with the radio selector. Nothing. The radio had been shot out.

I pulled away from the oxygen station. Sucking oxygen from the walk-around bottle, I passed Gise and headed toward the flight deck. The feat of Sconiers' braced my mind. If Oley or Gates were in trouble, I could help fly the ship home.

Red liquid, similar to hydraulic brake fluid, seeped down between the cracks and over the metal wall plating into the catwalk. As I stepped up from the walkway, I saw Gates' left hand clenched around his armrest. As I had so many times before, I stood facing the cabin, behind and between the pilots' seats.

The flight deck had received a direct hit.

It was a rear quarter attack. The blast of cannon entered from the left side, the explosion crashing across the cabin.

Winds rushed in through the blown-out windows. Broken safety glass, hanging by plastic thread, tinkled as it slapped against the frames. Electrical fires crackled on the instrument panel and, below, sparks rained from the servicing conduits. Smoke climbed, fanning through the cockpit, splitting and curling against the surfaces. Torn canvas and dangling wires flapped from the ceiling, hitting me in the face. And everywhere, I saw splattered blood and bits of flesh and hair.

In the crushing howl of the wind was a pitiful silence. The words hung in my heart: "Oley, get out of your goddamn seat . . . Norman, unfasten that belt . . . c'mon . . . let's get out of here."

But they weren't coming. Not then. Not ever. My Commander and Copilot slumped in their seats, crumpled in death. The yellow-white lambswool exposed in the seams of their clothes was soaking in blood, and only the stiff leather flight suits constrained the masses of fragmented tissue.

JESUS. Moments ago they were talking and now, they're . . . they're . . . hamburger.

Numbed, without comprehension, I stared at the bloodied steering columns. Uninterrupted, they moved in unison, the yokes clicking back and forth.

Acrid fumes from cordite smoke and vapors from burning filaments were choking me as I felt my body begin to cook in the intense heat from the smoldering bulkhead.

Resisting the finality, my hand reached out. To wake them? Quickly, I pulled it back. Nothing could help them. There was nothing I could do. Oley, Gates and Snoozy II would never make it back to the White Cliffs of Dover.

Suddenly, the sun went by. We were starting a flat spin of descent. I had to get out. FAST!

With the wind drowning human voice, I pounded hard on top-turret Wissenback's foot and hurried back to my compartment.

In the nose, I pulled the Klaxon horn and pushed the warning button. Neither worked. In the confusion and despair I knew what I had to do—protect the Norden bombsight from the enemy. With the Colt .45 in hand, readying my ears for the crash, I dramatically shot out the sight. There was a shred of good feeling in that performance of duty, before all shit hit the fan.

I tossed the gun back in the tray—it would be useless against an army—and grabbed the pack of Lucky Strikes. We could get out. After all, our plane held the Squadron's record; sixteen seconds to abandon ship. As I started toward Gise, the worst possible happened. The sun went by the nose again.

I was caught in a spin of centrifugal force that smashed my glasses to the floor, ripped the tube from the oxygen bottle and hurled me against the right side of the bulkhead. Flattened to the wall, my ribs were sucked into my spine, my head nailed to the spot. My eyeballs bulged as the sockets were drawn into my skull. The skin was pulled back from my face so tight that I struggled to keep my lips touching, afraid to let them part for fear I'd never get my mouth closed again.

Plastered to the walls all around me were maps and papers. Even my gloves, palms down, looked like they were hands trying to get out the window.

Seated in his chair, his back to me, Gise held onto his desk. If he let go, he'd fly into my lap.

Over on the table, I saw the gun had caught on the lip of the tray. My gum was still stuck on the hinge.

Immobilized, the pressure so scathing, I was sure, if it continued, the flesh would peel away from my body. I was going to die. Before me passed the ledger of my life. In seconds, I lived it again. I didn't put the nickel my father gave me into the collection plate at Sunday School. I saved it and bought a mile-high ice cream cone instead. Oh, God, forgive me. Being the littlest guy in junior high, I was elected to squeeze under the locked accordion gates and toss out apples and gum from the corner market. I siphoned gas, just enough to get me to the football game. Sure, I helped set off the fire alarm and I know I wasn't smart to stand there and ask, "Where's the fire?"

Please don't count all the bad things, I did some goodies, too. I helped my step-mom and she wasn't very affectionate with me. I broke the pole vault record in high school and please remember the touchdown I made in the Rose Bowl when I played in the Milk-Fund Game. I wasn't lazy. I worked. I had jobs all the time . . . even Easter week, I went down early and got a job in the Balboa Pharmacy. I washed all those glasses; those sticky, rotten glasses from marshmallow Cokes. I knew some of my friends were stealing, tucking a carton of cigarettes into a newspaper and leaving a dime when I was on the other side of the fountain.

Memories careened through my mind. I was back making Balboa Punch in the bathtub, mixing together whatever booze anyone brought, some of it stolen. "Gin and whisky, sorta risky . . . whisky and beer, have no fear . . ."

The nose let down. The ship assumed an attitude that eased the spin. With my hands, I grabbed a protruding rib in the bulkhead and, crossing one foot over the other, pulled myself forward. Gise moved around. We looked at each other as the spin tightened again. I waited. The ship mushed again and with all the strength in my arms, I pulled hard. Again the ship whipped, holding me fast. The third time the spin relaxed, I lunged forward, reaching Gise.

He was white and in shock. I could see blood around his neck. I didn't know how badly he was injured.

I put my arm around his shoulder and, hunching together, we dragged ourselves, bumping from side to side, through the catwalk. It was only four feet between the nose bulkhead and the escape hatch. It seemed like a mile. When I finally reached down to pull up the lid, it didn't budge. I kicked it. It was frozen. Oh, God, we've got to go all the way back to the bomb bay.

Getting sleepy, I pulled Gise and started walking around the hatch when a sudden assault of air hit my back. I turned around. The hatch door had been sucked out of the ship.

I motioned for Gise to jump. "Go ahead."

He shook his head and pointed at me.

I shook my head and waved him out. "Please go."

He shook his head and waved me out. I didn't want to be selfish and neither did he. Gentlemen to the end.

Jesus Christ! The whole world was shooting at us, the ship was on fire and there was death on board. "Goddamnit, get out," I screamed. I pulled him and pushed him out. Oh, shit, I thought; I've killed him. He's wounded and won't pull the ripcord.

The centrifugal force began again.

I threw myself forward in a dive, cracking my head on the side of the hatch. It revived me. I placed my hand on the square handle that dangled on my shoulder, balled myself up and tumbled out. It was my practice jump.

I blacked out.

17

HONEST JOHN McKEE

With John Olson's plane in a spin of descent, John McKee in Rose O'Day was now miles behind the protection of the formation. He was vulnerable and he knew it. He pushed the throttles forward, unleashing the power of all 4800 horses, in the attempt to rejoin the homeward-bound Fortresses. Just a few minutes, that's all he would need.

An ailing B-24 gave McKee the time. The damaged aircraft, limping below the B-17, became the next choice, an easy "kill" for the German fighters. The Focke-Wulf 190s closed in on the Liberator as McKee closed toward the 306th.

In his rush to catch up, McKee did not pull off the power and overshot the formation. Diverting the plane into a "dog leg," the turn enabled the ship to reduce its speed to that of the other aircraft. Rose O'Day tucked into the formation and its safety like a chick under the wing of the mother hen.

The German fighters, trying to determine the vulnerability of this new aircraft, continued to survey the B-17s and intermittently attacked. A FW 190, attempting to attain a diving range, pulled up, but did not have enough speed and stalled out right in front of John McKee. He was so close that anyone could have "leaned over and hit him with a monkey wrench." The gunners didn't move. They gaped at the German, spellbound.

Ahead, McKee could see the coast and the approaching Spitfires. The Spits, having refueled, were returning to cover the withdrawing American aircraft and engage the pursuing German fighters.

From one of the "Spitties" being chased by a Focke-Wulf, the gutsy English pilot radioed over VHF frequency to McKee: "Aye say, Yank, would you lead that son-of-a-bitch? I'm catching all of it."

The Fortresses needed the protection of the RAF. The mission had exposed the weakness of the Flying Fort. She was not a racehorse. Maneuverable and dependable, the B-17 was no match for the fast FW 190 or the Messerschmitt 109.

McKee had seen the FW 190 stand on a prop and go up right past him. He recalled Wendover Field and the conversation he had had with the representative from Boeing Aircraft.

"Being that I'm 11/10th coward," John mused, "what if you get into trouble?"

"If you get into trouble in the B-17," the factory rep answered, "just hit those turbo superchargers and climb. No fighter can keep up with you."

Christ, McKee thought, now there's an intelligent son-of-a-bitch. I wish he'd been there.

Over the Channel, the tautness eased from the body of McKee. He was nearly back to the safety of the base, to the Key Club, to scotch, to women. Yes, the maiden mission was nearly over.

But the pain of war was just beginning. McKee thought back to the morning, back to a few minutes after the pilots' briefing, less than three hours ago. Oley had pulled him aside and, in a voice filled with resignation, said, "Honest John, I have a premonition, this feeling. I'm going to get it. Today is the day."

"Ah, hell, Swede," McKee protested, "you and I are too tough, too ornery. Why shit, you're crazy. They'll never get us."

At Thurleigh, ship after ship landed. Ferrying down the flight line, they pulled onto their pads. All of the crews of the 306th returned except for John Olson's. The empty revetment of Snoozy II wounded the sight.

John McKee described the reaction to the loss. "Everyone felt it. Nobody said anything. Nobody wanted to say anything. They were gone. We knew it. We kept it inside."

Darwin Wissenback, waist gunner in McKee's plane, saw Olson's craft hit and notified his pilot, John McKee. With the other gunners on his ship, Darwin fired at the attacking fighters. Then he watched Snoozy II, with his twin brother in the top turret still firing, go down. All Darwin Wissenback could do was hope.

McKee could not get Oley out of his mind. He saw Swede's face. He heard the easy laugh.

The ache in Honest John's gut had started to ferment. Squeezing, tightening, twisting, his mind was a cavern of disbelief; his armor of youthful immortality, luck and Divine protection was bruised and blurred. In the ensuing grief, John McKee shut the door.

Before his tour was finished, Honest John McKee would effect a courageous career.

Seventy-two days later, on December 20th, after bombing the Aerodrome at Romilly-Sur-Seine, with three engines gone, John McKee and his crew parachuted from the crippled Rose O'Day. McKee landed forty-five miles east of Paris. Accompanied by an agent of the Belgian Underground, wearing civilian clothes and carrying Basque ID papers, Honest John made his way to Spain. On December 24th, as he departed an express train in Paris, John bumped into a German officer. His mind filled with Christmas Eve, John said, "Pardon me, buddy." Hurrying off into the crowded station, McKee didn't wait to find out if the officer understood English.

On New Year's Eve, at nightfall, he began walking over the west side of the Pyrenees. The soundless straw slippers he was wearing disintegrated in the pouring rain. In stocking feet, with frostbitten toes, he arrived in St. Sebastian, Spain twenty-four hours later—on New Year's night, 1943.

John McKee was the first American bomber pilot to escape from occupied France. His story was filmed by Hollywood director and producer Norman Z. McLeod, who entitled the movie, "Johnny Comes Walking Home."

McKee returned to the ETO and became Operations Officer, serving as Command Pilot for the 92nd Bomb Group. In 1946, he retired as a Lt. Colonel.

"Hero? My ass!" John said. "It was just that you had one more ounce of pride than you had fear, enough so that you stood by the wheel of the plane until your crew got out. You'd rather be killed than have someone say, 'He's got no guts.' "

Single and a "loner," Honest John McKee would remember that morning of October 9th the rest of his life.

"I decided then that I wasn't going to take any more of that shit. Swede and me . . . we were buddies. After Swede got killed, I never got close to anybody again."

He never did.

18

GOING DOWN

God may have been someone else's copilot, but he pulled my ripcord. I remembered nothing until the chest buckle on my parachute harness cracked me sharply on the chin, jerking me into consciousness. That was one way, the hard way, to find out my parachute and harness was on wrong. The shoulder straps of the harness were riding about six inches above my shoulders, encasing my head like a vice. I was unable to look up or down or turn my head in any direction. I could not move.

The winds were strong and slapped me around wildly, so forcefully I felt I was being dragged. The gut fear was that my chute was hung up on the ship's tail surfaces. Oh-h-h-h, but worst of all, the chute's harness was pulled high on my body. The straps buckled on each leg reached my navel and gnawed back and forth against my scrotum.

I felt I was being sawed in half. The pain was excruciating. Moaning in agony, my legs and arms dangling helplessly like a rag doll, I was pitched and tossed by forces I couldn't see, 20,000 feet above ground.

I cursed myself for not paying more attention to the courses in cadet school, courses I thought trivial, like the one on parachutes. Then, incredibly, just as my instructor had promised,

> "Your mind will speed 'oer the track'
> To bring you back
> What 'ere went out of your mind."

A

Etched in my memory was page eighteen of the parachute manual, ". . . if your chute harness is not on properly, if it is worn too loose and the result is it rides high on the body, follow directions 1, 2, 3 . . ." Oh, thank God for that instructor, the greatest man that ever lived, cramming that course at me.

Slowly, battling for every inch, I eased the harness like a girdle, down, until the hammock that had been in the middle of my back became low enough for me to pull it under my hips and sit in it.

Not only did the acute pain in my groin lessen to a tolerable throbbing, but also above me I could see, billowing freely, twenty-two feet of white silk.

Safe in my chute, I wondered, "Where is Gise? Had I killed him?" I struggled to look around. I knew he had to be behind me since I had jumped after he did. I reached for the shrouds and, turning my head to look under my arms, I searched the sky. At about three o'clock, I saw him. He was falling rapidly. He reached a position where his parachute was outlined against a dark background and I could see one of the panels in his chute was missing. But he was O.K. He was going to make it. Thank God.

Below him I saw an OD-colored aircraft, the props still going, in a wide left turn, drift out of my vision. Directly under me was a profusely burning mass, trailing black smoke. Either one could have been Snoozy II. I hoped Wissenback made it. I didn't think anyone else could have.

My head was a pounding ache. My neck was seared and wet. My face stung hotly. But I was alive! I counted my fingers and wiggled my toes. Not only was I breathing, but I was in one piece.

Sounds from the war carried on behind me. I reached up and twisted the risers to the chute counterclockwise, swinging myself around to face Lille, miles away. I could see boxes of aircraft in formation and fighters darting in and out through the smoke-dirtied air. Ugly red-orange balls of flame burst on the ground. Thumps from explosions and staccato from machine gun fire radiated from the battle, reverberating against me.

But from my distant observation, the drama's significance was muted. Its existence may well have been a play set on a miniature stage with animated toys. The war, like the struggles I had just endured, seemed no more than shadows, a vague dream, as I wafted in the air in total tranquillity.

Reality was this peace and solitude. I was a spirit, a bubble, a balloon, an echo of trailing laughter. I had transcended time and mortality. I was part of the universe, deeply quieted and soothed. Somewhere birds were singing, and more calming than any sound of my life, the shushing whisper of a tender, gentle wind as it must sound when it caresses the highest treetops. Floating, I was a soul transported in the winds.

The contentment was so insulating that I was only a spectator to the parachute that was hovering off to my right, almost even with my body.

Finally, I wondered, whose chute *is* that? I didn't see anyone. There *was* no one near me. I was confused. What was a chute doing out there? What the hell is this? I didn't grasp the situation until I saw the sunshine bounce off the silver-white shrouds that led to me. It was *my* parachute.

Oh! That's not right at all. The wind had pulled the chute to the side of me. Euphoria was gone. I was again very mortal. I didn't need a book to tell me that I could fall into my own chute. And if I did, it would be ZIP!

With vivid recall, I began to slip air, pulling down the lines on one side and then the other, timidly, remembering the box on the bottom of page 19: "WARNING: TOO MUCH OSCILLATION AND YOU MAY COLLAPSE YOUR CHUTE." It took time and a hell of a lot of restraint to bring myself back into position.

From my two frames of reference, the chute and the horizon, it seemed to me I was traveling laterally as much as I was traveling down. The vertical winds aloft were so strong that I was falling about 1,000 feet a minute, probably one-half what was normal.

I had barely adjusted myself, when I became aware of a new danger. The battle's sounds from Lille were carried by air masses in front of me and now, to my rear, came the constant drone of an airplane motor. It was a single engine plane, a fighter—I tied onto that.

Once again, I grabbed the risers above me, yanking them around in a half circle. When I let go, the seat turned around to catch the chute.

A plane, the wings slightly tilted, was heading towards me.

A recent headline from the Pacific War Zone flashed through my mind. Japanese pilots used the guys bailing out of their Flying Tiger P-40s for target practice, shooting them right out of the sky. I searched my mind, grasping for the pages on plane identification. It was either a Messerschmitt or a Spitfire. The plane had an inline engine. But which one had the air-scoop on the right and which on the left? I drew a blank.

Groping for some protective device to save myself, if I had to, I thought I would slip air from the chute as I had done before, alternately, thereby pulling myself out of the apex of his fire. If the enemy picked up that maneuver, I would slip twice in the same direction, one right, then right again, then left, then . . . I was kidding myself. All the pilot had to do was kick a rudder and fire. Screw it. He'd get me anyway.

He came closer; close enough that I could see the pilot's goggles catching the sun's reflection as they rested across his helmet. He came as close as the German fighter that went by the nose of the ship. Oh, he's going to throw some lead at me. I stiffened. To be ripped by machine gun fire would be quick.

Oh, Christ! What team was he on? Willing to cry and not daring to breathe, I kept hoping.

The elliptical wings flipped up on their sides as the ship took a slight dive around me.

Naked against the bright blue sky, the brown, OD-colored aircraft was clearly definable. It had two wavy yellow lines across the trunk, camouflaged to resemble a path when the plane was on the ground, and on one wing tip was the MAGNIFICENT red, white and blue roundel of the English Spitfire.

I was drinking Coke again. I had just won another war. I had my life back.

As he performed a pylon turn, the pilot looked up at me. He flew at my level, circling me twice and then took a quick dive to fly around Gise, stealing a lot of altitude in a hurry from any German planes that might be around. Nearing the ground, he turned abruptly and hedgehopped toward England. Oh, what a peach of a guy, protecting us that way.

The lower I came, the milder the winds. I had more control over the chute. People on bicycles and in small groups watched me.

Another surging fear. Where was the enemy? There didn't seem to be anyone in uniform. But what about the civilians? One of them may have lost a loved one in a raid a day or two before and maybe was just mad enough to shoot anyone coming out of the sky.

I searched for the Underground's signal. Two blue things with a pair of pants in the middle, or was it the other way around? It didn't matter. Everyone in northern France washed that day. The clotheslines were full.

I tugged the shroud enough to get me over a small reservoir. Stupidly, I had left my orange Mae West somewhere back at the base. I didn't want to land in water, not in a tree, nor in a hedgerow. I undid the buckles of my harness, leaving only my weight to hold me in the swing. Guiding the chute to a clearing beside the water, I came down in an uncultivated field, landing on one leg, facing the wind, the parachute blowing off behind me. It was like the book described, a perfect landing.

Now, where the hell was I and how could I get home?

A

Al's escape picture, to be used for phony passport, if shot down
and rescued by Allied Underground.

19

VINE, VOMEN AND SONG

The first imperative was to bury the chute. In the open countryside, I had no time for an excavation project. Gathering the sprawling white silk, I hurriedly shoved it into a shallow grave and threw a few leaves over it.

Per POW briefings, I took off my non-identifying outer garments and, leaving the heavy winter flight jacket next to the parachute, I carried my OD coveralls.

From nowhere in the uncultivated farmland, people started to gather. Older men and women and children watched me, being careful to maintain a distance from me and from each other.

It was my first exposure to a suspicious, subjugated people.

Who was a German? Who was a traitor? Who, for an extra meal, would point their finger and talk?

In my uniform, not the blue uniform of the Luftwaffe, not the green of the Wehrmacht, with no swastika to label me, in my twill suntans, they trusted I was not a German. I immediately became the recipient of a bottle of wine, a loaf of bread, some green root vegetables and a couple of eggs.

"Thank you, thank you. I'm American."

They regarded me with puzzled expressions. In this hinterland I was an oddity, a stranger in a peculiar uniform. What America was I from? South America? Central America? Canada? From America, USA? Then, I was a wonder from utopia.

The peasants that brought me the food did so quickly and

then disappeared. Other spectators, on bicycles, on foot, and one on horseback, arrived to view me with curiosity.

With my arms filled with food, I determined to walk to the closest farmhouse. It had laundry on the lines and the woman who stood outside had a kind face, not the face of an SS Trooper.

The pretty, young woman, standing on a knoll, looked down at me and spoke cautiously. No one else was willing to get involved, but she was nervy enough to try and flap a little English—school English that she could read better than she could speak.

I told her I wanted to go east, in the direction that Gise had landed.

"No, no," she answered, "Boches, Boches!" Pointing west, she said, "You go that way. Go. Go."

"England, England," I pleaded, "which way to England?"

Glancing at the people around us for possible informers, she shook her head and repeated, "Go, go."

I retraced my steps back to where I had landed.

Amid the furtive inspection of sightseers, someone called, "Second Front?"

A Second Front? What the hell was that?

It was the first time these people had seen Fortresses. They were looking, hoping for an invasion, for a landing force to relieve them. They thought the Front had begun. They were two years early.

People broke away, a sign that Germans were in the area.

Wanting something between the enemy and me, I hid behind a hedgerow, a thick, gnarled rooty growth, a windbreak ten feet high that had trees growing through it. I forced myself to sit down and plan a course of action. My body did not want to rest. It wanted to move. The powerful impulse was to run.

With the food arranged on the dirt beside me, I opened my escape kit. Inside, I found a map, a compass, French franc notes held together with transparent paper, a 3½-inch saw blade, some gum, an envelope of Nabisco cookies, two crackers with cheese and a concentrated chocolate bar. The blade was so dull it couldn't cut butter and the compass, possibly hit by flak, was hung up on the south. This was an escape kit? More like a trick or treat, a practical joke. It must have been assumed I would meet with the Underground.

Within a half hour, an old man and a kid appeared. The gray-bearded man wore a dark jacket and pants with a cap pulled low over his forehead. The child was in knickers and carried my parachute. No more than six, he was fascinated with my throat mike, which I forgot I had on. I gave it to him. Such grateful affection beamed from his face that I gave him my leather flight helmet and the chocolate bar as well.

"Allons."

I looked at the old guy.

"Come."

Leaving the food, I followed them, past the reservoir of water, over small hills, through a wooded area, to a weathered, frame farmhouse. Inside the single, large room, were beds at one end and a massive fireplace at the other.

"I am American. Here are some French francs. Get me out of here."

The women smiled at me, but did not speak. They prepared scrambled eggs, fried potatoes and a green vegetable. Having served them to me, they left.

I spread the map on the table, trying to figure out where I was. After some minutes, the old gent poked his head through the open door and again said, "Come."

Outside was a cart made of wood slats and big, wooden wheels. It was loaded with kindling. People clustered around the cart, their faces inquisitively asking, "Who are you?"

Directing me to a seat below that of the driver's, the old man, sucking on an upside down pipe, planted himself heavily above me and jerked the reins. The gray-and-white-spotted horse plugged forward as my feet dangled inches above the ground.

By the sun I could tell we were traveling west and north, not exactly the direction I wanted to go. But I trusted the old guy. His timing was right, waiting until I was hidden behind the hedgerow and then, like a puff of smoke, he was there. His actions were methodical and charted, as though our route was pre-planned.

As soon as we were out of sight of the farmhouse and the civilians, he stopped the cart and burrowed a hole in the back for me to crawl into. Covered by the lattice crisscross of the long, thin, wooden sticks, we continued our journey. Partially hidden, I could see people working in the fields. No one paid attention to us. The farther we traveled, the safer I felt. Still, I knew only too well, I had to be on guard at all times. If I heard guttural noises, I would drop down and crawl off the road into the field.

At a border, having passed through an open gate in a hedgerow, a young man took over the driving. A red-and-white-striped pole that was topped in black and a sign that began "ACHTUNG, ACHTUNG" signified the border checkpoint. Attached was an arrow pointing behind us, in the direction from where we had come. It was marked Tournai.

We rolled over the dirt road, passing roaming cows and pigs. Most of the trees had turned color and were dropping their leaves. Some distance beyond the border was a white signpost with an arrow pointing ahead, marked Kortrijk (Courtrai).

The light from the noonday sun was beginning to dim in a film of cirrus clouds when the young driver stopped the cart. Leaving it on the road, the intelligent-looking young man accompanied me through a wooded groove to another farmhouse, where he, too, left me.

The house was a replica of the first one, from the scurrying dogs and chickens to the nurtured plot of green grass that cushioned its entrance. With the exception of a small partition and a large iron stove, the interior was also the same.

There, as before, two women were preparing food. They were husky looking and wore dark hose, wooden shoes and long, white aprons. They smiled as they served me fried potatoes and a hot herb tea, yet they did not speak.

I was not hungry. Food was of no importance to me. I had other problems. Things were happening fast. This was a new life. And, I hadn't been in my last one very long.

I studied the map, but could not estimate my position in relation to the map's central point of Lille and the Channel. North and east did not seem the way to travel. Perhaps west? That direction was heavily wooded.

Into the room walked a tall, blue-eyed Scandinavian. In a dark pea coat and pants, high boots, peak cap and black turtleneck sweater, he spoke with authority. He was either going to throw me to the wolves or be my best friend. He was serious, but friendly. He didn't hurry, but there was urgency in his voice. He wanted to tell me something and get the hell out of there. In a few English words, he set the scene.

A British Lysander, a small aircraft that had the ability to get in and out of rough, narrow terrain, would be coming in that night. Flares would be lighted in a nearby field where the plane would land, deliver contraband and shuttle me back to England.

This was a person who could tell me where I was, but when I looked up from the map, the trim, athletic blond was gone. So were the women.

Well, everything was going to be O.K. I was taken care of. I was damn lucky. And that Underground! It was astonishingly experienced and organized. Just to think, I would be back in England that very same night.

Relaxed, I ate the fried potatoes and munched on a piece of French bread. The thought of doughnuts went through my mind. I wondered what kind they were. Were they cake doughnuts like my mother made? They got hard awfully quick. Maybe they would be that new "raised" kind. I hoped that there would be some left. If Butterball ate more than five, I'd bop him one.

Assured that I had nothing to worry about, I did not pay attention to the voices that were coming from the side of the house: "Oui." "Non." "Oui." Pacified, I thought that the Lysander had arrived early. When the volume of the voices increased and the guttural replaced the romantic, I looked out the window. Seven or eight people stood talking. Among the bobbing heads were the pink cheeks and funny round faces I had seen in magazines at home.

JESUS CHRIST! GERMANS!

There were the green uniforms of the German Army and the long trench coats and slouched hats of the Gestapo.

Swiftly, I crossed the room. Halfway across, I heard shots from hand weapons. It was no time to stop and see what happened. Grabbing only the map and a hard-boiled egg and tucking them in my pockets, I ran out the back door and down five stairs without touching one of them. My feet were going around like a fast Ferris Wheel, but my body seemed anchored in slow motion as I headed across the fifty-yard clearing towards the woods. I would be safe in its dense growth of fir trees. Protection was just beyond me. With my youthful stamina and one hard-boiled egg, I could hide there for at least a week.

"HALTEN SIE."

I kept running.

"HALTEN SIE."

I heard the slide of a pistol. The weapon was cocked. A shell was in the chamber, ready to fire.

I stopped. Putting my hands up, slowly I turned around.

My eyes fell on three sights: those of two guns—a Lugar and a P-38—and the face of my captor. I couldn't believe it. He had the same face that was characterized on the cover of the June 13th issue of *Literary Digest*.

Chubby, jowly, pink cheeks, little black mustache, he was comical, funny, friendly, squinting his face into a smile. There was so much meat, he *had* to squint.

Walking up to me, he said, "Ach, lucky for you. For you, das var, der Krieg, is offer."

I *was* lucky.

He wore the billed garrison cap (squarely on top of his head), the long, blue jacket and jodhpur-styled pants, the leather boots and gloves of an officer—an officer of the Luftwaffe. If I had to be a prisoner, that was the way to go, not as a prisoner of the Elite SS Troops or Hitler's Jugenen. After interrogation, they would just as soon chop you to pieces RIGHT NOW.

"Yah," he repeated, "das var is offer. Now you vill have vine, vomen and song."

I stared at his big, toothy grin, flickering with gold fillings. Searching his face, I asked, "Goddamn, haven't I seen you before somewhere?"

He was happy. His look was, "Ha, ha, I got me one."

I was happy. My feeling was, "Ah, he didn't shoot."

After searching me for weapons, we went into the house to wait for transportation. The other Germans recognized that I was his prisoner. He had the guns to prove it.

Before the arranged transportation arrived, the officer who spoke to me in tolerable English told me he had been a butcher in Pittsburgh. In "Amerika." He was proud of the fact. The rest of his story was not as explicit, but apparently he had returned to Germany for a visit with relatives and had been retained for the war.

A French taxi arrived.

An Unter Offizier searched me. Padding his hands over my uniform, he took the map, cigarettes, Ronson lighter, both Air Force and 2nd Lt. collar insignias, dog tags, watch, and even the hard-boiled egg. He asked for my ring, which I twisted in a half-hearted effort around my finger. I pretended I couldn't get it off so he let me keep it. The Sergeant was particularly impressed with the cigarette lighter and watch. Fondling them, he exclaimed "Gold?"

The Luftwaffe officer and I climbed into the back seat, the Sergeant and driver sat in front. The Gestapo and other men drove off in another car.

The ride to a small business district was short. I was taken into a converted commercial building where a Wehrmacht officer sat at a solitary table.

"Setzen Sie sich," the butcher from Pittsburgh ordered.

Taking a seat in one of the chairs that lined the wall, I watched the officer depart. "Auf Wiedersehen," he bid me goodbye.

From the rotund figure, my eyes fell to a chair close to the front door. Its contents shocked me. There was my parachute and heavy winter flight jacket. The Germans had me under surveillance from the beginning!

What about the old man? The little guy? My throat mike and helmet weren't there; maybe he got away. The women who cooked for me? The blond Scandinavian? He left some time before I heard the voices. Was someone shot? I didn't see any bodies, but then I didn't walk around that side of the house. The Gestapo hadn't taken prisoners.

People killed because of me? Another ramrod of despair!

20

OH, NO!

The chair was large and cumbersome, of rough construction. I hated sitting in it. I walked back and forth and over to the guy's desk. He tolerated me for a while and then he yelled, "Setzen Sie sich!"

Squirming in my seat, I watched people file into the room, waiting in line for passes, for special permits, for food coupons. German soldiers came in and sat down. They looked at me. Some smiled. They talked between themselves and seemed pleased.

Hours passed. I was bored and uncomfortable. I leaned back in my chair and poked my fingers into my back pockets.

MY GOD! It was like a piece of DYNAMITE. A BOMB! A bomb went off in my mind. Just that quick I knew what it was that I had touched in my rear left pocket. THE TISSUE-THIN AIRMAIL LETTER I HAD WRITTEN TO PAPPY LUTZ YES-TERDAY! I had forgotten to mail it!!!

OH! I pulled my hand out real quick like it had shit on it. OH, NO! The letter contained all the information the Germans could have asked for: my Group, my Field, my Squadron, my Air-craft, my APO number . . . OH! Congress and the Air Force would have never forgiven me. If the Germans had that letter, it would be the end of my world. I could never go home!

If someone had been watching me, watching my face, they would have caught on. But no one was. The soldiers had left, the guards were posted outside and the officer was busy at his desk. I wanted to eat the paper. My fingers felt hot, as if they had actually been burned. My rear left cheek prickled from a concentrated heat. What could I do?

Composing myself, I waited. During a lull at the desk, I walked up to the officer and said, "Toilet?"

"Toiletta?" he asked. "Pissen or scheissen?"

What the hell difference did it make? I pretended not to understand. "Uh huh."

He called for a guard.

The green-uniformed soldier came into the room, clanging like cows coming home from the pasture. He was a walking display of a hardware store. The Wehrmacht wore their whole life around their gut.

A big leather harness climbed straight up their spine and split over their shoulders. It supplied the metal fasteners to carry their equipment. Each man was a self-contained unit. They carried a forty-six ounce can containing a gas mask, a metal canteen, a first-aid kit, keys, chains that attached to their bayonet, a knapsack over the right hip and a leather pouch of ammunition.

The guard stood at attention. His tin cans didn't. After their conversation, the guard turned to me and muttered, "Pissen or scheissen?"

"Uh huh."

He took me around through the back door to a little room that had a real toilet; not the usual privy, but a real flushing toilet.

I closed the door, afraid he would hear me as I unbuttoned my back pocket. Slowly, ever so carefully, I pulled out the letter. Less than an ounce, the letter felt like it weighed two tons. If I dropped it, it would explode. I was holding the world's biggest secret. If the guard knew, he would shoot me right through the door.

Bit by bit I tore up the paper and dropped the teeny shreds into the toilet.

The cans on the guard clanged as he moved from one leg to the other. He butted the door with his rifle.

Letting the paper soak in the water, I grunted to hide the soundlessness and then I flushed the toilet. I waited. In my fear of being discovered, my mind featured in gigantic disproportion the disaster of finding even one piece of the letter.

The guard banged the door again.

I flushed the toilet a second time. I never did pull my pants down. If I had, I might have taken a grand whiz. As it was, I didn't care.

The guard looked at me suspiciously when I opened the door. Impatiently, he walked me back to the central room. Sweating with relief, I was glad, now, to sit down.

21

TRAVELING ABROAD

Only a short time after disposing of the letter, a young, handsome Luftwaffe officer came in and walked importantly to the desk. The officer receiving him stood up attentively. They spoke and turned to look at me. The blond pilot, faultlessly groomed, with his hat tucked underneath his arm, came over and addressed me: "Herr Leutnant La Chasse? Hauptman Hartmann."

I stood up and pulled my hand from my pocket, pressuring him to shake it. He held onto his gloves and left my hand hanging. I felt he wanted to shake hands, but for appearance's sake he was going by the book.

With a small smile, he excused his English. "Mein Englisch ist nicht gut. Verstehen sie mich, ah, understand . . . mmm . . . you . . . me?"

I gave him a big smile. "Uh huh."

"You . . . ah . . . Peelote . . . Bumberr, Flugzeug? Short Sterling . . . Englaender? Ja? Ja?"

I knew little of the Short Sterling aircraft. I wanted to ask if he was the pilot that shot us down. I felt he was, but I didn't know the word for shoot.

We looked at each other questioningly.

His eyes softened. He ran his hands over his face and asked, "Ver vundet?"

I didn't know what he was referring to. I felt my face, the stubble of a beard and a numb covering like dried mud.

The Captain touched my shoulder while he inspected the back of my neck. The skin that had been exposed below my leather helmet felt like a weeping blister.

Sympathetically, he inquired, "Sie sind krank?"

Whatever his words, I knew he was asking if I was all right. As long as my head was still attached to my body, I was fine. "No, I'm O.K."

He gave me a smoke from a light blue box. It was an English Player cigarette, probably part of the large English stores that fell heir to the Germans at Dunkirk.

Hauptman Hartmann had poise and integrity. Beneath the cool composure, he cared. I liked him. I kept on smiling.

He was perplexed that I was as happy as I was.

"Sind Sie froehlich? Sie haben getrunken?" With his hand, he imitated drinking.

I didn't have to drink to be happy. Sure I was happy. Happy that I had all my faculties and all of my extremities. I had survived, not once that day, but many times. Not the least was disposing of Pappy's letter with all the incriminating information. It would have sentenced me as an informer. Damn right I was happy, more so because I was taller than the adversary standing before me.

The pilot clicked his boots in a salute, spoke a few words at the desk and departed.

The officer at the table, who had been relieved earlier, returned. The afternoon, darkened by an overcast sky, turned black in the evening. Despite the approaching night, the flow of civilians through the room continued. They filed in through the side and back doors, waiting patiently in a long line.

Lapsing from inactivity, I was aroused when I heard conversation. From hours of watching the cold reserve of the officer behind the table, I knew from his animation that he was dealing with one of the Belgian "swifties," obvious in her trade by silk stockings and lipstick. Sure enough, he was squeezing the girl's arm, verbally pursuing her.

I had resigned myself to sleeping in that chair for the night and was about to ask to go to the toilet again, when three Luftwaffe officers, popping their feet over the wooden steps and floor, banged into the room. They conferred with the Wehrmacht officer, who pointed to me.

One of the men said, "Kommen Sie." With his hand he waved for me to come with him.

Socked into that room for so many hours, I felt liberated as we climbed into a German jeep and drove off into the night.

The Germans did not know where they were going. They made stops, turns and backtracked in their search for an unfamiliar destination. At one point they consulted a map. Finally, on the outskirts of a town, we parked in front of a big, brown building. As we got out of the car, I heard the staccato of machine-gun fire somewhere in the distance.

We climbed up a long flight of stairs. It was dark in the enclosed stairwell and the steps had an unnatural overhang, so that I stumbled several times. Though the Germans also tripped, it embarrassed me. I wanted to look smart, not foolish.

The small, plain entrance gave no clue as to what was waiting for me. I felt another "first time" anxiety, the ever present danger in the uncertainty. All the briefings and all the books could not duplicate the personal experience. I found myself wary, flinching like an animal.

Once inside the building, I felt easier. It was an old, beautifully appointed nightclub with a handsome interior, rich in wood paneling. The empty room was warm, with a central stone fireplace and hand-carved scrollwork ornamenting the circular wood bar.

The four of us sat in overstuffed chairs around a low cocktail table. Plush and comfortable, we appeared to be old friends enjoying an evening at the Club. But in the quietness there was a tremor of expectancy.

For the Germans, I was an enjoyable challenge. For them this was no ordinary duty. Besides the pleasure of going on leave (transporting a prisoner was a utilization of available manpower), with me they had an opportunity to elevate themselves. To obtain information would be a victory. Behind the manipulated smiles was the intent for personal glory.

For me, too, this was a challenge. For the first time, I faced interrogation. Could I field their questions effectively, giving up nothing but appeasement? Could I protect my determination, my toughness, with a harmless veneer? Was I knowledgeable enough to appear innocent? How clever was I?

A waiter stood with a tray in hand as an officer asked me, "Vas trinken Sie?"

"Bourbon."

"Bourbon? Vas ist das?" The three men searched each other for an answer. Groping for a moment, they quickly recovered the smug profile natural to the "superior race." The officer, agitated, repeated, "Bourbon, machen Sie schnell." The waiter hurried off.

Well, I thought, here comes the wine, now for the women.

We sat in silence. Why the procrastination? I was ready to flip a coin so we could get on with it.

Timidly, one of the officers began, "Verstehen Sie das?"

I didn't answer.

"Understand Sie mich . . . ah, mm, verstehens you mich?"

"Verstands you . . .?" I repeated.

"Ja, understand you mich?"

"O.K."

"You, Bumberr? Vas fuer ein Bumberr?" He looked at me intently, trying to pull an answer with his eyes.

I shrugged my shoulders.

The officer turned to the other for key English words. "Ich veiss nicht . . . Ich veiss nicht . . ."

I had learned enough German from my grandmother to decipher the phrase, "I don't know." Hell! That's why they were hesitating. These guys couldn't speak English!

The drinks were served.

The three men lifted their glasses and toasted, "Sieg Heil." Taking a gulp, they licked their lips in approval. They were having a good time. "Trinken Sie . . . trinken Sie . . ." they urged me. The lukewarm alcohol made me gag. It was clear colored and poisonously raw. Compared to it, straight Scotch was like a glass of milk. I could barely tolerate it. Good old S-2 didn't have to worry about their boys getting drunk and spilling the beans over here. No guys would willingly touch the stuff.

The next officer began, "Verstehen Sie . . . vas ist ihr Flugzeug, ah ihr Bumberr, der Namma, Namma, verstehen . . . unterstand?"

Picking up the drink, I toasted him, "Here's lookin' at ya." With my nose closed I took another swallow.

"Bumberr . . . gross?" He held his arms out in an estimate of size. "Bumberr, Junker 88? Halifax? Lancaster? Stuka? Short Sterling?"

"Stuka ME??" I shook my head.

The officers asked the same questions. "Bumberr?" "Tage?" "Nacht Bumberr?" "Gross?" "Verstehen Sie mich?"

Each, wanting to impress the others, held his moment eyeball-to-eyeball, hoping that if he didn't get the information in words, he would by osmosis.

They were not geared for this job. This was all new to them. Fumbling for English, they joked between themselves. The interrogation was a farce. All I had to do was play with words, for time and for more cigarettes.

I could not differentiate rank, but I knew these were officers by the style and cloth of their uniforms; by their leather gloves, blue shirts and black ties; by the silver eagles on a field of yellow felt. They were not rated to fly for they wore no wings.

But these officers, older than myself, behaved like school kids who hadn't done their homework. They showed no smartness, certainly not the confidence of the Luftwaffe pilot I had met earlier. These men, giggling and giddy, were to me, screw-ups. Every service had them, even the U.S. Air Force.

The "screw-ups"—those men who attained rank by knowing the right person or by having an influential relative and, most offensive, the men who bought themselves desk jobs at Pinetree by refusing to fly.

These were the Luftwaffe "incompetents." And, like so many in the U.S. Air Force, they probably were not familiar with their revolvers. Their weapons were securely buckled into the holsters. I could kick them in the nuts and be gone before they could even draw. But where could I go? The streets were dark and I could easily get trapped in an alley. These guys would not hesitate to kill me. With no identifying dog tags, they could claim I was a saboteur. No, I would have to wait, perhaps for a sign from the Underground. The game of words continued and I decided to play.

"Vo varen Sie in England?"

"No," I answered. "I'm from the United States."

"Ja, ja," they agreed. "Vereinigten Staaten, ja. Vo varen Sie in England?" they asked again.

I knew they wanted to know where I was stationed. Ignoring them, I added with calm significance, "I'm from California." I could see by their eyes that I had made an impression. Was it true here, as it had been since bombardier training, that the word California commanded the magic? I played it for all it was worth. "Yes, I'm from Glendale, near LOS ANGELES."

"Ach, so."

"Yes, near HOLLYWOOD. You've heard of HOLLYWOOD? You know, where the stars live? ERICH Von STROHEIM, MARLENE DIETRICH?"

"Ach so."

In rapt attention, the Germans studied me in a new light. Not only was I from America, but I was from HOLLYWOOD and I knew the STARS. It was written all over their faces. The questions diminished as I parried places and names of the movie capitol, names projecting glamour that awed the imagination, even of the men in Hitler's Third Reich.

Alone as I was, I felt *I* was on top. I had guided them into my comfort zone, a space where I could gather myself, where I could take a breath and get ready for what was coming next. The session had been a rehearsal. I hoped I could play it again.

The Luftwaffe officers checked their watches as if a deadline had been prearranged. They ordered more drinks for themselves, but made no attempt to get me drunk.

Having spent less than two hours in the Club they drove me south, to a newly constructed jail. It was a big building, as big as a football field. On either side of the huge entry were halls that contained small rooms. It was a holding tank, a detention center.

As we entered the compound, an announcement was made, one that followed me everywhere: "Ein Amerikanischer Kriegsgefangener."

Heads turned. The inquiring faces evaluated mine. The soldiers acted as if they had never seen an American before.

In the new bathroom of flushing toilets I accomplished what I could not do in Snoozy II that morning—I relieved myself. There were no mirrors, but I was able to wash my hands for the first time since leaving the 367th barracks at Thurleigh.

In cell number 9, I mechanically ate the cheese and fruit which had been given me. The reality of the eternity before me crowded my mind, but I was too tired to wrestle with it. Gratefully, I made my last escape of the day. I lay on the cot and went to sleep.

Awakened around 5 a.m., I was taken in a '37 tan Ford (I'd always wanted one) to a railroad station. With two of the officers from the previous day and a Gefreit (corporal) we waited for an interminable time, but no train showed.

God Bless the Limeys. Had a successful RAF raid taken place? We drove to another Belgian train depot.

Many civilians were waiting behind the boarding gates. I was marched along the front platform. In my suntans, uniquely quiet among the clashing colors of the Wehrmacht and silver braid of the Luftwaffe, bearing myself in the casual carriage of an American GI, without the strutting or the goose-step or the knife-sharp attention displayed between German ranks, without a helmet, a weapon or decoration, and followed by a brown bag of meandering silk, I was a curiosity to the civilians, and a favorable one. My presence kindled a friendly enthusiasm as the word "Amerikaner" leaked through the station.

They waved and smiled. Anonymous voices called, "Hi, Yank." Someone yelled, "How are the Brooklyn Dodgers doing?" Another countered, "How about the New York Yankees?" Camouflaging their actions by picking their noses or scratching their heads, the people made "V" signs.

Oh, I could melt into that crowd so easily. What a great way to escape.

The train backed into the station. Isolated from the passengers by the Germans, I rode in a roofed flat car on wooden benches.

The train was jammed. Some passengers rode standing up. The frequent stops and starts indicated destruction due to strafings and sabotage. We passed work crews along the tracks and, occasionally, billboards advertising Coca Cola, Shell Oil and General Motors products.

In Brussels, the afternoon was filled with more friendly faces. On the platform, several hundred people waiting behind the huge wrought iron gates and fence gave me smiles and implied friendship with their "Vs" for victory.

The guards moved me forward to the station's front offices where they talked with the stationmaster. He was a cocky, chunky little man who wore a uniform garish in gold braid, glorifying his position as the station's "fuehrer."

Uniforms seemed to be important. Even the street sweeper, pushing a trash can on wheels and carrying a broom, was attired in an outfit dripping in gold epaulets.

While the guards checked the train schedules, I reveled in the commiserating bodies no more than twenty feet away. With my eyes, I embraced them.

Abruptly, the stationmaster came out of his office. Walking over to me, he slapped my face. He was about to slap me with his other hand when the German officer raised his arm and stopped him.

"Nein, nein," he rebuked him. "Das ist ein Offizier."

Stunned, my surprise turned to anger. Even as a child, I nourished hot resentment for such a humiliating punishment. Daring the bastard to slap me again, I put my hands in my pockets and glared directly into his eyes, reciprocating his look of hate. The German officer walked the stationmaster away.

In the delay of the train, while other transportation was being arranged, my guards and I had our pictures taken. The photographs were made inside a room with barred windows. Some shots were stills. Others were made with a portable motion picture camera that rested on the cameraman's shoulder.

A bakery truck arrived. My parachute, coat and I were shoved into a back corner. The Germans jumped in behind me.

We drove about ten miles south and east of Brussels to St. Gillis, near Waterloo. It was the same prison where Napoleon had tossed *his* political prisoners. St. Gillis was a nightmare.

Inside, the air was heavy, latent in a pungent stench, streaked with disinfectant. Equally oppressive was the sound of a tense, confused humming.

I was deposited into a small room. Two walls were solid. The others were of a thick, interwoven wire about six feet high with diamond mesh extending to the ceiling. Standing on my toes, I peeked through the open screen.

"Hi, Yank."

"Hi."

As I grew accustomed to the darkness, I could see what I had formerly sensed. Eyes stared back at me. Blue eyes, green eyes, eyes of all colors in haunting intensity pierced the shadows. A mass of men and women were packed together in a wire cage. Their tired, sad faces were lined with resignation, their bodies breathed together in waves of sighs.

"Yank, Yank." The whisper spread. The people pressed forward to see me.

I heard something breaking like cracking cement. It was then that I noticed, above my head, a walkway that ridged the cage. Two German guards, carrying whips, hovered above the prisoners. What I heard was a whip cracking.

Was this for real? Do people really do these things? My God! This wasn't a stage where some cowboy was snapping a horse lasso. The Germans were trying to nip those guys!

Despite the whips, the agitation increased. Within a few minutes I was removed from the prison by the three officers who had brought me there and was driven to another location for the night's custody. St. Gillis was one more horror that I tried to block out of my mind.

Convenient to St. Gillis was a military station, a Wehrmacht training and assignment center.

In the large hall where I was taken, the walls were mounted with instructional posters. One, close to me, was a layout of the post, designated "WACHEPLAN." Another, with cutaway illustrations of collars and sleeves denoting braid, stripes and insignias, was a list of the Services' ranks in Germany, England and the U.S.

Following my introduction, "Ein Amerikanischer Kriegsgefangener," I was left in the charge of the trainees.

Intrigued, they crowded around me. "Sind Sie hungrig?" they asked. "Kommen Sie." They led me to a food counter at the side of the hall, where I was brought soup, cold potato pancakes, bread and an ersatz coffee. "Essen, essen," they urged me to eat.

Under the microscopic attention of twenty faces, I was careful to use my best manners, though it was difficult to be smooth, since their cutlery was awkwardly large.

"Mehr, mehr?" Leaning around me in a circle, the men offered me more food.

I was not the enemy here. I was a novelty, a surprise package. I was from another world and they wanted to know all about it.

A few questions about my "Flugzeug" and then they asked about *me*.

"Universitat? Namma? Namma?" "Vie alt sind Sie? Jahres?" "Spielen Sie Baseball?"

In a lengthy charade, I described the game of football and sold California as the Eighth Wonder of the World.

Between them, the young Germans attempted the translation. "Kalifornia, schoen. Das ist richtig." "Ja, Pazifische Ozean." "Sierras gross Berg, Mohave . . . vust heiss . . ." Ja, ja."

They were captivated by my ring. I spread my fingers out and twisted it around.

"Vas ist das?" they asked, pointing to the garnet. On the side of the ring was an outline of a plane. "Flugzeug? Ist das Gold?"

Outfitted in new tan and green uniforms, these were spirited young men. Untouched by battle, they were curious and friendly. It was hard to believe they were indoctrinated in the concept of "Deutschland über alles." Rather, at that moment, unobserved by officers, we were joined together by our youth, by the confiscated freedom to enjoy that youth and by our uncertain destiny.

In that room, if it had been left to us, there would have been no war.

The following morning, after a comfortable night's sleep on a couch in the Center's recreation room, I was taken back to the train station. Waiting there was a RAF airman who had been picked up and was now going to travel with us.

At once, I felt a strangeness about him. He had no insignia, although neither did I. His accent was British but he flapped several languages, including German. He was so at ease he made me nervous. Between us, we said little. Who knows? Perhaps he was as suspicious of me as I was of him.

As I stood on the platform, the Gefreit who was carrying my parachute and coat held them out for me to take. I did not say anything. I did not take them. He shoved them at me. I took the heavy winter flying jacket and put it on. As for my parachute, he could leave it. I was still smarting from the slap I had received the day before. I felt that if I accepted the parachute I would lose status. I had to take a stand.

The angered guard pushed the silk in my face.

"No," I insisted, "I am an officer."

A Luftwaffe officer interceded on my behalf. In Belgium, at least for the time being, I enjoyed the Luftwaffe's respect for rank.

A crowd of people began accumulating outside the boarding gates. Biding time, the guards lit cigarettes and talked among themselves. The RAF airman conversed with them.

No one was watching me. Positioned on the platform next to the boarding train, I slipped, unnoticed, inside. I walked through the empty train, outside and across a pair of tracks. Passing a string of cars, through another empty train, I arrived at a third landing. I was free.

All hell broke loose. "ACHTUNG. ACHTUNG." Whistles blew. Where were the crowds of friendly people now that I needed them? I jumped into an empty car and crouched down, determined to sweat it out. Guards ran around with their rifles pointed. There were shots fired. Though the bullets didn't come close, they made me more of a chicken.

A switchman gave me away. Royally uniformed, he pompously led the Germans to me. With several rifle barrels butted into my spine, I was roughly pushed back to the front platform.

The crowd, waiting to board the many trains, began whistling. First one, then two, until the morning was pierced by a sustained shriek.

The German officers looked perplexed. Were the people jeering them, their leaders? They were discomforted by the kinship the crowd showed for me. The Germans were red in the face, especially the new ones who had just come on duty. Embarrassed and angry, they pushed me into a compartment on the train away from the sympathetic civilians. It wasn't going to be a pleasant ride with these guys.

Once we began traveling, their tempers cooled.

One of the younger officers brought me a piece of bread. It was of a variety that the Germans vacuum wrapped and distributed to their front-line troops. The flavor was molasses and reminded me of canned brown bread; a luxury that when it was served at home I thought my father had come into money. They also brought me some chicory coffee and a fruit drink that the younger men preferred instead of dark beer, and they lit cigarettes for me.

During the trip, I was ogled by passengers as they passed the compartment and by my accompanying guards. As I caught them looking at me, they would quickly avert their eyes. Sometimes I winked at them, evoking a startled response.

It was a tedious ride. The train backed up as much as it went forward. We made frequent stops as passengers got off and others boarded. We made stops other than at stations.

Traveling through Belgium, by train or by car, we would be required to wait for varying periods of time. For what reason, security or repair work, I was never told. None of the delays could compare to the one we endured when we crossed the border into Germany.

At the border, the train was searched. The Frontier Police swarmed all over the cars and us. There were so many guards at the border, it was evident they were there not just to keep people out, but to keep the German populace from escaping. The guards were sullen and harsh with their own people. They acted like losers who, given a uniform, became heady with power.

The anticipation of moving again soon paled in the lengthy passage of time. Confined to the small space of the compartment, in a soup of smoke, the Germans mumbled to each other while repeatedly checking their watches. Word came that the train was to be detained longer. The guards took me outside.

The tiny station, left over from a previous century, was somber. It was a mood I was to discover as symbolic of the whole country. Somewhere behind us, a curtain had fallen.

The German military and civilians waiting at the depot bore no smile or sparkle as did those people in the subjugated countries. In the country waging the war, the faces were pinched, the feelings dulled. The promises of greatness had faded. For four years, the German people had been impelled to give their energy and possessions to the war effort. The strain had gutted their lives. It was as if life had been vanquished; only duty remained. The look on the faces of the assembled crowd waiting for the train was, "Oh, hell, we're going home again."

From the platform, looking up at the train's passengers, I could see the expressions of the Germans and conscripted Belgians and French were just as grim.

In the old-fashioned depot, tucked in the lap of an earth bursting of autumn, there was no denying the ominous. Even the engine, puffing steam and pausing on the brink of a trestle, seemed to be gathering nerve for the trip ahead that was, for everyone, the end of the show.

When the search seemed to be nearly finished, we reentered the train. On our way into the compartment someone took another picture of us.

Seated next to the window, facing forward, I was separated from the RAF airman by two guards. Across from us were four more Germans. One of them, a Luftwaffe officer, had just joined us. He looked and acted like he had brains. His face was pleasant. He wore glasses and spoke with a quiet voice. Judging by the attitude of the other men toward him, he held a higher rank. He didn't smoke and, from the time he sat down, no one else did.

The air in the compartment was close and reeked of damp wool and body odors. Except for the officer with the glasses, the uniforms of the men around me were coarse and tacky. The cloth must have contained some wood fiber, for when they slid down in the mohair seats it sounded like a scraping washboard. And *all* of us were sliding, fidgeting, trying to rearrange our bodies into the narrow seats.

I learned to commit myself to space when settling down with the guards. As soon as I took a seat, I staked out the armrest with an elbow, but I had to fight for the floor. The guard who always ended up directly opposite me had long legs and big feet. They sprawled across the floor under me. My feet were set next to his, like two boats going upstream. While I looked out of the window, I moved my feet forwards, stubbing the guard's boots. On each contact he withdrew his feet until I commanded my fair share of the floorboards.

And still the train did not go. It became another agonizing wait, long enough that we walked around the station a second time.

KÖLN, depicted in prominent white letters, was the night's destination. The train depot was filled with Wehrmacht in platoon fronts waiting for transport. In helmets and carrying rifles, they looked threatening and dangerous, ugly in their resolution. Their commanders were distinguished by long, sweeping coats. The coats of green leather denoted higher ranks. The officers were gruff with their troops and with each other.

Around us, I could hear troops marching and trucks screeching to halts. The road nearby was lined with the subdued lights of motor vehicles driving toward the station.

Bombs had battered the protective coverings over trains as well as the main building. The roof and ceiling had numerous patches, and the glass was gone from the partially boarded windows.

Inside, the large waiting room was packed with military. The young men, mostly in green uniforms with little or no insignia, sat on all the available surfaces, benches, tables and luggage receptacles. They smiled as I passed.

I was led to the back of the large room and into a small, adjoining L-shaped closet. Between the guards and me, there was standing room only.

A stream of soldiers stole glimpses of me through the half-opened door. I could smell food cooking and heard, far away, as I had every night, the thunder of bombing.

While the other guards took breaks, one of the older officers stayed with me. He spoke English. He never questioned me. Instead, he talked about Germany. He told me what a beautiful country it was and how good the German people were. He made clear his dislike for England, but he was complimentary about America. With so many Germans in America, so many relatives of German citizens, he could not understand why America had sided with the English instead of with Germany. He poured out his feelings, his frustrations and disappointments. He lectured me on Germany and its politics. In the middle of his catharsis, as I stood propped in a corner, I went to sleep.

The morning promised fatigue as we crossed the tracks, back to the elevated station platform. Once again, we were to be dogged by the railroad's illusive timetable.

More urgent to me than the crawling seconds was my need for food. In more than thirty hours I had eaten only one piece of bread. Though I was strong and able-bodied, distressing pangs had grabbed my gut. Fortunately, Germany had its own Red Cross. Girls in long, gray skirts and Red Cross armbands and hats were offering soup to the men in the station. The aroma, so salient to my nostrils, did not tempt my guards. The officers had aides who carried briefcases of food for them. The enlisted men carried their own supply of sausage, cheese and bread in a hip pack or backpack.

My mouth began to salivate as two young women approached me.

"Suppe, Suppe," the first girl invited.

"Suppe, Suppe mit Greaze!" the other tried to mix in some English to let me know she had a soup with a meat base, a rare commodity.

The thermos bucket containing the soup was of unpolished silver metal. Stamped on the front was a black swastika on a white field encircled in red. With a metal ladle, she spooned the soup into a porcelain cup and handed it to me.

"Thank you." I was truly grateful.

In the early dawn the station was a maze of activity. Among the assembled troops, HEIL HITLERS harped monotonously. Especially in the Wehrmacht, while addressing ranking officers, the pledge was fervent.

In the corner of the depot, apart from the military, was a small group of men and women waiting for trains. They were not dressed like the peasants in the neighboring countries, but wore sophisticated suits and hats. Uncommunicative, their dark clothes depicted the prevailing gloom. Similarly, dogs drooped around, their tails between their legs.

At the far end of one of the platforms, a ranking officer commanded the attention of a large entourage. His figure was of extensive proportions and he wore white. I did not know then, that this was the uniform worn by Goering.

Feeling as though I was growing roots in the cement, I counted helmets, officers, long coats, anything to pass the time. Suddenly, my guards, the RAF airman and I were directed to a large car. Sinking into the back seat, I considered it a welcome deliverance.

From Cologne we drove south along the Rhine.

Not meant as a taxi for prisoners-of-war, the overripe command car was used by generals and staff officers to review troops. Three seats spanned the width of the car and were capable of carrying more than fifteen people. Akin to a baby buggy, the big military touring car stood high off the ground, without doors, and tarp that was folded like an accordion behind me. Grime fogged the tan paint and the interior had an odor of canvas and leather saturated in human sweat. A band of soil edged the seat and glistened from the polishing of its changing cargo of passengers.

The car, probably built by Mercedes, drove like a giant jeep. Tripped by every crack and pebble that pockmarked the macadam, and bumping over dirt roads, it jostled me until my bladder pained for release.

22

DULAG LUFT

It was midmorning when we arrived at Dulag Luft in Oberursel near Frankfurt-am-Main. The same Dulag had been used as an interrogation center in WW I, but it was so well maintained that it looked new. A road divided the center into two areas. On the left was a group of large, white buildings where the screening and interrogation of prisoners took place and on the right, encircled by a high fence of barbed wire, was the transition camp. As we drove up the road, men gathered on the walking perimeter of the camp to watch us.

Inside the central building, while the guards and the English fellow were still standing in the reception area, I was ushered through a hallway into a single room. The door closed and locked behind me.

The cell was about eight-by-ten feet. There was just enough space for a table, a chair and a bed. The bed's wood frame base had hemp webbing that supported an excelsior mattress. The single blanket was Australian. From Dunkirk? A metal heater that appeared to be new and resembled a steam radiator, squatted beneath the window ledge. The window and opened transom above it were of milk-colored glass and were covered with bars. The floor was wood, the room a stone white. Above the door was a single, unlit light bulb and in the door, a slit of one-way glass. I was surrounded by fourteen inches of concrete. For a guy who liked people, this was shit!

Buoyantly, I reasoned that this was all part of the routine—some formal interrogation and then a release to the camp. The questioning wouldn't be long, because, well, cripes, I didn't know anything. With every corpuscle lagging, I lay down on the bed and instantly fell asleep.

Minutes or hours later, I didn't know which, I heard the heavy door being pushed open. The guards, their rifles slung over their shoulders, threw some clothes at me.

Where was I? I sat up. It took moments for me to associate my situation with the imprisonment.

"Auf, Auf," the guards yelled at me, motioning for me to change. They waited in the doorway, muttering to each other and insisting I give them all my clothes including my underwear and shoes.

I pulled on a baggy pair of pants that gathered and tied at the waist. The angry blue wool bit and itched like small ants. I was thankful the crotch hung to my knees. A coat of the same material buttoned to my chin. The back of the jacket had a gaping hole and was caked with dried, flaking blood. The uniform was still marked with the insignias of the Polish Army. With my feet encased in wooden clogs, the guards directed me to go with them.

In an oversized uniform, with my feet stumbling, I began to feel humiliated about my appearance. This was hard to take. My cocky resilience, my precious American know-how, began to ebb. I was being degraded and there wasn't a damn thing I could do about it.

I shuffled along between the guards, down a hallway that curved through the U-shaped building like an endless tunnel. In the dim recess, the filaments from the overhead light bulbs poked at me like the eyes of gargoyles.

We turned and went through a door into a bathroom. The room was white and gray with round, opaque ceiling lights and a skylight arched at the peak of the roof. There was a row of pull-cord flushing toilets and facing them, three washbasins under a long mirror. Having given me a razor blade and soap, the guards remained with me. They were not going to give me a chance to kill myself.

Not since the morning of October 9th, had I looked into a mirror. I gasped. I truly felt sorry for myself. Besides the beard stubble, my hair was bushy and matted. My nose and cheeks were crusted in blood. I nimbly began to pick off pieces of flak that were half submerged in my skin. Some of it was deeply embedded under scabs. To shave such a tender surface was a painful prospect, but the razor blade (made in Japan) was a punishing joke. It must have been used by every prisoner before me, so dull it couldn't cut a throat much less a beard.

After stroking the blade back and forth against the mirror, I put it in one of the empty razors that lay scattered on the shelf. With cold water and a harsh clay-like soap, I gently sawed at my beard. I took as much time as I could. The room down the hallway looked a little too permanent. Regardless of the time and care, I was aware of a raw, sore face for hours after.

I hadn't been back in my cell long when I heard a large, heavy object squeaking down the hall. The ungainly motion stopped and started over and over. I could hear metal scraping and dishes clattering. With a rap on the door and a declaration, "Essen," a guard set a type of Bakelite tray on the table with the noon meal. A large mixing bowl contained less than half a cup of soup. Accompanying it was a big, useless tin spoon and a large mug half filled with an ersatz tea. There was a piece of bread with a slab of "marge," a butter substitute made from coal. The bread was heavy, dark and rich. It contained many types of flours, including barley, oats, wheat and, as an adhesive, twenty-five percent pulverized white pine.

In the afternoon, a soldier came in to interrogate me. Showing undisguised boredom, he was there as the initial contact to make the preliminary probe. In a heavy German accent, his English almost indecipherable, I protested, answering that I didn't understand him. But I understood what he wanted to know. He ended the session by advising me to give the necessary information so that they could notify the International Red Cross, who, in turn, would notify my parents that I was alive and well. It was implied that it was my humanitarian obligation to answer.

"Albert La Chasse, 2nd Lieutenant, 0-726044."

The German sniffed, handed me a Red Cross form, and left.

Well, I thought, that wasn't bad. If they were all like this guy, it would be a cinch. The interview reinforced my hope for a momentary release.

I looked over the outline he had given me. The folded, two-page, legal size document was white with red printing and bordered in red crosses. At the bottom of the first page was an official "Printed in Switzerland." The questions were: What kind of aircraft were you flying? How many motors on your aircraft? How many firing positions on the ship? Who were your pilot and copilot? What was your mission? How many in your crew? Their names? Where is your organization stationed?

They had to be kidding. Filling out that form would have been worse than handing them Pappy's letter.

Hours passed. Time dragged. What was taking so long? Why didn't they get the interrogation over and let me out? I needed something to do. Why not the crapper? I pulled on the handle of the door that released a metal weight on the other side which fell and bonged against it.

A guard came and asked, "Pissen or scheissen?"

With the amount of food I'd had, the trip was hardly necessary, but it was a walk and I welcomed it.

At dusk, the same tank as before, rattling of plates, came creaking down the hall. The same one-half cup of soup, piece of bread and ersatz tea came on the same Bakelite tray, with portions so small they merely whetted my appetite.

What were they having back home? Spam? At Thureigh? Giblets and gravy? And doughnuts.

During that long stretch of time, from a closet in my mind, from an alcove hidden and suppressed, came the figures of Oley and Gates. I could see Oley, open and friendly. There was Norman, studious and shy. I could not stem the vision of Oley in a nightclub, drinking rye whisky, grabbing the microphone and off key, I could hear him singing, "H, A, double R I . . . G-A-N spells HARRIGAN . . ." And Norman, quiet, thoughtful, as he rechecked the ship's instruments. Dynan, Kaylor, Wissenback, Wilder, and who was the guy who replaced Talbot? Nicholson? I never even met him. Young kids, all of them . . .

With the feeling of cement piling in my gut and iodine tears burning abraded skin, with my back to the door, I creased into the chair.

It was so unfair. Sweet guys, just like that, GONE.

Hate engulfed my emotions when I thought of the lines of guys who waited outside Colonel Overacker's office, jumping at the chance when he asked if there was anyone who didn't think he could take it, that he couldn't fly. A nice guy, Overacker, but not tough enough. Imagine the Marines on Corregidor, sweating it out, facing the invading Japs, deciding they couldn't take it, that they wanted out. They would have been shot for desertion.

So futile . . .

If only Gaston had been along. If only we'd had more practice, like Terry requested from the general. Oh, if ONLY we'd had more formation flying. And turning back over the target with those goddamn P-38s leaving us there. Christ, we didn't have a prayer. And Oley, he would have been a Group Commander. Now he's gone. They're all gone. No distinguished medals, no ribbons, no victories, no homecomings, no reunions, no applause.

> " . . . It was the first big fight encountered by American Forts in this Theater. And it was a good one . . . Captain Olson . . . was the only plane that we lost . . . (the mission) was a noteworthy success . . ."
>
> War Diary (p. 7)
> 306th Bomb Group (H)

The evening shadows draped the cell in mourning. Lying on the cot, steeling myself from the memories, I prayed for Oley, Gates and the crew, for sleep, and for that first day in solitary to be my last.

It wasn't.

23

POW #18

Dear Cousin:

A long time since I have seen you. A lot has happened in that time too. I have been here quite awhile. Al and I made the trip together and have had some pretty good times over here until a few days ago. There is not much more I can say—I do my drinking ALONE now.

Everything is different over here. The language is the same of course but the money system is different. Took us several days to get onto the price we were paying for things here but that is all straight now and I am winning a little at poker. Al was doing pretty good too until a few days ago. Then WE lost half of what we started with in Albuquerque, sorry to say, our luck was not running the right way.

I like it over here pretty much. I want to be where we can really do some good in this war. I am in the Battle for more than just a war now. We try to make every shot count for the guys who happened to go down first.

Well can't write much as all our work is pretty much secret. I will say Goodbye for A.W.L. I know he would have wanted me to. So

long for now and I'll try to see you again someday. Keep a prayer
that the war ends soon.

Always,
Kenny

The second day was tougher.

It began with soup and bread. I did some exercises—hand-
stands and sit-ups. It would be easy in that step-and-a-half of
space to become soft, to wither out of a conditioning that I had
attained in Hoover High School. I could see my track coach, Vic
Francy, more limber and enduring than any of us, leading the
vigorous routine. I was shocked that now my body seemed to tire
so easily. Fright fed my body more fatigue. I was beginning to
comprehend how carefully I had to maintain a physical reserve
and, more importantly, a mental reserve. Panic was the real force of
destruction that could cause me to waste away quickly.

I heard the whistles of birds, and in flight their shadows fell
across the window. I stepped out of my clogs and, pressing my
hands on each side of the window jamb, balanced myself on the
sill. Looking over the opened transom, I was able to see a narrow
angle of what was outside. There were rows of cultivated plants. A
man in an English battle jacket with a basket was picking tomatoes. Every once in a while he would open his jacket and throw in
a piece of the fruit. I felt a burst of exhilaration. Terrific! Stealing
from the Germans. We were winning. The man finally worked his
way out of my view, but I couldn't maintain that position for long
anyway. I was on my toes, stretching in a tedious posture. When I
was settled back on the cot, I looked up at the window, smugly
satisfied. To know that I could look out any time I wanted without
being seen was my own special secret. It gave me comfort.

On both the second and third days I was interrogated. The
young men spoke English reasonably well and they offered me

cigarettes that I butted out fast so that I would have smokes for later. I was allowed a box of matches of Japanese import.

The fourth day I felt that my release was imminent. I understood from the questioning, that they believed I had been the pilot of a Short Sterling Bomber. Prisoners in that capacity had been held before me, so what new information could I possibly have had that would be useful? No, it was probably some type of a systematic procedure from headquarters that was keeping me there.

Early in the afternoon I heard different footsteps approaching. They were unusual compared to the guards' shuffling and the young interrogators' quiet, quick pace. The steps pounding towards me were sharp and authoritative. Someone of importance was coming. I leaned against the wall and tried to look nonchalant.

A tall, dark Luftwaffe officer came into the room. The handsome structure of his face was blunted by a frozen expression. He clicked his heels and made a perfunctory "Heil Hitler." Introducing himself as a Lt. Colonel, he addressed me: "Good afternoon, Herr Leutnant La Chasse. Are you comfortable? Perhaps you would like something to read?"

Nodding my approval, I thought, geez, I didn't know they had something for me to read. The relief must have shown on my face because the officer relaxed.

"Care for a cigarette?" He offered me a French Elegant.

"Thanks."

With a cigarette lighter he lit first his cigarette and then mine. He sat on the table and remarked, "Good cigarette, don't you think?"

"Yes, very good."

His light blue uniform was made to order. The material was a fine gabardine and the tailoring emphasized the broad shoulders and trim build. His shirt was crisply collared and centered with a black, knotted tie.

"You and I, Herr Leutnant, we are both men of the air. In the larger sense we are comrades, yes?"

As I listened to his English, beautifully pronounced, I felt uneasy. I had finally met a pro.

"We understand our positions and we will get along well together." Firmly, he stated, "We will cooperate, each with the other, won't we?"

"Yes, Sir."

"Your name, L-A C-H-A-S-S-E, is it spelled correctly?"

"Yes."

"Your family . . . from France?"

"My father is French, my mother is English. Both are from St. Louis, Missouri."

"Tell me, I have forgotten so much of my French. What is the literal translation of La Chasse?"

"Translated, La Chasse means 'the hunt.' "

"Ah, now I remember." The Colonel stood up and asked, "You, you are from Glendale, California?"

He read that right off my dog tags. "That's right."

"Is Glendale near a Burbank, California?"

Oh, oh. "Uh, reasonably close."

"In this Burbank, do they have a manufacturing plant? Say, an industrial center that produces aircraft?"

It was "Oh-Shit" time. "Well, every city has some kind of industry."

"We know, Herr Leutnant, that your aircraft was built in Burbank." From his coat pocket he pulled a small metal ID plate that had been riveted to some section of an aircraft. Printed on it was "Lockheed Aircraft Corporation, Burbank, California." "The aircraft that you were in was a B-17, what you call a Flying Fortress?"

It wasn't red tape that was keeping me there, after all.

Not waiting for an answer, the Colonel pressed on. "The question you must answer is how did this ship get to England? Who were your crew members and what were their names?"

"Colonel," I pleaded, "my instructions are to give only three pieces of information: my name, rank and serial number. Albert La Chasse, 2nd Lieutenant, 0-726044."

"Don't have the idea that you're real smart and that you are not going to say anything, Leutnant, because . . . in a few days we will be bombing England to where all your comrades and all the English will no longer be there. We will, in fact, bomb that small English island right off the map. Then we will concentrate entirely on the Russian Front. We are right now winning in Stalingrad and on our way to Moscow."

His last statement was true. I had heard it myself over the Oberkommando radio at Thurleigh. From all indications, the Germans *were* winning the war. They were beating the hell out of the Russians at Stalingrad. They held all of North Africa, Sicily, all the islands in the Mediterranean, and the West Wall that we were trying to attack, was strongly entrenched. I had no reason to doubt that what this guy was telling me was inevitable.

Looking down at me with eyes of flint blue, the Colonel said, "So you see, you have nothing to lose." Taking a pen from his pocket, he tapped it against the tabletop. "I will tell you what we will do. We will not concern ourselves with your personal history. Honoring your duty, we will be satisfied if you fill out this Red Cross form . . . this for the sake of international relations. After that, you will be released to the camp." Pleased with his words of goodwill, he handed me the form.

"I've looked at it," I said, shaking my head, "and I can't believe anyone has filled this out before."

"Oh, but of course they have." From the door, he called an order to one of the guards, who, in too short of a time, came back with a hand full of the forms. They were given to me. The officer sat down in the chair, lit another cigarette and watched me.

Some of the entries had been made by Germans. The giveaway was the number 7 with a line through it. But one of the entries specifically caught my attention. At the bottom of the page, in one box, was the question: What was your civilian occupation? The written answer was "former safecracker." I may have flinched, but I kept from smiling. Slang! The Germans, with their superior attitude, would never admit they didn't know what you were talking about. It was a way to buy time.

"Oh," I dropped the words, "you don't want to know all this junk. Let's just say it was a 'fly-by-night outfit' and if I told you any more it would be a 'double cross.' "

He jotted some notes on a pad of paper. "Das ist richtig," he crowed. "Now for our records, fill out this front page." The Colonel offered me his pen.

"Colonel, according to the articles of the Geneva Convention . . ." I didn't know what the goddamn articles were, but he was so impressed with himself.

All pleasantness ceased. He straightened his frame seven inches over me and remonstrated: "There is nothing for you to hide. The Luftwaffe and our espionage forces can get the information we need. We have a complete network of agents extending throughout the world. We know *much* more than you think!" And with that he pulled from his pocket a pair of ID tags and dangled them in front of me.

They were Oley's.

The son-of-a-bitch. I was plain mad. "Then if you know everything," I shouted, "what in hell do you want with me? Why *me* then?"

Anger flashed across the officer's face. "Ah, so why me?" he repeated, irritated.

That was dangerous behavior on my part, talking back to a chosen one of the "Deutschland über alles," a member of the master race. That concept of superiority was to be understood and respected at all times. It was essential that the Germans felt they were in total command. On a whim, he could shoot me as a saboteur. I had been threatened with that from the beginning, but seeing my Commander's dog tags was heartbreaking.

"You, Herr La Chasse, take too much of my time." He threw his cigarette on the floor, then crushed and stomped it with his boot. "Some have called you a tough nut. It makes no difference.

You will tell us what we want to know or stay in here and rot. Heil Hitler."

There were no magazines. I received two books. One was a school text on the mechanics of construction, the other a novel, entitled *The Citadel*, which had large sections missing; the pages, no doubt, used for toilet paper. Hot damn!

In the following days I had two sessions of interrogations, one in the morning and one in the afternoon. The same young men conducted them, a total of six in all.

They seemed fascinated by me, not simply because I was an American but because my birthplace was St. Louis, Missouri. The latter was of special interest because some of the German personnel had relatives there.

The consuming question was the B-17. If it was made in California, how did it get to England? If it was being shipped (and no aircraft was known yet to fly over the Atlantic), then how were so many getting over when the German Wolf Packs, the submarines, were torpedoing the British Royal Tonnage to death?

The questions were fired with rapidity; some interjected out of context, trying to trip a response. Others were phrased in such a way as to goad me into a competitive defense.

"Your ship, does it have a tricycle landing gear?" "Does it have one or two turrets?" "Your parents, were they born in St. Louis, Missouri?" "Only two turrets on your craft?" "How many firing positions? It doesn't matter, because our Heinkel 111 has more than yours anyway." "You were born in California?" "Your fuel consumption . . . it must be great for such a heavy ship?" "Your ship's bomb capacity, smaller than our Dorneir?"

The questions were predictable and so was the food. Once in a while the menu was spiced with a sausage end or scraps of clip-cheese made from fish leavings.

Plagued by a shrunken, vacant stomach, I revisited all the restaurants and lunch counters I had ever been to, including the cafeteria at Hoover High School. My mind was glutted with the great food I would treat myself to when the war was over, which it would be—someday.

As soon as I got back to California, I would go to Yosemite National Park and the Ahwahnee Hotel. In vivid detail, I pictured the hotel's great kitchen where I had worked as a kitchen porter. I had been a privileged partaker of the culinary achievements that originated in its multiple-sectioned food center, each section devoted to preparing a specialty, with individual chefs and assistants. There was a roast man, a steak and chop man, a salad chef, a baker, a man who handled fruit and who had an assistant that did nothing all day long during the summer but scoop out melon balls. The eggs were dispensed from one area of the kitchen and, according to their weight, boiled to the exact second. Each chef prided himself on his creations, especially the pastry chef who built whipped cream confections like an architect. The soup chef simmered aromatic juices in copper cauldrons. He was so fastidious that he personally would oversee the washing and polishing of the massive containers after each use. It was the soup man, a Czechoslovakian, who gave me my first inkling of the coming world conflict. Literally crying in his soup, he told me of the concession of land, some 10,000 square miles, that had been given by his homeland to Hitler that same month of September 1938.

In those lean days of that year, my duty of stocking food supplies was a job to be envied. As soon as I acquired stature, which was the afternoon of the morning I arrived, my friends landed. One after the other, they wandered close to that haven of food.

"Wipe that hungry look off your face and act like you work here," I scolded, as I, on my way to deliver ice to the bar, grabbed a chop or a sandwich and stuffed it into my apron pocket for later distribution.

My mouth watered as I remembered the ravishing assortments of meat, vegetables, and homemade breads that were wielded on trays through the double swinging doors. Yes, just as soon as this thing was over, that's where I was going and I would eat, and eat . . . and eat.

Some days later I heard familiar footsteps. It was the Lt. Colonel again, but this time he was wearing a long, white smock that covered him from his chin to the top of his polished boots. On his left shoulder was a white patch with two red rings around a red cross. Encircling the border was INTERNATIONAL RED CROSS.

"Colonel," I said, "is it possible to be a member of both the Red Cross *and* the Luftwaffe? You are not on the ball."

Looking up from his clipboard, he realized he had come into the wrong cell. His eyes dropped immediately. Busily writing, he repeated, "Ach so . . . not on ball."

Several days after the visit by the International Red Cross, I was balanced on the window ledge, looking over the transom. The tomato plants had turned a bright pea-green against a gray and swollen sky. Across the field there were lights shining from windows. There was no movement, no sound, not even birds. It was strangely quiet, like all of nature was playing "statue" and God was about to touch.

I lay back on the cot. As big raindrops crashed on the roof and founts of water began to spout from the window casement, I daydreamed, pleased for once that I was inside and warm. Staring vacantly, I barely noticed the small white puffs, like tiny clouds, that began to float across the ceiling. It became dense before I realized that it was smoke and it was pouring from the heater. Someone had turned on the heat. I rolled onto the floor, over to the door, and reaching up, pulled on the handle. Nothing happened. No bong, no clang. I had pissened and scheissened my way to the can so much the damn handle had broken! On the floor, with my mouth pressed to get the air that came under the door, I pounded and kicked furiously. Someone was trying to ignore me. I screamed and yelled until two guards pushed the door open and me with it. They were so annoyed they muzzled the barrels of their guns into my face. Amid growlings worthy of obscenities, they finally understood it was the heater, not me, that caused the smoke.

For delicious moments, while repairs were being made, I was allowed to stand in the hallway. Everything I saw was important to me. Whenever I was taken to the bathroom, there was no other person around except the guards. Now I saw an English prisoner walking the hall alone, *without* a guard. German personnel came and went, some in skirts, which was more than stimulating. Parked just beyond me was the food cart or soup wagon. It looked as I had imagined, old and wooden, with heavy iron wheels. Two shelves stacked on top held wooden bowls and a helmet-shaped pan. Rags were tied to the cart's wooden handles. The cart had not been used that morning and as I thought back, I hadn't heard it for days. I watched, but no one came or went from any of the rooms in that part of the building. Was everyone gone but me?

By now I knew I had information to protect, information about the Fortress and particularly, about the bombsight. So far it had not been mentioned. I did not like being valuable. Locked back in the cell, I had unsettled feelings.

My life yawned on in solitary.

One morning I heard a buzzing. There above me, looping, circling, hovering in effortless flight, was a fly. It gave me enormous pleasure to think that I had company. From the bed, I watched it. I was envious. The tiny bug could walk under the door or fly over the transom. How long had it been here? What was it doing? What attracted it? Did it have a flight pattern?

I watched the fly for a long while. Its flight was erratic, its direction spontaneous. It would land and walk up or down the side of the wall at an angle. Stopping, the creature would then take off again. The light from the window seemed to lure it, although it liked the corners of the ceiling best. After a time, the insect swooped down and landed on the table. I went over slowly and sat down. I looked at the fly and the fly looked at me. His name was Peabody. Peabody was about three-eighths of an inch long, with pale black circles fading in and out of a gray body. His head was all Mickey Mouse ears—each eye like a pile of minute caviar. The veined, transparent wings were tinted with green, blue and gold. His legs were like those of a wrought iron table and seemed to be wearing black stockings. We stared at each other. I cupped my hands and tried to put them over him. He flew off. He stayed close to the ceiling. When he landed, I climbed on the bed and shooed him into flight again. From lunch I saved two crumbs from the slice of bread. Peabody was on the window, moving like a jaywalking pedestrian. He zigzagged across the glass in a hurry only to get to one side and then turn around and come back. Again I cupped my hands; this time I caged him from behind. I held tightly until the batting wings stopped. Slowly, I opened a cave between my fingers and Peabody scurried forward to the pad below my thumb. I moved him even with the tabletop, trying to introduce him to the crumbs. But before I could maneuver him further, he flew off.

All kinds of questions popped into my mind. Could I train him? Did he enjoy sex? What was his life span?

Through the rest of that day and the next morning, I over-loved him. By afternoon, I easily caught him. He would emerge and stand patiently on my hand. Toward evening, I noticed that Peabody was flying close to the transom. I held my breath. Just an inch or two and he would be over it and outside to freedom. That small pest of nature was overwhelming me with its superior capa-bilities. I stood on the bed and, once more, captured him. I brought him over to the table and set him down.

Without forethought, with an involuntary jerk, I pulled off one of his wings. The surprise of my action warped into revulsion and guilt. Why did I do that? Peabody was my friend, my only friend. I watched as the little fly with one wing tried to achieve flight. A couple of inches off of the table, he wavered as he reached for momentum, and then dove to the floor.

Poor fly. Poor me. Was I cracking?

In a morbid torpor, I watched Peabody, who, with his legs springing him off, managed small heights. From a tight circle he spun wider and wider until he dove once again, back to the floor.

I snapped back to my senses when I heard the sharp clicking of heels in the hallway. Picking up the struggling Peabody, I placed him carefully under the bed. I didn't want anyone stepping on the poor little guy.

The Lt. Colonel came in. Standing at attention, he roared a commanding "Heil Hitler!" In his Luftwaffe uniform, he had returned to retrieve his credibility.

"How are you, Leutnant La Chasse? Are you ready to leave here?" The Colonel took off his gloves, put them inside his hat and laid it on the table.

"Herr Leutnant, we have been talking to you for some time now, and you say you know nothing. I'm telling you, you might as well tell us what is necessary for you to leave here. The information you give is for your own good, for it will allow us to tell your forces, your family and your friends that you are safe. After all, you have been missing for a long time and it would be thoughtless of you not to reassure those people near to you. Yes?" He took a great deal of time lighting a cigarette.

"As I have told you, there is no piece of information that will be kept from us. We . . . we are everywhere." With his back to me, he fell silent for what seemed like minutes. "Herr Leutnant, do you belong to a Key Club?"

My face reddened. Abruptly, he turned to look at me. Not wanting him to catch my surprise, I dropped my cigarette and bent over to pick it up. "Key Club?" I asked weakly.

"Yes, you know, a Key Club. There are many of them. I belong to several. Do you belong to one?" Facing me as I sat on the bed, he put his foot on the chair and crossing his arms, leaned forward on one knee.

Wow, Key Clubs. So easy to infiltrate. All the dames around. All the guys in different uniforms. An easy source of information.

"Well, do you?" he demanded.

"Well, yeah..I went with some guys. They served a drink I've never had before. I think it was called Pimms."

"Pimms. Yes, of course. Very popular. I prefer gin and lime, myself."

"I like that, too, but it's so hard to get."

"We had plenty at the Club the other evening."

"You did?" I asked, in total admiration.

"Yes, we were at the Club in Bassingbourn. Do you know where that is?"

"No, I don't."

The Colonel inhaled deeply on his cigarette and sat down in the chair. "Of course, we arrived early enough so that I could choose a table near the bar . . . for the best service and for a position of observing the entrance."

It was as though he was teasing me about the Club in Bedford.

Pointing his cigarette at me, he bragged, "I had a very good cut of meat. Fresh meat, mind you, not Bully Beef. And it was prepared to my specifications."

I was hanging on to every word.

He nodded. "Very satisfying. And so were the vegetables. Green beans, almost overcooked, but they were fresh. There was no canned aftertaste." With regret, he added, "Too bad they didn't have cognac, but then there's a war on. Even we Germans must make sacrifices. Yes, the food was good and it was served properly. The English are clean and in some ways, practical. Their tea is excellent." He leered, "It should be. They excel at tea drinking."

Standing, he pressed his cigarette into the jar lid that I used for an ashtray. "Aber, but they live in the past. They have *no* imagination. Examine their Key Clubs. Very troublesome entrances. In order to close the front door, you must stand on the first step. There is no entry. And the stairs are so narrow and steep. When I walk into the Club, I nearly hit my head. The tables, too, they are small and the chairs uncomfortable. The bar is the size of a horse stall."

By now, I was positive he was talking about the Club in Bedford. "But, you," I soft-soaped, "and your fellow Germans, you are so much taller. On campus, Colonel, we would call you a B.M.O.C."

"Repeat."

"B.M.O.C. is short for Big Man On Campus. You would be considered very important."

The Colonel smiled and, opening a fresh pack of cigarettes, offered me an English Oval.

I was in a comfort zone and I wanted to hold onto it. "How do you like the English women?"

"They are useful." A rascal smile crossed his face, one that would have upstaged Errol Flynn. Arrogantly, he added, "The truth is the English people are insipid and weak. They have no convictions, no strength of purpose. Like Neville Chamberlain, they have no character. They could not even fight their own war. They had to beg you Americans to help them."

The Colonel straightened his jacket. "Now, Herr Leutnant, in the Key Clubs there is talk about your Flying Fortress. The opinion is that it is very strong, indestructible. Ah, but we know different." Wrapping his arms behind him, he lectured, "Daylight bombing, precision bombing, a fortress. Remarkable, but, oh, so foolish. The Armada of the Royal Air Force could not do it. The great German Air Command, the superior Luftwaffe, could not do it. So how is it that this B-17 aircraft can do it? You know what I mean? *You* are proof that this is not an indestructible craft. *You* are *here*."

"But, Colonel, you have highly-trained fighter pilots, so nothing is indestructible to you. You know that. After all, you have been fighting for years, since the Spanish Civil War."

Discomforted, he warned, "Aber, we are talking about *your* craft."

"Yes, Sir."

"Your craft cannot carry enough crew for proper defense? Or perhaps the firing positions are inadequate?"

"Yes, Sir."

"You know that the strength of the bomb load and the accuracy of this B-17 has not proved credible."

"Yes, Sir."

Sneering, he picked up his hat. "Leutnant, it is all over for you and I warn you again that, without the simple information we require, you will not be allowed to leave here. It is up to *you*. Heil Hitler."

The strutting footsteps faded down the hall. And with them all optimism.

The Germans, they knew so much! And I had been there so long. People had come and gone. I hadn't heard the food cart for days. Fright danced through my body as the possibility that they would shoot me turned to stark reality. Undernourished, isolated, so terribly alone, I fell into an abyss of despair.

24

AH, KAULIFORNIA!

For a racking day-and-a-half I had no contact with anyone but the dreary, lifeless guards. Then, on the second afternoon I was taken to the Kommandant's office. As I walked out of the enclosure, I felt an intense relief. My anesthetized body awoke in the sunshine and fresh air. On the path to the camp's headquarters, I looked back at the building I had been in. In one of the front rooms, probably an office, there were a group of men sitting and walking around. Their movements were clearly discernible through the milk-colored glass. What an ass I had been! Crawling around the windowsill, thinking I was secretly looking out of the window—anyone watching would have seen every silly move I made. I wouldn't do that again.

It was about one-third of a city block to the square, white building that contained the officers' quarters. East of the prison and uphill, it was a long walk for starving legs. Wobbling, I climbed the stairs to the entrance.

Inside was a succession of offices. The first one was the Kommandant's. After knocking and receiving permission, the guard ordered me inside. He closed the door behind me. In a comfortable stance of attention, waiting to be recognized, I drank in the room.

It was large and gray. Three white globes suspended by metal ropes hung from the high ceiling. A series of windows ran behind the long, polished desk. The rest of the walls were covered with maps. At one end of the desk was a row of filing cabinets that partitioned off a side of the room. On my left, the wall was papered with a large map of England. Underneath it were shelves of electronic equipment. On both sides of me, facing the desk, were rows of chairs.

Having allowed the necessary wait due his person, the Kommandant looked up and smiled. "Sit." He motioned me to a leather-bound chair that was placed a distance away and in front of his desk. "Cigaretten?"

I got up from my chair to reach it. "Thank you."

He lit his own and put the lighter down on the edge of the desk for me to use. I inhaled. Good Lord! It was an American cigarette, a Camel.

The Kommandant, seated in a high-backed, upholstered chair, had a round, dimpled face, gray-blond hair and a space between his two front teeth. He epitomized an older Ernest Borgnine. His Luftwaffe uniform, like that of the Lt. Colonel, was of a fine, silky material, tailor-made and garnished with lots of salad dressing, including the Iron Cross.

His desk was in perfect order. On the leather-bound blotter was an even stack of papers, envelopes, a writing pad, a row of sharp pencils, a manila folder and an ashtray, which was the base of a 50-millimeter cannon shell. Placed to the far right of the desk was a wicker basket of white grapes. Once I spotted the fruit, nothing else mattered. It became my sole objective.

After opening a folder, he looked up at me. "So, Herr Leutnant La Chasse, you from Kaulifornia?"

"Yes, Sir." I butted out my cigarette and put it in my breast pocket.

"From Los Angeles?"

"Yes, Sir." I leaned forward to take another cigarette and as I did, I reached under the chair and pulled it with me. I almost sprained my back.

"Ah, Kaulifornia. I vas dere."

"Really?" Who cares? Give me some grapes.

"Ja, und Hollyvood. I vas auch in Hollyvood. Ah, vunderbar stadt. I vas invited zu parties in Hollyvood. Many people dere mit glamor—schoen, schoen people." He leaned back in his chair and raised his arms in a heavenly exclamation. "Such talent—Marlene Dietrich, Sam Goldvyn, Greta Garbo, und Ernest Lubitsch." He pointed his finger at me, "Lubitsch—Deutsch. Otto Preminger—Vien, Deutsch."

I reached for a third cigarette and again pulled the chair forward. It was like trying to pull a car with the brakes still on. It was hard to look casual. The Kommandant didn't notice. He was basking in nostalgia.

"I vas in da Hollyvood Bowl, ach, such musick. Vunderbar."

The German officer did not want any remarks. Just having me there was enough. After all, where in Germany could he find a better audience to listen to all that crap? I smoked closer to the grapes.

"Ah, und Sunset Boulevard, grosse Häuser. Da same ve Vrigley's Island."

"You mean Catalina Island?"

"Aber, but of course. Catalina Island."

I had butted out enough smokes to make it to the desk. Looking directly at the Kommandant, I said, "Grapes this time of year?" He couldn't be a cheap chintz and not offer them to me. It was a set up. Besides, he had everything going for him, including a pair of ears from Southern California.

"Vollen Sie Frucht?"

I pulled the basket to me and began eating the grapes, stuffing them into my mouth, seeds, bird-shit and all.

"Und, Pasadena, da Neu Jahre Fest, very important. I saw de parade. Ach, so many blooms, und das in Vinter! Und da Rosen Bowl, das fussball spiel."

With my mouth full of grapes, I offered, "I played football in the Rose Bowl."

"Ah?" The German had become almost fatherly.

"Yes, I was the leader of the team, the quarterback."

"You, Universität?"

"Yes, Glendale College, my hometown team."

"Ah so." And still he went on. He talked about the mile-high lakes, Lake Arrowhead and Big Bear. He talked about San Diego, about the great seaport and the many boats anchored there. When he got to La Jolla, I had finished the grapes and had become acutely aware that my mouth tasted like tarpaper.

At the end of the desk was a round tray with a glass pitcher of water and some drinking glasses. I waited as long as I could and then asked for a glass of water.

Handing it to me, he summarized, " Ja Kaulifornia, like Gloria Svanson, haben vas you call 'it.' "

The bombs were about to fall. I lit another cigarette.

"Herr Leutnant, you know, you bist Amerikan Kriegsgefangener number eighteen. Ja. Das ist richtig. You kamst in Flying Fortress. Kamst you ober den Atlantisch? An der Qveen?"

"By subway." *That* popped out. Oh. I wondered if he knew what that was. It certainly wasn't the Red Cars he must have seen in L.A.

"Du verst lucky you vere not gesunken!"

"Yeah."

Standing up, he said, "Kommen mit me, Herr Leutnant." He picked up a doweling stick and walked to the large map of England.

Slowly, as slowly as I possibly could, I pushed the chair back. As I did, I noticed for the first time the three small flags behind the desk. One was the German national flag, the other two had air insignias on them. It was then that I realized there was no emblem of the Third Reich, no swastika in the room. The Luftwaffe couldn't be bothered. They were above all that.

He waited for me. With the pointer, he started rapping the map; popping from one point to another, he named cities, fighter and bomber bases. He watched for my response. When he hit Wellington, I looked twice at the map. It sounded like Ellington.

"Ah, du vas in Vellington. Yes, of course."

If he wanted to believe that was my base, it was all right with me.

Pleased with himself, the Kommandant leaned on the stick as if it were a cane. Moving from side to side, he boasted, "Ja, of course. Vir vissen alles. Ve know vo das ist." He went back to his desk and still standing, glanced over my file.

I sat down in the big chair, willing to stay forever, until I was dragged out.

The officer called, "Posten, Posten."

The door opened quickly. The guard looked like a union employee who couldn't wait to get home. "Kommst," he ordered me.

I snuffed out the last cigarette and put it in a pocket with the others. I had stashed away enough butts that I looked like I was wearing a brassiere.

The officer looked up from his desk and nodded goodbye.

As I was taken back to the prison, I could hear yelling and laughing from the guys playing rugby in the camp.

Inside the cell, the stillness, the unknown, overwhelmed me. My body felt abused by too many green grapes and cigarettes. I had a feeling things were not good. It was too easy. He bought too readily. I was stalked with anxieties I could not shake off.

It was usually about sundown when I was brought the supper tray. That day of the Kommandant's meeting it was long after twilight and no food had been brought. In my darkened mind I resigned myself that I might never eat again. I had reached a new low and I couldn't see bottom.

Then, I heard the most beautiful of all sounds, the rumpling, creaking squeak of the food cart. New prisoners had been purged into the wing. I was not alone. I had company. And, for the first time, the light went on in my cell, and with it came renewed hope. I was back in the ball game.

The next morning I was interrogated by a young man, new to his job, and unable to match wits with me, the old pro. Forgetting everything, including the little, dead Peabody lying on his back, my mind was shored in anticipation. Something was about to happen.

And it did. That afternoon I was taken from the cell, across the compound to the camp. The fenced fields ahead gave strength to my body and limbs. With an expanding chest, I began to take long strides. "Hey, you guys," I wanted to shout, "are you ready? Here I come." In the wonderful open air, at any moment the drums would roll and the bugles would play. "Hey everybody, look, I'm here, I'm free, oh, glorious day." As I walked through the gates, I expected to be embraced and kissed on both cheeks like the hero in a French movie.

Two English chaps in the nearly empty camp turned as I walked by and, devoid of interest, said, "Hi, Yank."

25

THE ANNIVERSARY

Hello, what's this? Neatly arranged on a bunk bed were my U.S. uniform and belongings.

A real towel? A warm shower? Depressing the valve, the overhead spray pelted down like warm rain. With the clay soap, I washed away Dulag.

If the shower was comfort, teatime was pure luxury. Thick apple jam, biscuits, hard tack from Canada, Peeks flat sugar cookies, round cans of cheese, sweet butter, tea, ground coffee, sugar, Klim powdered milk. It was a banquet to starving eyes. I was so hungry I could have inhaled it. I wanted to wolf it down, but I restrained myself. I felt my whole country was represented by me and I was going to give it all the dignity I could command, and I could command it. I could take it. Trying to be blasé, I took small portions and ate slowly.

"You had a tough go, what?" was the question from the camp's permanent party, the only men occupying the camp when I arrived. The liaison between the German staff and the British was obvious right away. The British appeared to have knowledge of how long I was confined and when I would be released. They were intrigued that I was American. U.S. anything was news. They had preconceived ideas that all Americans drank booze from the age of eight, wore ten-gallon hats and cowboy boots, drove huge, expensive cars, and that the American women were the most beautiful in the world with Lana Turner at the top of the list.

I was allowed to write four cards home. I sent a note to my parents, to Hank Rogers, Rita, and one to Captain Haberman.

> Dear Captain,
>   In case you don't know, I'm a POW and am in Dulag Luft at Frankfurt-am-Main. Please spread the word. I don't know how the crew made out. Would you please take care of my next-of-kin kit, my commissary dues and investigate my Key Club dues.
>
>   As always, Al.

There were no Key Club dues.

Dinner that night was another extravagant repast for a shrunken gut—fried potatoes and even a canned apple roll for dessert.

From the subdued conversation that evening, I sensed a tension among the English permanent party, a couple of whom had been caught in the air the day war was declared. Some of the men felt others were receiving more privileges, being able to go to town more often, to visit the dentist and to have dinner out. One of the RAF was disgruntled at the Queen because she had insisted that a group of English planes drop sweetmeats over several of the newly occupied countries for Christmas—a "bloody poor way to go down."

With a gramophone to play music, books to read and a field where I fouled my way through rugby, I was heady with freedom and activity. It was a powerful relaxation—away from the solitary, from the interrogations and from the worry about what was going to happen. For several days I was exuberant that I was, again, participating in life.

Prisoners dribbled in. With them began the "there I was" stories. In comparison, mine turned out to be very ordinary.

A top turret gunner was going down as his plane sank into the water. He opened his mouth for one last breath of air that was trapped at the top of the bubble. As he gulped, his false teeth popped out of his mouth. Without thinking, he went after them. Thrashing around in the water, he hit a mechanism that released the turret from the ship. Retaining the pocket of air, the compartment bounced to the surface like a cork. He was picked up by German Air-Sea Rescue.

One RAF pilot bailed out. When he came down, the ground winds were so strong they blew his chute out in front of him. It pulled him along, bumping, and scraping over the ground. When he came to a fence, he pushed his body into a jump over it. The kid was so stripped of skin it looked as if the burns had been painted on.

I had met one of the men purged into the camp before. After telling him the date that I was shot down, the RAF pilot, Flight Lt. John Dowler, described how that same morning his Spitfire had been damaged over Lille. Spotting chutes ahead and knowing the Germans wanted prisoners, he flew pylons around them for his own protection. When he got close enough, he hit the deck and flew home. John Dowler was the pilot who flew around Gise and myself that Friday morning of October 9th.

With the influx of prisoners, roll calls—Appels—were made six to eight times a day. Within two days the roll swelled from one, myself, to twelve to fifteen people. During one of the roll calls, the counter announced, "Herr Leutnant La Chasse, two steps forward, bitte. You are going back to the cooler."

The German Appel detail, four in front and behind, marched me back to the central building of Dulag Luft, where I was locked into another cell. I was going to be punished for being a smart-ass.

A man in a uniform heavy in black, sternly reprimanded me, saying that they knew all the time what a subway was and they knew I was not from Wellington. If I wanted out, I would have to make a broadcast back home. When I repeated my orders, he angrily dismissed me.

Sustained by the food I had so recently enjoyed, I was not alarmed by the imprisonment. Rather, I was impressed that the stay would be short by the fact they let me keep my uniform and by the constant shuffle of feet around me. They had a whole new group to squeeze.

The next day I was released. When I walked back inside the camp, the English met me with, "Well, lad, you must have told them a long story." They looked at me, the only American there, like I was a criminal.

Happily, two more Americans arrived at the camp. One, Nick Cox, was a copilot of the Liberator that was shot down the same day I was. Nationality tied us together like old shoes.

The stay in the camp was a short one and first-class to what was to follow. The day after I was released from Dulag, fifteen of us, all Dominion people and three Americans, no English, were marched in route step to Frankfurt. The approaching winter was bitterly cold, especially for someone with California blood. The two pieces of warm clothing that I had been given, a wool pullover sweater and a battle jacket buttoned to the throat, were thin protection. My goose pimples longed for the heavy, winter flight outfit, bulk and all.

In Frankfurt, we boarded one of what was left of the city's transportation system, a wooden-seated trolley car. Women occupying the sheltered ends sent us admiring glances. Seated in the open, central portion of the car with no buffer from the frost, I shivered. I pulled the sweater down over my hands. Adding to my discomfort was a passenger who stood directly over me, a member of the Luftwaffe. He was happy, smiling and smelly. Every whiff of cold air was tiered with his body odor.

In the Frankfurt train station, in a remote area of tracks, we boarded a train. It carried as many boxcars as passengers. Commuters stood and sat in the front and back compartments. We were kept together with other subjugated laborers in the car's central bay. Seated on hard, utility seats, protected from the cold by the enclosed car, we were all prisoners. Suspicions shaded friendships.

For hundreds of miles, it was a long, deadening ride. I walked the aisles to keep my blood circulating. Hunks of bread were thrown in to one person for distribution. Mugs of hot liquid were occasionally passed. There were delays while trains were reshuffled. Priorities were given to the ones carrying supplies to the Eastern Front.

We closed towards No Man's Land. There was no way to punch your ticket and get off. No whistle was going to blow, ending the game. Obscurity loomed ahead.

Sagan Station, Germany.

The East Camp of Stalag III was only yards away. The heart of a forest had been cut out for a rectangle of slat-sided buildings. Their dirty, olive-drab color blended into the hard, barren earth. The Camp was surrounded by a heavy, chain link fence fifteen feet high, by machine guns and coils of barbed wire.

Through the gate, ten yards past the two-foot warning rail, in the stone-cold sunlight, the air turned stale and time stalled. Was this going to be it for the rest of my life, a number, a slave in the German monolith? In the open dungeon, with no assurance, no comfortable conclusion, and no way to measure the war we were losing, there was no future. There were no goals.

It was November 11, 1942, the anniversary of the WW I Armistice on the Western Front. No one was celebrating. For more than nine hundred days, no one would.

26

JANUARY'S FORCED MARCH

Powdered drifts, winter's acoustical cushions, dimmed the sounds of the German motor convoys as they led the column far ahead. Distinctly audible in the barren, frozen terrain was the crunch of packed snow and the swish of feet in wet shoes. Panting steam, the thousands of POWs, all American Air Officers, four abreast and in route step, snaked over a forgotten road. Needles of the night's cold wind pierced our coats and sweaters. Beards were jeweled in icicles, noses burned in the glacial frost, eyes watered and blinked protectively. Behind us, near Sagan, about one hundred miles southeast of Berlin, sprawled the massive prison compound, Stalag Luft III, nearly empty and awaiting the Russian advance patrols, reported to be eight hours away.

Not far past the front gate I turned to look back at the South Compound where I had spent my middle twenties, but the camp had vanished in a thick smoke of fog. I knew I could handle the march. Hell, I'd not always been a glamour boy of the U.S. Air Force. I had been in the U.S. Marines! Still, the load I was carrying was heavy. The knapsack I had fashioned from the palliasse covering the mattress, pulled relentlessly on my shoulders.

And I had taken so little; the beautiful, gray wool blanket from Australia, the address book, the war log, the diary I had made out of tin can labels, the RAF cartoons, my shaving kit, soap, some packages of cheese. So much was left behind—the military insignias, the records, the books, and the letters. Leaving those mementos from home, that was tough.

How appropriate the show that evening, produced by our own South Camp personnel: "You Can't Take It With You." It was opening night, with the German Command in the front row seats, enjoying the performance. Then, during the intermission, the announcement that we were to report back to our barracks immediately, that we were leaving within the hour. The Germans filed out in surprise.

Stalag Luft III was over.

With Bud Gaston, Nick Cox, Don Eldredge and Chuck Lipsky, roommates since '42, we marched southwest, the distance ever expanding away from the three tunnels we had helped dig—Tom, Dick and Harry; from the "cooler" where I had spent time for attempted escapes; from the bunk where I had read Rheva's "Dear John letter," from our barracks wallpapered in pinups. The slogan, "At your door in '44" had changed to, "Hope we're alive in '45." Well, we were. And we sure as hell planned to stay that way.

The handmade garrison cap sheltered my face from the flurries of snow, but nothing impeded their assault on my overcoat. The crystals settled onto the khaki wool and melted into the fibers, the permeating wetness increasing the weight of the "greatcoat."

The optimism, the confused happiness that we had felt at the outset of the march, was deadened by the fear of the unknown ahead and by the hardships of the severest German winter in over one hundred years. Prisoner and guard alike labored to keep up. Heads down, hunched, we leaned into small inclines. Each man, burdened with his own body, knew that he, alone, had to make it. The exertion was obvious, especially for men who had suffered injuries and for guards who had long since been dismissed by the Third Reich as too old.

Two hours into the march and the lines in front started to jam. The rest break that had begun a half-mile ahead had finally reached us. I brushed the snow from a large rock at the side of the road and sat down.

God, what a relief to sit down! Yet, now, breathing had become acutely painful. How long had I been gasping for breath? I felt like I had just run a long race. My nose and throat ached. My insides strained for oxygen. But in the arctic air, every breath was a searing stab. The below-freezing temperatures were refrigerating my lungs. I took the angora shawl from around my shoulders, secured it under the garrison cap and crisscrossed it over my mouth.

Small fires flickered as men, burning anything available including cigarettes, heated snow in tin cups. When the liquid was hot, they mixed it with powdered Nescafé coffee.

In the short time before the march resumed, ice had formed around my shoes, the same GI high-top shoes I had worn the day I was shot down. The slush kicked off easy enough, but my feet were strangely numb. Man! I wouldn't sit down again. I'd keep standing, keep the circulation going. How easy to freeze to death, especially for someone weaned on California sunshine.

The snow was still falling as the artery of men, no longer in lines, continued to trudge southwest.

How depressing. Why couldn't the advancing troops have been American? We could have overwhelmed the Germans, who were as shocked and unprepared as we were. But who wanted to wait around for the Russians? Who knew what they would do when their artillery units came within range of the camp? The stories about them were all the same. The Soviets refused to respect the Americans as allies. Our guys who flew shuttle raids out of Italy and England and who landed in Russian territory, were treated like prisoners. They had to stay close to their aircraft, either sleep next to it or in it. And, the Russian orderly at the First Aid Station, he was friendly until he found out I was American. Then, with animosity, he described the U.S. war effort as inferior, manpower and machinery alike, including the Bell Air Cobra he was shot down in. While he took pleasure in mocking the war material we had given them, he dismissed the fact that without the U.S. equipment the U.S.S.R would have had nothing to fight with. Yes, the vibes were always negative. The Russians were anti-American.

It seemed like a fatal march. We were in a vice. An unfriendly ally was behind us and a now-desperate German enemy lay ahead. I accepted the inevitable, that I would be fighting soon.

In curves in the road, the men stalled in bunches. In the long stretches they thinned unevenly. Inventively, they fought the cold by slipping sleeve linings over shoes and sewing whole coat linings together to form hoods (the threaded needles were woven into their collars). Belts were used to secure backpacks; a piece of tied rope held up the pants.

I replaced wet gloves with wool socks and alternately slung the bag from one shoulder to another. Though the burden of my belongings and me was great, I was confident I could endure. But for others, the march was already proving too much. Packages of cheese, tins of Spam and Bully Beef, sweaters, underwear, and handkerchiefs lay strewn over the road. Some had already succumbed to a fact that would eventually face all of us: eat it, wear it, or get rid of it.

Oh! Tossing food away was incredible. I picked up a package of American cheese, only another eight ounces, and pushed it into my backpack. And to think of all the latest issues of Red Cross packages that we had to leave behind—the margarine, jam, sardines, powdered milk. Better to have left the Russians some soup, those rotten soups that began my very first night at Stalag. I recalled my initiation to them.

"How many do you have?"

"I haven't counted them all."

"I have more than twelve."

The large metal spoons clanged against the oversized bowls, skimming the gray-green liquid for the white kernels, I watched curiously as the men banked the hollow pellets around the rim of their bowls.

"What are you doing?" I asked the RAF kid across from me.

In clipped, brittle English he answered, "There's extra soup tonight and the one who counts the most maggots gets it."

MAGGOTS? My stomach went up and down like an elevator. Nausea shivered through my spine. I could feel the worms wiggling down my throat, swimming in my gut. I looked closer into the soup with its strange proteins.

"You mean those little things that look like rice are maggots?" I hoped not.

"It makes no never mind," the veteran prisoner had reassured me, "they don't have any bones."

The winds grew stronger, polishing the earth. Many, including myself, slipped and fell. The help to get up was your own will to survive. A discarded sweater, torn in half and wrapped around my shoes, gave better traction. The guards began dragging their rifles, then dropping them. We picked them up and handed them back. Better to let the guards carry them. If we needed a weapon, we knew where to get one. Intermittently, blasts of snow engulfed us, numbing the senses, distorting vision. I wondered if the guy who had huddled next to the tree or the one at the side of the road had frozen where he had rested.

For miles, the landscape was a vast nothingness, softening when scraggly brush began to appear along the sides of the road, when a light twinkled in the distance, or when we entered the warm covering of a forest. The trees, interrupting the fog, provided protection from a possible air strafing or a barrage of machine gun fire. Among the timbers, the snow fell softer. Every once in a while there was a waterfall of noise when the snow tumbled from the limbs and thundered to the ground.

The next day, there was a break in the clouds; the light reflected in the snow brightened the morning. The patches of sunlight fighting their way in seemed reassuring that something was trying to be good to us.

And it was. For the first time in years I smelled farm manure. It reminded me of the dairy back home. Real livestock! The nearest I'd been to an animal in over two years was a horse's head, boiled gray, with one eye hanging by gristly threads, being removed from a soup tank in Stalag's cookhouse.

At last, in the middle of a forest, at a crossroads, we were given the opportunity to rest. We had marched some twenty hours. As the villagers studied us, evidently pleased by our appearance, we crowded into their barns. In a hayloft, close to the ceiling and its captured heat, I laid out the greatcoat as a bed and, damp-drying my shoes, socks and gloves under me, I cuddled the chill from my bones. Though my breath still sprayed a frosty powder and winter knifed between the barn's wooden boards, there was a warmth, from the cows and horses harbored in their stalls to the two large, tallow lanterns that hung from the ceiling.

The roomy, handsome barn was roughly the size of the theater we had built in our South Camp. Like the barn, it was constructed of wood, had a peaked roof and the wooden Red Cross parcel boxes used for seats accommodated in excess of two hundred people. The officers, having nothing to do, became expert audio and lighting technicians. The materials we needed were supplied by the Germans who, on orders to keep us there, theorized, "Give these guys whatever they need to keep them busy," lessening the chance of trouble. Meanwhile, we diverted tools to the Big X (Escape Committee) when they needed them for work on the tunnels.

With the purges bringing in professional talent, the amateur skits gradually expanded into first-rate productions. Accomplished musicians who called themselves the Luft Bandsters scored them. The American senior officers gave our country's parole (promise) to borrow scripts, costumes and props from Germany and other foreign sources. The musical instruments were given to us by the International YMCA. In the early shows, guys were asked to participate. But when the productions developed into the professional level, everyone stood in line for a chance to try out. Some of them were persuasive hams. A little guy in a blond wig sang, soft and sexy, "My Embraceable You." The audience, gripped by their hunger for the sensual, dreamed of the sweet young things back home. Offstage, Aphrodite turned very mortal. Standing in his GI shoes and socks, with sweat pouring from beneath the golden curls, he chewed on a cigar.

The march resumed after a short, six-hour sleep. Without formality, without instructions, or breakfast, the groups of men unraveled from their shelters back to the road. Leaving my diary to the safekeeping of the barn, my pack was lightened by two pounds and my hands were warm in dry socks. They were my last pair. The others were drying in the inside pockets of my battle jacket. The socks were wool, the best I carried. I had received them in a Red Cross Christmas package that had arrived in June. They had been knitted by a lady in North Dakota. In the toe was a note: "I hope these keep you warm, even if you were a coward and gave up."

The sky was a mask of gray and it was a hellish cold, yet we acclimated ourselves to the march. There had been plenty of opportunities to die before then. Our bodies drew strength from an iron-willed determination.

What was at the end of the march? The question nagged us all. There was no use talking about it. No one knew anything. The scuttlebutt was that Hitler was going to use us as a pawn, a bargaining weapon. But with their world crumbling around them, how humanitarian would the Germans be? We knew they had shot many of the allied prisoners who had escaped out of tunnel Harry. And I had witnessed the impulsiveness of a German guard when he shot the emulated bombardier, Lieutenant Sconiers, through the mouth for standing during an air raid. We expected the Germans to get nasty and revengeful. But there was no place to go. We were in the middle of an empty, frozen land, in the middle of nowhere. Besides, the farther south we marched, the closer we came to our own invasion forces. So we kept singing "Fuck Them All" and prayed that there really was a light at the end of the tunnel.

Before the night's stop, the march was made easier. A guy in our group fashioned a dragging device, Indian style, out of sticks and a blanket, where we stacked our packs and took turns pulling it.

We descended on the next village and its barns like a horde of locusts. The civilians looked at us in friendly surprise. These were the terrible bastards of the air? They seemed relieved that we were members of the human race. And, despite Hohendahl's (the ranking German guard) admonishments, they were eager to trade with us. We traded cigarettes and Canadian soap for their hot soup and sausage. The sausage, hard, spicy and delicious, was not the kind we had at Stalag that oozed jellied blood. That night in the barn proved especially warm. I slept between my buddy, McKorkle, and Bud Gaston.

Al sent this photo to his mother from Stalag Luft III. Left, Lt. Bud Gaston, 3rd from left, Al, and 4th from left, Lt. Don Eldredge.

Gaston's last mission was in November '42, only a month after we had been shot down. They had made their bomb run over the sub pens at St. Nazaire when their ship was hit and forced back towards the Brest Peninsula by German fighters. Another B-17 and crew gone. It must have been a critical loss for the American Eighth Air Force, but for me, living in that ho-hum restraint of an English-dominated prison camp, I personally was exuberant, ecstatic. There, among a new group of prisoners being purged in, were the familiar faces of Gaston and copilot Eldredge. There was no mistaking Bud Gaston in his garrison cap and GI uniform, looking gallant and dashing with his carefree, jaunty strides; and Don, walking tall and erect, appearing strong and healthy. Besides, if they were here, could Butterball Jones be far behind?

"Hi, young man." Bud greeted me in his usual affectionate manner.

"Boy, do you look good," I said. They were scrumptious to behold. I wasn't alone any more. "What got you?"

"We ditched," Gaston answered. "Any sports?"

"No baseball diamond."

"We'll take care of that."

Surveying the dirt and cell-like blocks, the compound's depressing future was immediately apparent. No crybaby, Eldredge asked, "How do we get the news?"

It was a long, tough wait while they were assigned barracks and debriefed. Finally, I had them to myself.

"Why did you have to ditch?"

Gaston was casual. "We lost an engine. Don put out the fire, but the ship wasn't responding. The bomb bay doors malfunctioned; we had a friction drag. We couldn't stay in formation. We lost altitude."

Eldredge added scornfully, "Those Germans herded us in like a stray cow."

"Sons of bitches . . . but . . ." I wanted to know everything.

"As we headed out over the Channel they surrounded us," Gaston explained. "We were close enough that we could see their goggles riding high on their helmets and their thumbs pointing down."

"Yeah," Don affirmed. "They kept firing bursts over the nose. As if we didn't know what they meant, they kept dropping and raising their wheels."

"At least," Bud said with great satisfaction, "they didn't get our ship."

"God." The questions were flipping through my mind. "Did you hear about us?"

"Yes, McKee told us."

"Did any of my crew get back? I know Gise got out."

"Nope. We didn't hear a thing."

At last, of course, I had to ask. "On your last mission, uh, did Kenny Jones fly with you?"

Don Eldredge told me as simply as he could. "Al, Kenny had an accident. He went out of the plane without a parachute."

A gunnery sergeant told me what happened. On the way back from a bomb run, unable to switch the bomb bay doors shut from his position in the nose, Kenny went down to the bomb bay to manually close them. He was hand-cranking the gearbox, inching the doors towards each other, when suddenly, over the Channel, the motor electrically activated. The force of it ejected Kenny. With no parachute there was nothing to save him.

In the morning, the march continued as January's iceberg held on. Shoes cracked and wore through. Feet were wrapped and tied in rags. Injured skin had turned purple. Clothes were damp, rations few. Crackers were exchanged for cheese, cheese for crackers. Cigarettes were exchanged for food. The best-fed people were the guys who didn't smoke. Rest breaks depended on the Germans' own rate of exhaustion and the conditions of the road. There were no better conditions, only bad and worse. Still, the snowball, the rolled up pair of socks, the shoe, was tossed back and forth in a game of catch, and the songs outclassed the whine of the wind. "Nothin' could be fina, than to be in your vagina in the mo'o'ohr'nin." The German guards, blanching under the same rotten conditions, continued to be puzzled by our spirit.

The Americans were different. They had an unconventional way of living—casually sloppy, resilient, indifferent to the system. The POWs, unimpressed, teased the Gestapo, whose very presence struck terror into the German civilians themselves, and who periodically invaded the camp, searching the barracks for tools and weapons. The group of secret police pulled a large sack down the center aisle and filled it with contraband, including some of our food. Every time their backs were turned, one of us would reach into the bag and pilfer the stuff right back. A new German guard would be met with a raised hand and a "Fuck Hitler." Eagerly, the German would return the national salute. The Appels, the roll calls, were always screwed up, with the Germans making their counts over and over. Some POWs were necessarily missing. Inevitably, the roll call came out even, because the little guys in the last row were running back and forth, shouting "here" for the bodies that were not present. The confinement produced an ingenious makeshift by the Americans that amazed the Germans, spurring plots and schemes of an outlandish nature—anything to harass, distract and generally confuse the detaining power. Among the achievements were banners delivered by flies.

In summer, huge horseflies were attracted to the trash-filled trenches that edged the camp's walking perimeter. They were a husky anomaly, so large that it was discovered they could be used for transport. Catching them, we hung a piece of thread between the body's segments. Both ends were tied to a piece of toilet paper inscribed "Fuck Hitler." Released, the insect would eventually rise to the "goon" towers where the guards would get the message.

Because of its proximity to the woods, the fence bordering the south side of the compound was considered the most likely place for an escape (subsequently, it was never used). In precaution, the Germans hung tin cans containing several rocks all along that wall of barbed wire, presuming the noise on contact would alert the guards. After saving enough string, the GI tied a rock at one end and, with the expertise of a fly-casting fisherman, looped it through the fence seventy-five to a hundred feet away. Hopefully, it would unroll and secure itself on the wire. The guards in their towers were too far away to see the string that lay over the warning rail. At midnight, from the barracks, the string was pulled with such technique that the cans banged and chattered in warning, "Someone got away." As soon as the camp's alarm had sounded, the POW jerked the string, breaking it, leaving no evidence. Meanwhile, the flap was on as the Kommandant, the guards, dogs and lights went searching into the forest for the escapee that never was. When string was unavailable, the athletes with their great throwing arms simultaneously tossed mud-filled cans into the woods, resulting in the same pandemonium.

And the sports ability of the Americans was fascinating to the Germans, who enjoyed watching the dazzling performance of those who excelled. But the Germans and English alike, could never quite understand the ritual of haranguing over baseball's declarations of "ball," "strike," "safe," and "you're out!" It was true, even as we marched, that we remained an enigma to our captors.

Prisoners at Stalag Luft III. Al, front row, 3rd from right.

Miles passed. We sucked snow and shared nibbles of chocolate bars as each one of us described his favorite restaurant and its menu in delicious detail. As we moved through the countryside, we could hear military training units marching and singing. Once we passed a training camp and saw the "troops." They were young kids—twelve, thirteen, fourteen years old—Hitler's last task force.

Where was Hitler? Was he alive or had he been assassinated? Maj. Joe Glass, the makeup artist from Hollywood, recognized that different men posed as Hitler. By comparing pictures cut from German newspapers, it was easy to see that in one the ears would be lower than the nose, in another the eyes would differ or there would be less chin. Some pictures featured bushy eyebrows, others thin, as if plucked. It was obvious that one man could not be in so many places at once, if, indeed, he was alive at all. The photographs were prized. We cut the "papes" (cards) for them. The lucky guy would then have the pleasure of using Der Fuehrer's face as toilet paper.

How satisfying, demeaning the Third Reich, wiping their faces in it, especially the Gestapo. Oh, how they must have wanted to shoot us after that inspection in the North Camp.

During roll calls, each of us took turns hiding in the barracks for purposes of Intelligence. On occasion, people of special expertise received the duty. During one Appel, the auto mechanics were given the assignment. It was a surprise roll call of all British and Americans ordered by the Gestapo. Ignoring the Kommandant's warning, the Gestapo drove through the front gates into the camp. The men in the long raincoats left the two cars in front of the barracks and, surrounding us with machine guns, for eight hours they supervised the Appel and searched the barracks. Meanwhile, the mechanical experts relieved the cars of all usable equipment. The stone faces of the Gestapo must have cracked in embarrassment when they found their automobiles had been rendered shells. Besides needing to have the cars towed away, a briefcase filled with priority material had been taken. That night the Kommandant issued orders demanding that the briefcase and contents be returned for the safety of all. And it was. But each paper marked for Berlin was stamped with the Allied Seal (molded out of thick Jell-O) and carried a signature of approval by each senior American and British officer. The Kommandant and that party of Gestapo probably ended up on the dreaded "Ost" (Eastern Front).

Sanctuary, the last night of the march, was a glass factory. Operational, it relayed heat and light though the glass brick floors. They were hot enough to dry some socks I had rinsed out and laid on them. Some guys couldn't take the roasting and chose to remain outside. In that village, as in all the others, there were no young people. The civilians were friendly and traded sleds for our cigarettes.

Another day's march. The month had turned to February, the snow to rain. There were rumors of "black feet." I kept wiggling my toes, making sure I could feel them. The guards were fewer and farther between. During rest breaks we mingled with them, sharing food and cigarettes. After all, they did not belong there. They belonged at home with grandma. Ahead of them, if not death, was defeat.

Our chances were better. We were a large group and one to be reckoned with. Closing south, our mood shifted to one of anticipation. We were stealing some warmth from the rain and from the direction where Patton was advancing.

And at Spremberg, a new ingredient was added to the march, a feeling of importance. In a bankrupt transportation system, we were going to be moved by rail. We knew nothing about the doomed mass transportation and the ensuing atrocities directed towards the Jews, so we had no fears of the boxcars that we were being herded into. The fact that the Germans were going to use their precious energy to transport us, impressed us with our value. The forty and eight cars, so named during World War I for accommodating forty men or eight horses, were each filled with more than fifty men. Most of the manure had been shoveled out and we were able to push the doors open three inches, which allowed us a relief station. Subsisting on allotments of bread and marge, for days we took turns standing and sitting. We shared hammocks, blankets strung from the ceiling. Sleeping in one of those was startling cold and an education that floorboards were insulating. Among the remnants of manure, we could smell our own clothes and bodies, so dirty that I, with amazement, could peel a gray matter from my skin, an accumulation of oils and body excretions that had been covered up too long. By talking, joking and singing, we kept ourselves "up" even when we were strafed by our own aircraft. We smothered anxieties as to the question of our destination. Within the week we would know the motive, a moot possibility:

"One hundred miles south of Nuremberg lay Munich, not far from the Austrian Alps and in the general area where Hitler planned to make his last stand, 'holed' up in the mountain vastnesses he called 'the Last Redoubt.' "[12]

The most valuable resource left to Hitler, the American Air Officers. Hostages to barter with?

27

OLD BLOOD AND GUTS

The boxcars jockeyed back and forth for dozens of hours until they were positioned in front of our new compound, Stalag 17A. We were damned happy to get out of those giant crates and into the open air once again, but our jubilation was soon cut short by the hellhole before us.

The screening process through the "goon's" building was expedient. The maps hidden under my belt and the compass I carried in a pipe were easily smuggled past a complacent Wehrmacht. The bulkier contraband, wrapped in newspaper and carried by others, was tossed down the incoming lines of GIs where at the end the parts needed for radios and other intelligence equipment were thrown next to the fencing to be retrieved later.

The camp, named Moosburg for the nearby Bavarian town, was located between Munich and the Danube River and held thirty-some thousand prisoners. Stretching farther than I could see, it was divided into sections and contained all Allied nationalities. Excluded by barbed wire at the northeast perimeter of our compound, Turks, Indians and Egyptians, swathed in light-colored turbans and robes, milled in rainbow confusion. We were separated from all other prisoners in the camp, a compliment that the American Air Officers had the brains to organize and the ability to influence.

Exhausted by our transportation and the stress of expectancy, we headed directly across the field to an edge of buildings, eager to turn into a bunk for sleep. The barracks were large, open bays, bunk stacked upon bunk, with an attached room of unheated showers and a toilet. That single convenience was to be used by ranking officers and anyone who was unusually ill. The rest of us shared "Moosburg's Library," an abort with rows of toilet seats. The barracks were foul, smelling of body odors and waste matter. They were damp, cold and filthy. But worse, that night began the battle of the fleas.

Deeply asleep, I was awakened when one of the insects lumbered across my back like a Model-T Ford. As I turned over, I felt the scurrying, the prickling of pinhole borings on my chest and arms. Crap! It was a major invasion. In my extreme tiredness I began to endure the parasites like a dog, and between drillings, caught pockets of sleep.

We had dealt with vermin before. After every purge into Stalag Luft III, the barracks were scrubbed and deloused with every available chemical, the Germans giving what help they could, which was always too little. But next to the infestation at Moosburg, Stalag Luft III was medicinally antiseptic. After two nights, it was intolerable. I took a cold shower and, shivering in the freezing temperature, rubbed GI soap around my wrists, ankles and neck, sharply snapping out my clothes before putting them back on. Adding insurance, I slept outside where wedges of snow still clung to the ground, the cold prohibitive to insects.

In those first days at Moosburg I made a near fatal mistake. At Stalag, during air raids we laid on the floor of our barracks. At Moosburg, the protection was slit trenches. With the wailing sirens and hum of the approaching aircraft, I dove headfirst into the nearest trench. The seven-by-six foot hole filled up fast, the bodies crunching one after the other on top of me. An elbow poked my right eye, a knee my left. The air I was breathing had been someone else's, that of my friends, whose shoes and faces were pinning me into the dirt. I was trapped. Groans passed between my lips. My muscles strained, protecting bones that could easily have snapped. Shit! I'd rather stand and see the bomb blast me than be squished like a bug. It was a thirty-minute lesson that would never be repeated.

Hunger was constant. There were as many days when we did not receive food as days when we did. Though we bordered Switzerland, Red Cross parcels were nonexistent for more than a month and the Germans, unprepared to feed so many, had to stretch meager rations of bread, soup and potatoes. Soon we were asking, "How do you know when you're starving?" During an air raid I found out. Trying to run out of the building, my legs were like hollow poles, there was no feeling. They were numb. Yet, I watched my legs move, my feet touch the ground, as they carried me through the shower room and outside. I had been transported by two prayers that had been answered.

The food we had, that we had saved or scrounged for, was shared among our mess in razor-even proportions; a thin boiled cat, a single fresh egg. Snails were rendered in a communal pot, the goo and slime raked from the simmering juices. Far from escargot, they chewed like rubber. Cigarettes were highly valued and with them we traded for dried fruit from the North Africans. We became experts at making prune pudding.

During the acute shortage of food, when a chocolate bar could command a hundred-dollar promissory note, several guys started to steal. They would walk through the barracks in the middle of the night and lift from a knapsack a piece of bread or potato that some kid had saved. Even in piss-poor conditions there was no excuse. It was the worst kind of offense. The one grace of our captivity was the deep affection we had for each other; an affection that precluded anyone who had not experienced our imprisonment. Yoked together, there was no pettiness, no jealousy, only the desire to do something for the other guy. An integral part of that devotion was honor. When the duty pilots caught the guilty parties, they were court-martialed. We considered them to be as dirty as if they had cooperated with the Germans.

February passed. Thank God. In March, Red Cross packages

began to dribble in. The thirteen-pound parcels brought a measure of relief from the drab, dreary existence.

In the extreme cold and rains, sports activities were fractional. Inside the tents and barracks, among the insects, we played cards and waited turns for dog-eared books. Through it all, through the bugs, cold and hunger, time ticked slowly. Day crawled after day in an exasperating drag. Liberation never left our minds. It couldn't happen too soon, our rescue from that filthy monotony.

Sustaining us, calming our impatience, was the knowledge that among the Allied forces crossing Germany there was that one man. Unpredictable, competent, inspiring, he was the shining star, the light down the road. From newly purged POWs we learned of his advance. All of our concentration and hopes culminated in the one figure, PATTON.

Gen. George Smith Patton, Jr., bold, dashing, flamboyant, captured the imagination of everyone. Even the guards communicated through German-speaking Americans, their admiration for that single General. The slapping incident had been rumored through Stalag Luft III, even though his drive through Sicily and his sweep through France had been minimized, the BBC too busy touting Montgomery. But the speed and daring with which Patton had dispatched three divisions over one hundred miles of winter ice, breaking the German lines to relieve Bastogne, was news we'd all heard before the end of January. We were convinced then that the Master of the Battle of the Bulge was going to liberate us.

With maps and contraband radio our Intelligence followed him, estimating his arrival by the pace he was traveling from town to town. Resistance was reported to be heavy. The Germans fell back, regrouped and attacked again. They fought from behind rocks, windows and doorways. The story was that in one town, white flags of surrender greeted Patton's troops. As they marched in to occupy it, they were hit with sniper fire. In retaliation, an angry Patton ordered the next town leveled.

By March 23rd, Patton had crossed the Rhine.

April 4th, he was in Frankfurt.

In the climbing, agonizing anticipation of the General and his Third Army's 14th Armored Division and 99th Infantry, our happiness was fused with fear. Situated in a camp that was between retreating and liberating forces, we did not know whether we faced a battle or an evacuation. It was great to be in the path of approaching Americans, but if the Germans made a stand on the camp's borders, we would be caught in the crossfire.

Yet we felt there was a modicum of safety in the camp. A mass of men rushing down the road would certainly risk the chance of the advancing troops shooting first and asking questions later. Should we stay inside the barracks or outside? About twelve of us chose the latter in case we had to make a run for it. For a measure of protection we encircled ourselves with benches, boxes and pieces of wood, none of which would have stopped a 30-caliber, yet the arrangement allowed us to get some sleep.

As Patton advanced, the German guards gradually disappeared. One of them tossed his rifle over the fence. With all of his earthly possessions on his back and in his pockets, his girth was large, so bulky that he had to heave the gun into the air three times before clearing the wire. Afterwards he waddled off down the road. Many of the guards in those last days asked us to sign notes commending their care of us.

In late April, the end began. It was evening. To the east and south of us there was the rattling and clanging like a mass movement of Wehrmacht gas mask canisters. Someone familiar with tanks recognized the sound of the retreating German armored units. All during the next day, gaggles of German aircraft, including their new Messerschmitt 262 jet, were seen hedgehopping south. For two-and-one-half days the retreat continued, its extensiveness obvious. Someone was getting close.

April 29th we stood together, waiting for the usual morning roll call, for the German cadre to march in as they had every day.

EDWA

We waited and waited. Feeling the air and ground war, we expected some kind of announcement, even if it was from our own senior officers. Nothing. And still we waited.

All at once, out of the east and west, flying at about 1,000 feet, came U.S. lightweight aircraft. Weaving patterns north of us, they spotted the routes of the retreating German tank units. Within minutes of their reconnaissance, the clear skies were torn with the SWISH of shells, an intense volume of rockets that creased the air, leaving vapor trails. The heavy artillery, exploding one-quarter to one-half mile away, shook the ground where we stood. We didn't know there were such weapons. The battle for our liberation was on.

Tears ran freely as we grabbed and hugged each other. The Germans were GONE, the long years in prison were OVER.

The shelling increased as Patton's force, already having crossed the Danube, began to flank the camp in preparation of taking Moosburg. Jeeps, personnel carriers and marching troops headed towards the town, the tanks driving over the compound's fence, crushing the wire into the ground. We yelled, clapped, screamed, stomped, whistled. Moosburg's church steeple, in full view of the camp, began to chip away from the armored fire. As shells continued to break off the white mortar, the Nazi flag at the top exploded into dust. And then, shortly thereafter, yet it seemed almost instantly, the American flag was raised, the RED, WHITE and BLUE, the STARS and STRIPES.

OH, GOD! The moment was paralyzing, branding itself into memory; never, never to be forgotten.

All hell broke loose. We ransacked the camp's administrative offices and officers' quarters, but the Germans had stripped them of blankets and food, of anything that could have provided us with some bodily comfort. Only some medical records were left behind.

Who cared? We were going DOWNTOWN. Lighthearted, in careless abandon, we stepped over the beaten-down coils of barbed wire and headed towards Moosburg. FREE! That's what we were. The thought of it made me giddy. I gained weight with every step.

Savoring the excitement, I never thought of snipers. Fear had passed along with yesterday. Moosburg was my oyster and I went searching for its pearls.

Infantry, marching five to six feet apart, filed through Moosburg towards the Front. Many of the troops were new, replacements, their uniforms and boots respectable, apprehension in their faces. The seasoned soldiers were fatigued and rumpled, some splattered with blood. Men, who had been relieved, lounged around the streets.

"Hey," they called, "you from the prisoner cage?"

"Yeah."

"How long you been here?"

"Since '42."

"That long? Hell, I didn't know the war was that old. You guys hungry? Here, have a chocolate bar. You wanna cigarette? Go ahead, keep the whole pack."

"Where you from?"

"Cleveland. Where do you hail from?"

"California."

"YOU'RE KIDDING! WHY I'VE GOT AN AUNT IN SAN FRANCISCO."

The troops shared their food with us, giving us front-line rations, which they hated but we loved, and passed around cans of beans, corned beef hash and custard so that we all got a taste.

Some of the war-weary men could have cared less about us; one was downright unfriendly.

I spotted a pair of shoes in the middle of the street. Boy, did they look good. I sure could have used another pair. Picking one up, I admired it; yep, about my size, beautiful, handcrafted, not a GI issue.

"DROP IT."

A deep, snarling command turned me around to see a monster of a guy, a real dogface, aping at me. His eyes were ferocious. Shouldering guns and a bayonet, his clothes were patched, his helmet dented. He'd been on the front lines for a long time. OH! I dropped the shoe REAL QUICK. I didn't want them anyway. All I wanted was for him to be my friend.

There wasn't a hell of a lot to the town of Moosburg. Like Bedford, it began and ended quickly. Though splintered here and there, it had been spared real damage. The stucco and wooden buildings still faced each other over the stone and dirt street; the occupants secluded behind closed doors and boarded windows.

Command, attired in spotless uniforms and ties, had already established headquarters, their keen edge of experience evident in the smooth transition of the town's occupation. Milling around headquarters were war correspondents and combat photographers. News was not the POWs. The story was PATTON. Ogling the panorama of Moosburg and the occupying Americans, I was fascinated, engrossed. Nothing, however, was more impressive than the tanks. All around the edge of town they were being driven like kiddie cars.

Orders had come down that the sandbags carried as protective padding were to be removed. Their weight caused the tanks to use too much gas. The armored units, at top speed, without a waver and in perfect alignment, brushed the sides of trees, dislodging the bolts that secured the rows of filled gunnysacks. Sand went spraying everywhere.

One tank stood off, roaring back and forth in place, the dirt spewing from beneath the cleats. At peak momentum, it dashed for a house in an all-out charge. On impact, the walls were flattened, the roof suspended over the tank, camouflage for the night.

Close to evening I was still searching for some luxury, some food to take back to my guys. In the commercially quiet town I followed the foot traffic up to a second-story room that was serving bread, cheese and beer. The beer was horrible, but in the corner of the room I found my treasure, just what I had been looking for.

It was a basket of eggs. For cigarettes, I haggled them away from the proprietor. Having wrapped them in a piece of burlap, I CAREFULLY carried them back to camp.

Warmed by burning fence poles, we shared our day's collected wealth and feasted on a dinner of Bully Beef, potatoes, powdered milk and scrambled eggs, every one of which had been stamped with a swastika.

On April 30th, the camp was charged with activity. The Red Cross wagons had moved in and set up stations offering coffee and the front-line newspaper, *Stars and Stripes*. At the south end of the camp, where the fences were still standing, trucks were unloading German men and women. GI guards who were armed with machine guns were lining up the Luftwaffe and Wehrmacht prisoners. Investigated before being purged into their own camp, some were singled out and told to "get going." A distance away from the camp they were shot. The men marked for execution were SS Troops. I wandered around the camp, witnessing such an execution. The GI said, "You can't trust those sons of bitches." And handing me the gun, said, "Here, go ahead, take a shot."

Russian generals who were a dime a dozen, were comfortably barracked on the west side of the compound and were privy to the unusual company of some very attractive, high-heeled, silk-stockinged women.

The sounds of the war were moving south; the POP of sniper fire was constant. The fighters, flying in groups of two, three and four, flew low over the camp and waggled their wings. It was fun watching the show. Our cocky pride was returning.

May 1st. After a bountiful breakfast, there was a shout, "HEY, GENERAL PATTON'S HERE." The news spread like wildfire.

Directly in front of me, through the central gates, maybe 200 yards away, came a spearhead of people. Behind them lumbered two tanks, the first of them a huge machine with great snouts, the largest I'd ever seen. Leading the men and machines was none other than General Patton. Straight as a board he marched towards us. The sun ricocheted in a blaze off his lacquered helmet. In concise strides, his aides lined up behind him, first two, then three, four, five, six, like an expanding V. Towards the gaping, thrilled POW audience, the General marched closer. I was riveted on him, his paratrooper jacket, the jump boots polished like patent leather. My mouth was dry as I stood frozen in his approach, the bullets glistening around his belt, the ivory-handled revolvers in the holsters. In front of our barracks, he spread his legs apart and holding his swagger stick, paused.

I couldn't assimilate him all at once. It was HIM, "Old Blood and Guts" Patton, the reincarnate of ancient battlefields, the man who said, "Compared to war, all other forms of human behavior shrink into insignificance. God, how I love it." This was the General of whom aide-de-camp, Codman, wrote:

> ". . . none . . . can even remotely compare with General Patton in respect to his uncanny gift for sweeping men into doing things which they do not believe they are capable of doing, . . . which in fact, they would not do unless directly exposed to the personality, the genius . . . of this unique soldier . . . Here in France as in Sicily, an entire army, from corps commander to rifleman, is galvanized into action by the dynamism of one man. Even his military superiors find themselves irresistibly, if reluctantly, drawn into his magnetic field . . ." [13]

To ascending applause and newsreel cameras, Patton announced, "I think I'll go in here." He walked into our barracks. I ran around to the back door. There was nothing but butts in my face so I dove into the window. Worming my way over the floor, under guys who were stacked five and six on top of each other, I made it to the aisle. Two bunks from me, a POW captain stopped Patton. "Good Morning, General. We've prepared some food for you." On a wooden board, serving as a tray, was a piece of toast, a blob of our best jam, a cup of hot, real coffee and a bowl of apple and current cobbler topped with whipped KLIM. It was our best effort—food that any German or any one of us would have loved.

"What's this?" The scorning Patton assessed the tray and its contents. With his swagger stick he pushed the dishes around, finally knocking one onto the floor. Aware of the attending press, he roared, his yellow, crooked teeth detracting from the aura, "THESE ARE MY MEN. MY MEN DO NOT EAT THIS CRAP. GET THESE MEN SOME DECENT FOOD." Outside, ignoring the senior officers who were straining to talk to him, he and his aides climbed into the waiting cars and, with the hulking tank following, drove off. The next morning, each of us was given one-quarter loaf of white bread.

"Thank you, General."

Prisoners at Moosburg shortly after liberation by General Patton.
Al, standing on the right, wears the jacket of one of his captors.

28

ONE LAST MISSION

"Is that margarine?"

"What do you think we are, some half-assed outfit? It's real, dairy made." The mess sergeant smiled as he handed me stew and a hunk of bread thickly spread in the yellow butter.

"No, Sir," I assured him, the aroma of the meat flirting from the bowl. "Any outfit that can lay a bridge like that one has gotta' be first rate." The pontoon bridge that spanned the Danube was a technological feat, a construction that cowed my imagination.

I sat down on the running board of a truck, next to a corporal. With a bread sponge, he mopped his mess-kit pan for gravy.

"How long have you been here?" he asked.

"Since '42."

Swallowing the bread in a bolt, he shook his head. "NO SHIT? In '42 I was still in high school. What outfit?"

"Eighth Air Force, 306th Bomb Group, 367th Squadron." Pride swelled within me as I spoke.

A private sitting on the hood of his jeep, enjoined, "I didn't even know we were over here that early."

"Yes. It was our first mission, over Lille, France. We were the first crew in the 306th to go down. The first Clay Pigeon."

Excited, the kid asked, "Did you parachute? What's it like being an angel?"

Another engineer crowded in. "Was it bad? I mean, how tough was it? Did the Germans really hang guys out by the hands and let dogs chew on their balls?"

The men around me having mess all wore the red-and-yellow insignia of the Third Army's Corps of Engineers. They were experienced, experts, as vital as the front-line troops. They were close enough to the action to carry weapons, but bored by their routine they were hot for the war's dimensions.

A private in a dirty apron, on mess detail, came over to me, "Where ya headed?"

"Back . . ."

"Well, be careful. There's still enemy activity around. Last night one of our lieutenants got it."

"Really? So far from the Front?"

"Yeah. He was making it with a German girl and damn if she didn't pull the pin on a grenade . . . BANG! One minute they were . . . the next they weren't."

"Oh, Christ . . ."

"Do you want anything else? Coffee? More stew?"

"No, no thanks. It was all just great." I had devoured the food and was burping efficiently.

"You really liked that stuff?"

"Loved it."

"I don't believe my ears. What have you been used to?"

"Uh, cat bone marrow."

A sergeant commanded, "Give this guy a bedroom. He deserves it."

Before going into the house, a private, sitting on his helmet, yanked at my coat. "You guys, you guys were great. The air war made it possible. All the fighters . . . bombers around, they made it bad for the Germans. Lots of thanks goes to the Air Force."

In a war-ravaged country, the house that the Engineer Unit had chosen as headquarters on the south side of the Danube was extremely well preserved. More, it was in perfect repair. The floors were polished. The windows and their ornamental glass were intact. No doubt the country manor belonged to a person of distinction. The land around it was extensive. The wooden grounds dipped gracefully, cresting behind the house at the top of a hill. It was centrally located, the road from Moosburg to all points north easily accessible. From the porch could be seen the thin chinks of blackout lights as vehicles passed steadily in the night, some waiting in line to cross the single-lane bridge over the river.

It was a generous gesture for the sergeant to give me his room. I couldn't thank him enough. Upstairs in the back of the house, for the first time in years I was alone. A private room! If the guys could see me now. Oh, to be away from the smell, the stink, the congestion. I was surprised Gaston hadn't hitched a ride, so many were available on returning vehicles. Evacuating all those guys . . . impossible. It would take weeks. Besides, I wanted to see the news, see it happening, in Paris, maybe London. More important, my base—I had dreamed about that. The real pull was Thurleigh.

I took off the greatcoat and climbed between the quilts of the four-poster bed. They were down, like Elly's in Scotland, not as much fun, but damn, it was comfortable.

The bombing, machine gun and rifle fire boomed and spit over the countryside, incessant blisters in the May 2nd night. But with my guys all round me, I felt like I was surrounded by God. The safety of it lulled me into a sweet sleep.

The smell of bacon frying awakened me. God, LIFE!

The morning was beautiful with shafts of sunlight streaming through the woods, trees in shades of lavender greens and tiny blue flowers sprinkling the grass. The self-sufficient portable steel kitchen set up in the latticed garden house was steaming in breakfast, in eggs, pancakes, in gobs of good food. I washed up with the other GIs in the outside water basins and curtailed my appetite. It would be easy to overeat. The officers in the group hardly spoke. They were too upset, numbed by the death of the lieutenant, an incident that never should have happened. But the noncoms couldn't ask me enough questions and I, well, I gorged myself on being free again; watching a tire being changed, water pouring out of a spigot, a flushing toilet, sharing a birthday cake from home.

Gradually, my audience, who still had to get the job done, drifted away. I walked back to the road towards the river, thumbing my way as I went.

A truck stacked with the *Stars and Stripes* newspapers stopped for me. "Where ya going, Mac?"

"North."

"Hop in. What outfit?"

"I was just liberated from a POW camp."

"The hell you were!"

Rolling over the pontoon bridge was just as smooth as if we'd been on a concrete highway. The anchored rubber life rafts wired to each other were symmetrically placed, straight as an arrow, so taut that our passing weight did not cause a ripple in the Danube's blue-green waters.

Burned-out tanks, jeeps and cars were strewn by the way of battle. There were large pits in the earth from bombs. The 10x10 truck rolled over potholes, cracks and repairs as vehicles and pedestrians induced slow progress. The traffic was heaviest near the Front, the congestion waning as we moved north. In a straightaway we were approached by sirens and flashing red lights. Immediately, we turned away from the road and pulled to a stop, high on the hillside shoulder. Accompanied by a front and rear motorcycle escort, a great machine the size of three merged fire engines, pulling two trailers and a hoist, consuming the whole highway, screamed by us. The tank retriever was scary. Emergency equipment was the only speed merchant, the satellite sirens warning: "Get the hell out of the way."

At the truck's destination, I discovered there, as in all other Allied-occupied towns, that the Army mess halls were a ready source of food. Especially responsive were the sergeants in charge who would supply me with food even if the scheduled mess was over. With fresh fruit—oranges and apples—I walked north.

It takes only a few days to become a ground soldier, learning to get out of the way not only for equipment but for details of former front-line soldiers—no messing around—they were TOUGH.

A jeep gave me a lift.

"Pile in. Where ya from?"

"I've just been liberated from Moosburg."

"NO! What was it like? Did they . . .?"

We rode past villages, crops of cabbage and beets, over sections of the masterfully constructed autobahn, through the growth of newly planted forests, out of the bush to an open stretch of road. POP!

"Someone had a flat," I yelled, happy that we weren't swerving.

Coolly, the Sp. 2nd Class kept on driving. At the next town he examined the jeep. Between the back seat and fender, three inches below where my right cheek had been, was a bullet hole. We had been in the sights of a sniper!

By walking and hitching rides, I made my way over the southern route of Patton's advance to Frankfurt. There were many POW cages along the way, large spaces easily controlled, prison camps filled with Germans. From the distance, the Wehrmacht uniforms in a wave of gray-green looked like a field of Hawaiian pineapple. At all the camps, women and children, kin of the prisoners, crowded together outside the warning rail. Close to one of the camps I saw some of the youth I had seen on the march from Stalag. In their teens, their faces were forty years old, made haggard by the long struggle. They were relieved that it was over and that they were in the hands of the West, not the East.

Troops bivouacked near motor pools that were still under camouflage. Stacked among the equipment were tires and other parts cannibalized from disabled vehicles. Lightweight aircraft patrolled heavily guarded fuel dumps. Fighters still frequented the skies, the bombers having finished their job of high altitude, daylight precision bombing.

The more north, the more wartime Germany was returning to civilian life. The children, men and women were cleaning up the towns. Burned-out military equipment had been stacked to the sides of the roads, the armored cars and jeeps tossed by a winch ten to twenty feet in the air. By their color, by the ratio of German dirty green to the U.S. khaki olive drab, there were no spoils to the victor. To the end, the German Command went down in a sensible battling, in a running retreat. Not like the East Front where, flanked by Russians and winter, they had to make a stand and lost it all.

The Army Station Receiving Hospital in Frankfurt had portable water tanks, an outside facility of spigots and troughs that allowed me to wash up. The smell of food pulled me past the parked Red Cross trucks to an inside kitchen area of the circus-sized tent. I grabbed a tray and shared the line with others in purple bathrobes, white coats and Class A uniforms. There was no tap on my shoulder as I sat down at one of the tables arranged on the grassy dirt. In my British greatcoat, my B-10 jacket and bullshit hat, carrying my duffel bag, I had generated interest all the way from Moosburg, but here no one seemed to care. They were used to all kinds of military, including POWs who had already straggled in from other camps. While surgery was in progress, only partitions of canvas away, I lapped up the marvelous food, fresh vegetables, meat and milk.

There were scads of WACs around, an Army improvement since my early days in the war. Between bites of pot roast and mashed potatoes, I asked one next to me, "How far is Oberursel, you know, where Dulag Luft is?"

"You detained there?" she asked, without interest. "You must be Air Force."

"Yes. I am."

"You've got a fighter strip just over there." She pointed through the tent entrance in the direction of aircraft activity. The field's tower was no more than a mile away.

It was a chance, a possibility, my best opportunity. With luck I might get a lift. But I was so tired. I had walked most of the night. Just a short sleep, that's all I needed. On one of the cots lining the tent I laid down. An afternoon nap would do me good.

With the smell of ham and eggs wafting above me, my eyelids, weighted by a deep sleep, opened to the surprise of morning. Shit! I'd slept all through yesterday. Well, what the hell. Why should I care? I had all the time in the world.

Or did I? A stethoscope bounced by at the end of my cot. The man wearing it shot me an acknowledging glance. Two other men slowly passed as they made notations on their clipboards. The distraction concerned me. If the hospital wanted credit for the night's billet or a doctor ordered an examination, the required signature exposed me to responsibility, to some military procedure. I knew the minute I signed my name I would be on orders. Forget Dulag. Get out, QUICK. In one fluid motion I rolled off the cot and, pulling my duffel bag behind me, crawled under the tent flap.

Through Frankfurt, I walked toward the air tower that poked out of the morning fog. So early, yet the battered city was already busy, the MPs directing traffic, the civilians, dressed in shawls, caps and pieces of uniform, sifting through the rubble.

The air base was light scaled, of portable construction. The runway was made of steel mats. It was mainly a fighter base, although some heavy bombers were parked on the apron. Most of the boundary fencing was gone and it was lightly guarded, the area once secured so long ago. The three guys in the tower were rushed and busy with the air traffic. No information there. I took up a position central to the field's headquarters. Maybe, and I had no reason to believe it, but just maybe, someone would give me a ride.

Our eyes locked as he walked past. I looked back. He stopped and turned around.

"Hey, you look familiar. Where you from?" The dark hair was thinning, the build was slight. On his leather jacket were pilot wings marked with an S. They looked like the insignia on the radiator of a Model-T Ford.

"A POW camp. I've just been liberated." I stepped close to him. Yep. I knew him from somewhere.

"Really. How long?"

"Since '42."

"That's a hell of a long time. Where's your home?"

"California, Glendale."

His sharp, beady eyes, the kind all good pilots have, studied me. "What's your name?"

"La Chasse. Al La Chasse."

"Funny name. Well, hell, sure I know you. You, all shit and shinola." His face, patchy from adolescent acne, lit up. "You were one of my students at Joe Piloser's flight school. You remember the Civilian Pilot Training Program at Grand Central Air Terminal in Glendale?"

"Shit, yes. How the hell are YOU? Where are you going?"

"I'm taking a war-weary Fort over to Villa Coublais."

"Where's that?"

"Near Paris."

"Have you got room for one more?"

"We'll make room."

The Fort was tired all right, a shaky baby, one that had been stripped of instruments and was being readied to take back home on war bond drives. The guys around me, on just another repetitious hop, slept. But for me, it was a first exposure and the nose of the B-17 was a front row seat to the drama of an injured continent, hop-scotched in craters by trains of bombs, bald where forests had been, scratched with debris. It was a graphic history lesson; a message paid for by men like John Olson and Kenny Jones.

There was no sign of a city when we began cutting engines. My former instructor was stopping at his favorite restaurant for lunch. The fine, old establishment in Valenciennes, on the border of Belgium and France, was expecting us. In elegance, we were pampered with steak and red wine, all fifteen of us. It was a royal way to go, doing PR work for the war, a capacity that was a credit card to everywhere.

Following lunch we leisurely made an air tour of Paris, a city that from the air gave a false impression of being musty and medieval. The afternoon had been a complimentary treat. At Villa Coublais Field it ended quickly. I had no money. Where to go? My newfound friend, to whom I was grateful, reassured me. "If you're looking for a place to stay, check at the office of the International YMCA. Don't worry about transportation and food, your uniform is your ticket."

I boarded a tram at the field. Motoring downtown through Paris, we were stopped at an intersection by a white-gloved gendarme directing traffic. Standing on a curb right next to me were three Air Force officers. I did a double take. I couldn't believe it. One of them was Phil Haberman, the S-2 officer to whom I had sent information about the Key Club from Dulag.

"Phil, Phil Haberman."

The Lt. Colonel squinted as he looked at me. "Al? Al La Chasse? You! You son-of-a-bitch. What the hell are you doing here?" We shook hands through the open window.

"Patton just liberated us."

Quickly, Haberman scribbled a name and phone number on a card. "Here, Al," he said. "Call this friend of mine. He'll take good care of you."

Paris was in ecstasy. The kidnappers had been banished, the hibernation expelled. The city, uninhibited and serenaded by spring, whirled in a spiraling celebration. Everyone present was caught in the kisses, the hugs, the mental embrace of its liberation. Schnapps and wine flowed—some of it in emulation of our WW I fathers—from gals' high-heeled shoes.

Military personnel, mostly Army staff officers, rear-echelon people stationed in Paris, hosted me to drinks and nightclubs. We traded stories, my POW life, for news of technological advances like trucks that could swim and electronic bazookas; progress, it seemed to me, of a future century. The infantry major, the colonel attached to SHAEF (Supreme Headquarters, Allied Expeditionary Force), even the captain who pushed a pencil, chose his own story and would have shit in his pants if he received Front Line orders, were gratifying company. The conversation at a Place Pigalle nightclub was more interesting to me than the act, "A Wedding Night," a dry screw performed on stage by two people in G-strings. Although the nude waitresses who literally "snatched" tips from the end of the tables were easy to watch. I admired their muscle control.

The excitement bubbled all day and all night. At two in the morning, on my way up to the tiny (but mirrored) room that had been assigned to me by the YMCA organization, I had to have one more drink with the happy group in the hotel's bar. And, though I didn't think it would mean anything, before I left I had written my room number on the wrists of three girls.

Only an hour's sleep and I heard the lift as it squeaked upward. It ground to a halt on my floor, the iron-grilled gate rattled as it opened and closed. Before I could answer the tapping on my door, she had opened it and walked inside. "Yank?"

Plump, soft, dimpled, her baggy eyes noted my wealth, the foodstuffs on the table, on the way to my bed, two feet from the door. She must have liked what she saw for her clothes parted quickly. The bra, with seamed openings exposing her nipples, fell as she pulled off my shorts and nuzzled me with hot kisses in a "round the world treatment."

The bed was small and in the warm weather I perspired, a lather she carelessly shared while exploring my anatomy. From the beginning, she was in total control. She pinched, scratched, nibbled, dawdling when I began to climb. An expert strategist, she controlled the slow acceleration, massaging my neck, the small of my back, my groin. I was puffing, near pain, when at just the right moment . . . CONNECTION! Ohhhhhh. She could have put me in a paper bag.

For a man used to two-and-one-half years of nocturnal emissions, it was a sixty-minute game of hard football that I could have played in five. Mechanical, uncluttered by romance, she had been all business. And now she was going to get paid. With her hands she pushed the bed, bouncing a couple of times like she was getting ready for a ski jump. One shove, she was off the bed, touched the floor with her feet and made a perfect three-point landing on top of the portable john. She scooted herself as she sat atop the waterless bidet into a position in front of the table where she took stock of my inventory. Hurrying, she dressed, and with a loaf of white bread and cans of GI rations, she backed out of the door. "Merci, merci."

May 8th. With some other roaming POWs, I took the Metro to the Champs Élysées, to Red Cross headquarters. I had decided to borrow thirty dollars. Emerging from the underground transportation system to raucous noise and honking horns, we happened into, right there, square in front of us, the sensational spectacle, VE DAY!

As if the cork had popped, the champagne of colors, bands and figures poured into the morning. Four flags, so huge they denied gravity, hung from the middle of the Arc de Triomphe, silky tapestries of the major powers—U.S., England, France and Russia. Behind the Arc, formations of fighters, light and heavy bombers, gathered in Vs from all directions, suctions of aircraft in salute. The French National Anthem, in glorious beat, drummed through the air as men and women and children sang and marched to its direction. Women of all ages were dressed in flounces and ruffles predominant in colors of red, white and blue, their hair dyed the three shades to match. Twirling pedals of bicycles revealed shapely legs and lacy undergarments as they followed along with the great procession of tanks and Allied troops. Vendors dispensed food. Wine bottles clinked. The souvenir shops were loaded with junk labeled "Made in Paris," much of it satin pillows and cases stamped with "Mother," probably mass-produced in New Jersey.

It was an irresistible jubilation, one that drew me with the crowds from one side of the street to the next, down the Boulevard, around and through the base of the Arc.

Victory in Europe was a festival that went on for hours, long after I had taken out my loan from the Red Cross.

In Paris, I quit worrying about food. Quartermaster Supply, like the U.S. war machine, was rolling at top efficiency. The Army's menu was readily available. Every Allied mess, wherever they were, in and outside the city, opened at exactly the same time every day. One of them, Willow Run, was said to have been capable of feeding 4,000 military per HOUR. In the ballroom-like building, men curled around the stair-linked balconies to the main floor that was used as the dining room. At lunch I passed one of the officers' bars, twenty-five feet long, lined end to end with ice-filled glasses. And the war was still going on. It was an easy life, but bourgeois by contrast to that of the ranking military.

When I contacted the friend of Haberman's, a car was sent for me in an immediate invitation. I was delivered to a street that resembled an embassy row, to a gorgeous, white, U-shaped building. Its foyer was lighted in chandeliers and its walls were carved in relief. The verandah that encompassed each floor had a commanding view of the Eiffel Tower. My host was a warrant officer (the highest ranking non-commissioned officer) who occupied the entire third floor and possibly the whole building. Muscular, short, pleasant personality, he had a mind like a calculator. He had to. It was his job to see that the Red Ball Highway, the one he had helped organize, operated effectively. The highway was the direct supply line from the Channel-docked ships to the Front, a priority express, off limits to all other vehicles and personnel. A battery of men aided him in maintaining the network of stores and provisions ready to meet the demand of the Front and to insure the cooperation of the towns along the highway's route. Masterfully mobile, the highway nevertheless contributed to the Black Market. Many ploys, a woman lying nude or a crying baby, were used to stop the convoys that would then be highjacked. The profits involved were enormous, enough to risk life and commit murder.

The apartments of the warrant officer were plush. Even his own closets were stocked with good booze, sugar, coffee, beans, rice and clothing. Anything that was impossible to get and desirable to have, he was the man in charge. His phone rang constantly. After one call, he said, "That's the sixth time one of his aides have called asking for perfume. That goddamn general must have a harem he's screwing."

The officer gave me, along with carte blanche to his residence, new underwear and a good, used uniform. I showered and shaved in hot water, napped and helped myself to a refrigerator full of food, bowls of meat, cheese, milk, fresh fruits and vegetables.

Late in the afternoon, most of his staff, who had been going in and out like ants, had left. Another group, Allied military government people, American military personnel, worldwide war correspondents, and other warrant officers, about twenty-five in all, began to arrive. They were a select few; heavy with brass, smelling of leather and perfectly dressed. They all knew each other. I felt out of place; I wasn't the sharpest looking there, but my POW introduction paved the way. They all wanted to know the gory details.

The party evolved to a sit-down dinner prepared by a WAC major who had cooked the prime rib right there in the apartment's kitchen. The meal was tops, with a selection of French wines and REAL pastry.

After dinner, with a fresh scotch over ice, one of the war correspondents and I sat on the floor next to a coffee table and talked. He wore a Class A Army uniform, his job identified by the war correspondent patch on his sleeve. He was distinguished, soft-spoken, with graying wavy hair.

"I caught your conversation about the food earlier," he said. "How was their treatment of you?"

"I have to say it wasn't too bad. As a matter of fact, I was kind of happy. I had all my parts. And, since I was so new, the Germans who were used to the English and Dominion people, showed me around for purposes of propaganda."

"How new were you?"

"October 9, 1942."

He wrinkled his face in thought. "I forgot there was any strength here that early, only token forces. Of course, now that I think of it, the Air Force has to have the earliest and largest amount of prisoners. They were the only combat unit ready; the first, too, in North Africa, at Tunis and Oran. Then you were lucky. I've heard some pretty gruesome tales about the treatment that was dealt by the Germans."

"Yeah, but there's a big difference between combat prisoners and political prisoners. The German military made every effort to rescue combat people, among other reasons for interrogation. Most of the horror stories that came in later were about atrocities committed by the German civilians, the people who lived in and around the city that had just been bombed. They were the ones who ran the kid through with pitchforks, hung a guy by his own chute, tied men's limbs to the train track to be sawed off. I know these were true stories from the crew members who were picked up and saved by the Luftwaffe."

"You mean the Luftwaffe were a decent sort?"

"On the whole, yes, although I do know one guy, a kid named Townsend that I went to college with. He'd been picked up in the Underground and when he came into camp he told me he had been beaten with a rubber hose until his head was twice the normal size. But there again, I think that was Gestapo. They'd do anything to get information."

"And he lived?"

"Yes, but he acted like he had barbed-wire psychosis and was in the process of going around the bend."

"Did you ever try to escape?"

"Yeah, one Christmas night, the guard was relaxed. I climbed over one wall."

"Over barbed wire?"

"I had gloves on."

"Of course. Go on."

"The second wall was at the north edge of the North Camp and it's kind of funny, everyone had the same idea. Such a jam of us. We were all caught. The attempted escapes were 101 percent of the time."

"Were you punished?"

"Only solitary."

"We heard so much about their Intelligence. Was it as good as they say it was?" His voice was calm, persuasive, receptive to knowledgeable answers.

"Unbelievable. So sharp that when I was interrogated they knew more about my outfit than I knew myself. Within a couple of months after I was shot down they had the actual bulletins off our board at Thurleigh."

"Amazing." He rubbed his hand over his forehead. "I wonder how they did it?"

"Oh, their information shocked me right away."

"Tell me, as a POW were you able to follow the war's progress?"

"Yes. We had our own Intelligence. Actually, we had three sources. First, we had our own contraband radio, second, we bribed some of the German guards and third, and most important, were the new POWs that were purged in. They had dropped all over military Europe and had seen firsthand the military maneuvers, the strategic stockpiles, motor pools, fuel and ammunition dumps— information that our organization dispatched back to our own forces."

"That's astounding. I would never have believed you were so well organized."

"Oh, yes. We even knew what was going on back home and, I'll tell you that when we heard about the coal miners' strike, well, when we heard about that one, our whole life sank to a big, fat zero. God, if the people at home didn't care, who did?"

We sipped our drinks.

He asked one more question. "You must have had firsthand reports on the raids?"

"Sure. Absolutely. One of the kids I interrogated coming in had been shot down on the Schweinfurt raid and . . ."

"Interrogated?"

"Standard procedure. There were incidents when Germans came into the camp posing as Americans."

"Oh, I see."

"Anyway, this kid, Peachtree Murphy, a professional musician—by the way, he had less service time than I did and he was already a major—he felt the raid was significant. His exec said, 'Without ball bearings there will be no war and that's what we're going after.' That makes sense. I believed it."

"My God. So well informed. This is fantastic. What a story you've got. Wish I could write it now. Here's my card. When you get back to the States, call me. We'll get together." On the card was the name Quentin Reynolds.

The lingering holiday began to weigh on me. The booze, the gals, the open hospitality, I knew it couldn't continue. Every day the MPs were picking up more and more POWs. Soon *I* would be tagged as a RAMP (Relieved Allied Military Personnel), and sent to a hospital for observation. A purple bathrobe and cream of rice eight times a day would terminate the wanderlust. Then, as soon as my stomach had been stretched to what was considered normal size, I'd be shipped home. Though I maintained a low profile and stayed away from the tourist attractions, each passing day became more of a burden, the chances of getting out of the city lessening.

And what about the policy of the Air Force? At what point would I be considered Absent Without Leave? After all I'd been through, AWOL? Oh! What a horrible thought. But I wanted to make it to England, to Thurleigh. That had been my destination from the beginning, a kind of pilgrimage to say a prayer for the guys, for Kenny.

29

NO GOODBYES

From the activity on the third-floor suite, fortune smiled one more time. One of the warrant officer's partying guests, Wild Bill Casey, knew of a flight that was being readied for Bassingbourn. Wild Bill, an original pilot of the 368th Squadron of the 306th Bomb Group, had an established reputation, receiving a lot of press because he flew so long—into 1943—without a fatality. He finally ended up in Stalag Luft III and, like myself, had wandered from Moosburg into Paris.

The plane leaving for England was conscripted to bring eighty bottles of champagne back from Paris for a wedding. As soon as I heard about the flight, I knew I would be on it.

The Boston A-20 lifted from Orley Field into the blue perfection of morning. For the last time, I crossed the Channel. Its waters were calm and crowded with fishing boats. Most of the other aircraft crossing the body of water flew east towards France, probably sightseeing tours for rear-echelon and ground support people. In the gunner's compartment, I swung the radio dial around and picked up our pilot's voice as he announced he had VIPs on board. Sitting in front of me wearing a garrison cap and earphones, he looked very much like Oley, a haunting recollection considering he had been my Captain's replacement.

When we taxied to our assigned parking space near Bassingbourn's Air Tower, the commander of the 91ˢᵗ Heavy Bomb Group, Col. W. Terry, and members of his staff stood at attention to welcome us. Terry saluted as Wild Bill dropped down from the nose hatch and said, "Terry, you bastard. How in hell did you get to be a Station Commander?"

Terry's mouth dropped open. "I'll be!"

I dropped out of the rear hatch, all crumpled, my duffel bag tumbling after me. The lanky colonel looked at me, perplexed.

"Terry, I'm La Chasse, Al La Chasse. You remember, Oley's bombardier?"

Terry's youthful, fair-skinned face clouded. "Yes. I remember Olson. We were good friends. Too bad you were number 1." A smile erased the sentiment. "Al, how are you? Good to have you back." He shook my hand and introduced me. "Fellas, I'd like you to meet Al La Chasse. This guy was with the 367ᵗʰ, the first Clay Pigeon."

The first Clay Pigeon. Yeah. The first bird in the Group to be shot down. First fatalities. First place. Number 1.

By some quirk, some crazy chance, by an unpredictable fluke, a bullet didn't have my name on it. So I was in England again. At last I was purged from the Continent, from the months, the years of a life that hinged on strain and apprehension. I was finally safe. And free. It was wonderful, humbling, bewildering.

The wedding took place at noon, a large buffet and reception following. The base was filled with people; many high-ranking officers, some, like Terry and myself, from the original crews that started at Wendover. The groom was a bombardier, a major, who was still in high school when I had already been captured. To dress for the occasion, I was directed to a storeroom full of 'casual' clothes, unclaimed uniforms. I selected an Eisenhower jacket. I had seen some guys come into Stalag wearing them and I had thought they were so handsome.

The party was a jubilant affair, lasting all night, celebrating not only the wedding but also victory, the end of the war. There was music, dancing, champagne, and women. It was the kind of party that I, as a prisoner, had talked about, dreamed of, fantasized over. I took Benzedrine to stay awake, but I knew, my body knew, that I couldn't take very much. Like at the first Red Cross Station at Frankfurt, I ate a doughnut. For a gut used to limited rations, it was a sinker. I heard that one starved kid ate ten and dropped dead. No, I had experienced a lot in the past several weeks, from Patton to Paris, and I had little stamina. Every few hours I slipped off to a barracks for sleep.

We were several days at Bassingbourn. We played poker, threw darts, visited outlying pubs, and talked to the locals. Everyone was warm, friendly, and inquisitive. POW, Prisoner Of War, was a pass to instant hospitality and questions: "Did you know my buddy, Jack?"

But Bassingbourn was, like so many other bases, undergoing slow evacuation. And there was that one imperative, the "why" I had started out at the beginning.

"Hell," Wild Bill looked at me with surprise, "I know where there's a jeep."

Bedford was less than an hour's drive. We picked up some shavetail replacements who were hitchhiking. In the late afternoon, the hamlet of Thurleigh was already tucking itself in for the night, locking up the several business houses, warming up supper. The road was empty, with no sign of the heavy traffic that was routine on open post weekends.

Greeting the base was a big letdown. I didn't know a single soul. Bill did and made the round of handshakes. In the Officers' Club, a friend of his mixed us a drink. The ceiling of the building was filled with target names and dates. German air insignias hung from the walls. The bar was the same, though a bit more worn. The keyboard on the old, upright piano was covered and the stone fireplace with a mouth big enough to walk into, was dark, unlit. The base was folding up.

I left the Club and walked toward the apron of the field. A row of buildings intercepted my view of the Nissens and the runways that had paralleled the flight lines had been reset at angles. The field was practically deserted, the 306th having left sometime before to occupy a base inside of Germany.

Well, there I was. Back. Back where it all began. Lifetimes had passed, a hundred years and yet, it was only yesterday. In the dab of light left in the west and the moonlight reaching from behind some clouds, I could see the flight line where Butter had waved to us.

It was lonely standing there, the air cool and crisp like that morning of October 9th. A growing grief elbowed me. In the echoing silence I saw it, I heard it all again.

The revetments filled with B-17s, the ground crews nourishing them with affectionate care. The crews talking, waiting, set for the challenge, their bitching and laughter hiding the uncertainties. There was Gaston's plane across from Snoozy II and McKee with Oley, shooting the breeze. There were the tents, the bicycles, the whirring props and throbbing test of motors. Butter walked toward me rolling a silver dollar across his knuckles. For an instant, I half expected a hand on my shoulder and the voice from Alva . . .

Slowly, the moon pushed off its pad from behind the clouds and prying open the night with its fullness, threw streams of light over Thurleigh. The man in the moon was smiling. The prayer wasn't necessary.

"So long, guys." Goodbye is forever.

Albert William La Chasse
1917–1994

A search of the American Battle Monuments Commission's register of burials and memorializations and the complete register of World War II Dead maintained by the Department of the Army reveals that the remains of all the crewmen who perished on October 9th, 1942 in Snoozy II were recovered and identified. Their burial locations are listed below.

Capt. John W. Olson
0430684;
Plot B, Row 11, Grave 24; and,
T/Sgt. Thomas W. Dynan, Jr.
32190053;
Plot O, Row 4, Grave 7
Netherlands American Cemetery
Margraten, Holland

S/Sgt. Bert E. Kaylor
14077938;
Private Cemetery in Tennessee

S/Sgt. Bruce C. Nicholson
6937694;
S/Sgt. Truman C. Wilder, Jr.
18039746; and
2nd Lt. Joseph N. Gates
726221;
Section R, Grave 151
Fort McPherson National Cemetery
Maxwell, Nebraska

NOTES

1. Jerry Scutts, *USAAF Heavy Bomber Units, ETO & MTO 1942-1945* (New York, 1977), pg. 8.
2. Gen. Curtis E. LeMay with MacKinlay Kantor, *Mission with LeMay* (New York, 1965), pg. 210.
3. Ibid., pg. 142.
4. Ibid., pgs. 141-142.
5. Gen. H.H. Arnold, *Global Mission* (New York, 1949), pg. 157.
6. Ibid., pg. 349.
7. Ibid., pg. 350.
8. Ibid., pg. 348.
9. Jerry Scutts, *USAAF Heavy Bomber Units, ETO & MTO 1942-1945* (New York, 1977), pg. 7.
10. *Target: Germany, The Army Air Forces' Official Story of The VIII Bomber Command's First Year Over Europe* (New York, 1943), pg. 35.
11. Ibid., pg. 35.
12. Lt. Col. James F. Sunderman, U.S.A.F., *Air Escape and Evasion* (New York, 1963), pg. 51.
13. Col. Charles R. Codman, *DRIVE* (Boston, Toronto, 1957), pgs.159-160.

Printed in the United States
5922